THE END OF THE PEACE PROCESS

THE END
OF
THE PEACE PROCESS

Oslo and After

EDWARD W. SAID

PANTHEON BOOKS

New York

All rights reserved under International and Pan-American Copyright
Conventions. Published in the United States by Pantheon Books, a division
of Random House, Inc., New York, and simultaneously in Canada by
Random House of Canada Limited, Toronto.

Pantheon Books and colophon are registered trademarks of
Random House, Inc.

Library of Congress Cataloging-in-Publication Data

Said, Edward W.
The end of the peace process: Oslo and after / Edward W. Said.
p.   cm.
Includes index.
ISBN 0-375-40930-0 (hc.)
1. Arab-Israeli conflict—1993—Peace. 2. Israel. Treaties, etc. Munaòòamat
al-Taòràr al-Filasòànâyah, 1993 Sept. 13. I. Title.
DS119.76.S245 2000
956.05'3—dc21   99-044765

Random House Web Address: www.randomhouse.com

Book design by Trina Stahl

Printed in the United States of America
First Edition
2 4 6 8 9 7 5 3 1

To Deirdre and Allen Bergson

CONTENTS

ACKNOWLEDGMENTS

I AM SPECIALLY grateful to Deirdre Bergson for going over these essays with a critical eye, and for helping me enormously in getting them into shape. Patrick Deer also took time to look them over and make editorial suggestions: he has my warm thanks. With two exceptions all these essays originated in the pages of the *Cairo al-Ahram Weekly* and, in Arabic, in the London-based daily, *al-Hayat*. Mona Anis was my extremely helpful editor and friend at the former, Jihad al-Khazen and Dania Shamy at the latter. I owe them a great deal for their support and interest. Shelley Wanger in New York once again bore with me patiently as we prepared the text for publication. She is a dear friend and superb editor, whom I cannot thank enough. As ever, my assistant, Zaineb Istrabadi, prepared, collated, numbered, dated, and put all of these pieces in order. I could not have done any of the work in this book without her, and I am profoundly grateful to her. "On Visiting Wadie" and "West Bank Diary" were published in the *London Review of Books* by its gifted and ever-accommodating editor, Mary-Kay Wilmers, whom I am happy to thank warmly. Several of these essays also appeared in *The Progressive, Le Monde Diplomatique, Le Monde Dawn* (Pakistan), *Dagens Nyheter* (Stockholm), *El Pais* (Madrid), *The Guardian* (London), *Al Khaleej* (UAE), *Gulf Times* (UAE), and *The Nation,* to all of whom I am grateful for their support. Harvey Shapiro of the *New York Times Magazine* proposed that I write the last piece in this book, and Kyle Crichton skillfully saw it through the editing process. I am indebted to them both for giving me the opportunity to write what I did.

E.W.S.
New York
December 3, 1999

INTRODUCTION

EVER SINCE IT began secretly in Oslo and was signed on the White House lawn in September 1993, the Middle East "peace process" has seemed to me not only inevitable in its course but certain in its conclusion. Despite various apparent setbacks—from the 1994 Hebron massacre, to Yitzhak Rabin's assassination in 1995, to the various Palestinian suicide bombings and subsequent closures of territory, to, most recently, the destructive Benjamin Netanyahu period 1996–99—the sheer disparity in power between the United States and Israel, on the one hand, and the Palestinians as well as the Arab states on the other, has dictated that inevitability and its conclusions: the Oslo agreements would end in apparent success. As Avi Shlaim, the Israeli revisionist historian, puts it in a new book, *The Iron Wall*, it "was the assessment of the IDF director of military intelligence that Arafat's dire situation [in 1992], and possible imminent collapse, [that] made him the most convenient interlocutor for Israel . . ." With Ehud Barak's assumption of power in May 1999 things have certainly speeded up, so much so that a comprehensive peace between Israel, the Palestinians, Syria, and Lebanon will very likely be signed, if not completely implemented, within a year or so. All the parties seem to want it. The Arab states, Egypt and Jordan chief among them, have declared themselves willing partners, and what Israel wants it most certainly will get, including the additional military aid and support from the United States that Clinton gave Barak in July 1999. Yasir Arafat and his small coterie of supporters can furnish little resistance to the Israeli-American juggernaut, even though of course real Palestinian self-determination, in the sense that the Palestinian people will enjoy genuine freedom, will be postponed yet again. A "permanent interim agreement"—minus any resolution to the problems of refugees, the status of Jerusalem, exact borders, settlements, and water—is the likely result for the year 2000.

The essays in this book provide a personal attempt to chronicle the final official chapter of the Oslo peace process, to lay bare its assumptions, to detail its accomplishments and, much more, its failures, and above all, to show how despite the tremendous media and governmental attention lavished on it, it can neither lead to a real peace nor likely provide for one in the future. Written mostly for the Arab and European press, these essays, I believe, provide a detailed point of view rarely to be found in the U.S. press. My assumption throughout is that as a Palestinian I believe that neither the Arabs nor the Israelis have a real military option, and that the only hope for the future is a decent and fair coexistence between the two peoples based upon equality and self-determination. Already the Middle East accounts for 60 percent of the world's arms sales. Far too much of Arab as well as Israeli society is militarized even while democratic freedoms are abrogated, education and agriculture have declined, and the situation of the average citizen with regard to citizenship itself is worse than it was in 1948. The era of partitions and separations since 1948, the date of the Palestinian *nakba,* or disaster, as well as the date of Israel's establishment, has not produced wonderful results, to say the least, and can indeed be seen to have failed. The separation of peoples into supposedly homogenous states has imposed burdens on "outsiders" that are intolerable, both in Israel and in countries like Lebanon, whose fifteen-year-old civil war was based on sectarian exclusivism, and produced nothing except a more sectarianized country. Israel's non-Jewish, i.e., Palestinian, citizens constitute almost 20 percent of the state, so that even the Jewish state is not "just" a Jewish one. The Oslo agreements have built on, rather than modified, these unsound foundations. Insecurity breeds more insecurity so long as a whole nation or people feels deprived and manifestly treated as inferior on the basis of ethnicity or religion defined in advance as "other" or "alien."

These essays have been written as testimony to an alternative view, another way of looking not just at the present and past, but at the future as well. I maintain here that only by seriously trying to take account of one's own history—whether Israeli or Palestinian—as well as that of the other can one really plan to live *with* the other. In both instances, however, I find this historical awareness sadly lacking. The current Palestinian leadership has, in a cowardly and slavish way, tried to forget its own people's tragic history in order to accommodate their American and Israeli mentors. Consider a recent instance, the cancellation by the PLO of a meeting to be held July 15, 1999, in Geneva by the High Contracting parties to the Geneva Conventions on war, a meeting originally asked for by the PLO and accepted by the United Nations as a way of protecting the Palestinian populations of the West Bank and Gaza from further Israeli violations (torture, land expropriation, house demolition, imprisonment, etc.) of the Conventions. Instead of going through with the meeting on July 15, the PLO summarily canceled it as a sign of goodwill toward Ehud Barak after only one hour's convening of the group. And this before negotiating with a leader whose long history of enmity toward Palestinians is well known, and whose meager announcements have made it clear that he is not prepared to dismantle most of the illegal Israeli settlements established on Palestinian land since 1967. It is worth noting that there are 13,000 settlement units now under construction, and that no less than 42 hilltop settlements have been established in the West Bank since last year (1998–99). Barak has said that he plans to dismantle 13 or 14 of those, but after some resistance from the settlers he quickly gave up half of them. Along with the already existing 144 settlements and, including the population of annexed Jerusalem, there are about 350,000 Israeli Jewish settlers on Palestinian land. With leaders who refuse ever to deal frontally with this major problem, it is this sort of tampering with and manipulating of the Palestinian tragedy by our own leaders that these essays strenuously oppose, committed as I am in them to the facts of our history and not to fictions created at will by oppressive dictators.

As for Israeli history, one of the reasons I salute the New or Revisionist Israeli historians is that through their work they have exposed the myths and propaganda narratives that have attempted to deny Israel's responsibility in 1948 and thereafter for producing, in effect, the Palestinian catastrophe. I contend that unless this historical responsibility is officially borne by Israeli leaders and faced honestly by Israeli society and its supporters in the West, no paper arrangement, such as the one being projected now, can be transformed into peace. There are too many refugees still left homeless (four million at least), too many claims unsettled, too many apartheid policies still in place that discriminate explicitly against Palestinians on ethnic and religious grounds for us to accept such tinkerings as the Oslo peace process. It cannot succeed for long. Particularly after the NATO war on behalf of the Kosovo refugees, it seems ludicrously unjust not to apply the same criteria of right of return to people who were made deliberately homeless by ethnic cleansing over fifty years ago. But once again, I want it clearly understood here that I am totally in favor of peace by coexistence, self-determination, and equality between the Israeli and Palestinian peoples on the land of historical Palestine, and I am therefore exactly the opposite of an opponent of peace. The current Oslo "peace process" is an expedient and, in my opinion, foolish gamble that has already done far more harm than good. The facts must be faced, and in this book I try to face them. Peace requires sterner measures than Arafat, Clinton, and company have, or are ever likely to have, taken. And so some of us must try to make the effort that our leaders will not make.

Yet what the United States wants, the Arabs, alas, are prepared to give. More explicitly, as concerns the Oslo-Wye agreements it is absolutely clear that whether or not these agreements have actually helped or hindered Palestinian self-determination, no leader is prepared in any way to forego, modify, or renege on them. The Oslo agreements signed at the White House were first, two letters of "mutual recognition" exchanged between Israel and the PLO (though Israel only recognized the PLO as the representative of the Palestinian people) and second, a Declaration of Principles that laid out the interim arrangements for redeployment rather than withdrawal of the Israeli army from unspecified areas of the West Bank except for parts of Gaza and Jericho. The agreements postponed the really complicated issues—Jerusalem, refugees, settlements, borders, and sovereignty— to final-status negotiations that were to have commenced in 1996. Subsequent agreements at Cairo and Taba, and later concerning Hebron, were designed to set up the Palestinian Authority that was to administer Palestinian life under Arafat but retained security, border control, water, and most of the land for Israel. Settlements were allowed to continue. Far from ending, the Israeli occupation was simply repackaged, and what emerged in the West Bank was about seven discontinuous Palestinian islands amounting to 3 percent of the land surrounded and punctuated by Israeli-controlled territory. Even in Gaza, Israeli settlers held 40 percent of the land. I discussed the period until 1996 in an earlier book, *Peace and Its Discontents* (Vintage).

The Wye River agreement signed in October 1998, which was to give Palestinians about 10 percent more land, was never implemented by Netanyahu; he tried to modify or nullify all these agreements but in May 1999 was voted out of office. Ehud Barak has been greeted as the peace candidate, but given his background and what he has said and done so far, I am certain that his ideas are not different enough from Netanyahu's to warrant great optimism. For Barak, Jerusalem remains basically unnegotiable (except for giving Palestinians authority over a few sacred places in the old city and allowing Abu Dis to become their new Jerusalem); the settlements for the most part will stay, as will the bypass roads that now crisscross the territories; sovereignty, borders, overall security, water and air rights will be Israel's; millions of refugees will have to look elsewhere for help and remain where they are. Other than that, there can be a small Palestinian state without the reality of independence, and the Authority can continue its, at best, flawed rule. These things are implied in the agreement concluded in September 1999.

The real problem is that Barak does not seem inclined to visions of coexistence or of equality between Palestinians and Israeli Jews. He has clearly said that separation is what he wants, not integration. Perhaps he actually is a different sort of leader than Netanyahu and is capable of some tremendous about-face, but very little points that way, except the official optimism and hopefulness of the U.S. administration, its European allies, and liberal Zionists, Israeli and non-Israeli alike. The disproportion in power between Israel and the Arabs is so great that there is no room for optimistic speculation of the kind that will suddenly make everyone happy. Barak is a cautious man who seems actively to be seeking an unambitious Israeli consensus which, almost by definition, has a very low tolerance for real Palestinian independence and real self-determination. What he is being promised for his basically cost-free cooperation in return by the Arabs is full normalization, full peace, full opening of markets. He'd have to be a fool not to accept and go along with Wye and even a defanged little Palestinian statelet. If the last five years have taught Israelis anything, it is that Arafat can be trusted to do the job of policing and demoralizing his people far better than the Israeli Civil Administration could ever do it, so why stop short of letting him call his skimpy areas, 60 percent of Gaza included, a Palestinian state? If Clinton can force himself to do it, so can Barak and the rest.

None of this makes for pleasant days ahead. But failing a credible Palestinian opposition—which undoubtedly will be forming—the main matter before those of us who wish for peace and true reconciliation is what sort of strategy and tactics to follow. In the first place, I see no way of stopping Arafat and his people from continuing pretty much the same way in business dealings, civil rights, and peace negotiations. They have no real choice, either because none is offered them by their weakness vis-à-vis Israel, the other Arabs, and the United States, or because constitutively and structurally they are incapable of anything else. Habits are habits and, in addition, they are there doing what they do because it suits their "peace partners" perfectly. Corruption, police brutality, and undemocratic life will therefore remain. Arafat refuses to sign either a constitution or even a basic law of the land. The real question is how much damage this does to the long-term interests of the Palestinian people, insofar as there is still a strong desire for true self-determination. I myself think there *is* that desire: fifty-one years of oppression and bad, not to say disastrous, leadership haven't dimmed its flame, even though it seems occasionally abated by the sheer number of enemies, difficult obstacles, and detours. There is of course the strong possibility that Palestinians will be Red Indianized forever, but demography and the counterproductiveness and stupidity of Israel's official arrogance are likely (though not certain) to prevent that. People tend to resist efforts to marginalize and dehumanize them the more these efforts are made. Palestinians are no different, especially given the fact that by the year 2010 Palestinian Arabs and Israeli Jews will be equal in number on the land of historical Palestine. Yet caution enjoins us to add that we cannot absolutely guarantee success: history, alas, is a cruel arbiter of the fate of small, disproportionately weak peoples, so the role of will and purpose assumes greater significance for us.

One of the calculations made by proponents of the Oslo peace process is that sheer persistence and the longevity of the process itself will wear down resistance to it. This may be true, even though for the most part a majority of Palestinians in the working class and rural sectors have actually seen their conditions worsen (and their dissatisfaction increase) since Oslo. Unemployment since 1993 has risen dramatically; GDP has been almost halved; movement from one part of Palestine to the other is extremely difficult; Jerusalem is completely off limits; as yet there is only a highly controlled secure passage allowing through 40 percent of the Palestinians who apply between the West Bank and Gaza even though the Oslo documents specified that there should be a completely free one. It is the land of disadvantaged Palestinians that is being taken, their jobs lost, their standard of living reduced dramatically. They are the dissatisfied ones. They are the majority. A small number of businessmen and speculators have prospered, however, are written about in the international press, and are organizers of conferences with the Israelis and the Americans to further business and investment opportunities in the area.

All that is well known, as are the monopolies and scams that still bedevil life under the Authority, its stooges and hangers-on. What is less well known is that professionals, members of the better-off middle class, and many in positions of leadership have if not prospered then made an accommodation with the status quo. Let me say at the outset that it's easy to be critical if one doesn't have to worry about the future of one's family, job, all-over livelihood. So I can perfectly well understand the need felt by Palestinian doctors, engineers, academics, and economists living through the tribulations, punishments, and anxieties of years and years of occupation and uncertainty and desperation to make the best of a bad situation. And it really *is* a bad situation, with Israel on one side and the coarse rule of the Authority on the other. Very little reporting has been done on the day-to-day problems of Palestinians, so one has the impression that everyone manages. The question is how, and in what context.

Without at all wishing to underestimate the difficulties faced, I'd like to suggest that the professional class in particular—the class, that is, which supplies Palestinian life with its officers, teachers, physicians, architects, lawyers, engineers, journalists, and economists—has in effect made its peace with the present situation. The readiness of funders like members of the European Union, the Ford Foundation, and countless others like them have made ample money available to establish a large number of research institutes, study centers, women's and professional groups, all of which are extremely productive and do important work as (mostly) NGOs (nongovernmental organizations). The sad fact is that the Palestinian Authority and its various spokespersons have made no secret of their animosity toward these NGOs, which they see correctly as rivals both in patronage and influence; over the past four years various attempts have been made by the Authority to try to close them down, acquire or at least siphon off their budgets, and generally make their life difficult. Still, the NGOs go on so long as the funding and the will and determination of their members do not waver. That is a positive development.

Yet the question I raise here concerns the long-range strategy of these groups and the kind of thing they do. Put very simply, are they a substitute for a political movement, and can they ever become one? I don't think so since each operates in a bilateral relationship with the funders, each of whom makes it clear that money for work on democracy, health care, education—all important things—is forthcoming only within the overall framework of the current peace process. At least that is the implicit assumption. And these NGOs, necessary though they are to keep Palestinian life going, themselves become the goal instead of, for instance, liberation, or ending the occupation, or changing Palestinian society. The leadership vacuum, the absence of a political vision of the future, the general quiescence of Palestinian life, with everyone more or less fending for his/herself, have placed such secondary tasks as assuring oneself of funding, keeping the office staff at work, setting up meetings in Europe and elsewhere, ahead of the main task facing us as a people, which can be nothing less than liberating ourselves from our legacy of occupation, dispossession, and undemocratic rule.

This substitution of a short-range nationalism for a longer-range social movement is one of the intended effects of Oslo, in effect, to depoliticize Palestinian society and set it squarely within the main current of American-style globalization, where the market is king, everything else irrelevant or marginal. Just to have a Palestinian institute of folklore research or a Palestinian university or a Palestinian medical association is therefore not enough, any more than nationalism is enough. Frantz Fanon was right when he said to Algerians in 1960 that just to substitute an Algerian policeman for a French one is not the goal of liberation: a change in consciousness is. And the likelihood of that change is slowly being eroded in the current vogue for seminars, funding missions, and project reports. We need to concentrate our collective efforts on the collective destiny of the Palestinian people, however utopian and irrelevant such efforts may now seem. Unless the group spirit remains fixed on the attainment of real liberation and real self-determination—which themselves need to be clarified—we can quite easily drown in the global market with our flag proudly flying over us.

And yet there are encouraging signs that protest on a wide and impressive scale may be catching up with the profligacy and despotism of Arafat's rule. On November 28, 1999, twenty prominent West Bank and Gaza Palestinians signed a strongly worded petition condemning the Authority's corruption and abuse of its own citizens. Among the signatories were nine members of the Legislative Council, including Rawya al-Shawa, a strikingly brilliant and forceful woman who belongs to Gaza's leading family, and Bassam al-Shaka'a, former mayor of Nablus, a man genuinely admired and popular as much for his independence of mind as for the fact that he lost his legs in 1980 to an Israeli-set bomb in his booby-trapped car. Arafat responded by throwing most of the dissidents in jail. Yet the protests escalated, with thousands of Palestinians demonstrating on the streets, and literally hundreds (if not more) signing petitions in support of the original statement and its signatories. They had demanded new elections, a clear implication that Arafat's regime would not survive a democratic contest. As I write these lines, no one knows how the impasse will end, since neither side has backed down, but it seems obvious to me that the dispriting context of despair at the inequities and injustices of Oslo will continue to erupt into further confrontations of this sort.

The second problem of the present impasse is consequent on the first. Being or remaining Palestinian is scarcely an end in itself. It is perfectly in keeping with the colonial spirit of the peace process that Israel and the United States are at bottom delighted to give us symbols of sovereignty, such as a flag, while withholding real sovereignty, the right of return for all refugees, economic self-sufficiency, and relative independence. I have always felt that the meaning of Palestine is something more substantial than that. The struggle for Palestinian rights is first and above all a modern secular struggle to be a full, participating member in the modern world of nations from which we have long been excluded. It is not about returning to the past, or establishing a parochial little entity whose main purpose is to give the world another airline or bureaucracy or a handsome set of colored postage stamps.

Because the struggle against the repressive aspects of Jewish nationalism for non-Jews is so complex and difficult, I have also always felt that what we contribute toward Palestine is synonymous with a new sense of modernity, that is, a mission for getting beyond the horrors of the past into a new relationship with the whole world, not just with Israel and the Arabs, but with India, China, Japan, Africa, Latin America, and of course with Europe and North America. For this we require more, not less sophistication and knowledge, and especially an expansive, inquiring attitude toward other peoples and other histories. Only this can enable Palestinians to transcend themselves as a small people and to enter the ranks of the human vanguard along with the modern South Africans, who did so with such effect because they linked their struggle for justice to the entire world. For all sorts of reasons, we have for the time being lost that sense of confidence and worldliness, partly because we have had incapable, small leaders, and partly because we have become content with mere survival and the symbolic achievements I mentioned above. Our only hope is to be found among my children's generation, young people lucky enough to be crippled neither by the limitations imposed by the *nakba* nor by the dreadful lack of freedom and enlightenment prevailing in the Arab world today. Otherwise we might as well say that we already have a Palestinian state (declared, one ought to remember, in Algiers, November 1988), and so why bother.

Thus the next phase, with Ehud Barak and the others negotiating away busily, will go forward as planned. There's no point in being too enthusiastic about its narrow results, which are already clearly mapped out and are certain to be celebrated by the media and the White House. Beyond that, the process is considerably slower and longer-range. As I have tried to characterize it, it is where emphasis needs to be placed as much in terms of awareness as in terms of concrete steps. What needs more reflecting on is the relationship between this process in its Palestinian form and similar democratic and secular currents in other parts of the world, where once again the longer-term view is far more important and hopeful than anything the next political phase might succeed in fulfilling.

THE END OF THE PEACE PROCESS

Chapter One

The First Step

A SHORT WHILE AGO I was invited to present my views on the current "peace process" to an invited group of guests at the Columbia University School of Journalism. Aside from a small number of individuals from the university itself, and one Arab UN ambassador, the audience of about fifty people comprised reporters, news directors, and columnists from television, newspapers, and radio. What I had to say was described by the title of my remarks—"Misleading Images and Brutal Realities"—which argued that the picture given in the U.S. media as well as by the U.S. government of a wonderful progress toward peace in the Middle East is belied and contradicted by the worsening situation in the area, especially so far as Palestinians are concerned. I gave a documented and discouraging picture of how the Oslo agreement and its aftermath have increased Palestinian poverty and unemployment; how the worst aspects of the Israeli occupation—now the longest military occupation of the twentieth century—have continued; how land expropriation and the expansion of settlements have gone on; and finally, how for Palestinians living under the "limited autonomy" supposedly controlled by the Palestinian Authority life has gotten worse, freedom less, and prospects diminished. I laid the blame for this on the United States, which sponsors the injustices and inequities of the process; on Israel, which exploits Palestinian weakness to prolong its military occupation and settlement practices by other means; and on the Palestinian Authority, which has legalized the illegal, not to say preposterous, aspects of the "peace process" and presses on with it weakly and incompetently, in spite of incontrovertible evidence that Israel and the United States remain unchanged in their hostility to Palestinian aspirations.

A period of discussion and questions followed, most of it dominated by two or three supporters of Israel, one of them an Israeli employee of Reuters. The irony here was that all of them attacked me personally, speaking about my lack of integrity, anti-Semitism, and so on, without ever saying a single thing that contradicted the picture I had just presented. Both the organizer of the seminar and myself tried to push past the storm of insults and slurs, asking that people dispute with me on the basis of contested facts or figures. None was forthcoming. My crime seemed to be that I opposed the peace process, even though it was also the case that what I said about it *in fact* was true. My opponents were in every case people who described themselves as supporters of Peace Now (i.e., liberal Jews) and hence of peace with Palestinians. I kept raising the question of military occupation, settlement policy, the annexation of Jerusalem, but I received no response—only more accusations that I had missed certain nuances and important distinctions.

I concluded from this that in some very profound way I had violated the accepted norms for Palestinian behavior after Oslo. For one, I persisted in bringing up embarrassing questions and troubling issues. We are now supposed to feel that peace is moving forward and to question anything about the "peace process" is tantamount to being an ungrateful, treasonous wretch. For another, I spoke in terms of facts and figures, and I was unsparing in my criticism of all the parties to the peace process. But I found that I was expected to express gratitude and a general attitude of cheerfulness, which I had violated by complaining about concrete abuses. Lastly, I had had the nerve to speak about the situation neither as a supplicant nor as a subservient "native." This was particularly annoying to one of the individuals, who had become accustomed to Palestinians regarding her as a superior "expert" and foreign adviser. In other words Palestinians are obligated to see such people as somehow entitled to tell us what is good for us, for our own good. The precedent seems to derive from the

PLO chairman, who has surrounded himself with foreign advisers and financial experts, all of whom aid him in his private investments and commercial undertakings.

Although all the other members of the audience soon tired of my opponents, and expressed agreement with my views, I realized that the nature of the encounter I had just had with proponents of the "peace process" was the main thing that was wrong with that process: its total obliviousness to the interests of the Palestinian people, as well as its enhancement of Israel's position by propaganda and unstinting political pressure. Oslo gave Israelis and supporters of Israel a sense that the Palestinian problem had been solved, once and for all; it also gave liberals a sense of achievement, particularly as the "peace" came under attack by the Likud and settler movement. And this, in turn, made it unacceptable for Palestinians to express anything except appreciation for what had been done for them by Oslo, Clinton, Rabin, and Peres—even though unemployment in Gaza had risen at times to 60 percent, and closure of the West Bank and Gaza had demonstrated that Israeli occupation practices remained unchanged. When I was asked for an alternative I said that the alternative had been there from the very beginning: end of occupation, removal of settlements, return of East Jerusalem, real self-determination and equality for Palestinians. I had no problem at all with the prospects of real peace and real coexistence and had been speaking about those for twenty years; what I, and most Palestinians, opposed was a phony peace and our continued inequality in regard to the Israelis, who are allowed sovereignty, territorial integrity, and self-determination, whereas we are not.

Now that expropriations of Arab land in East Jerusalem are once again taking place—rather brazenly this time—I find myself puzzled as to why both the PLO and the Arab states allowed themselves to get in such an extraordinarily stupid position, that is, to sign peace agreements with Israel before even the most limited versions of Resolutions 242 and 338 had been complied with. After all, Jerusalem was annexed in 1967, shortly after which the expropriations and settlements were begun by successive Labor governments. In her recent book about the peace process *(This Side of Peace)* Hanan Ashrawi lifts the curtain on the mentality of those Palestinian leaders who were anxious to sign the Oslo accord with Israel before securing a satisfactory Israeli position on the settlements and Jerusalem. One of them told her, "We will sign now, then you [presumably he meant you inhabitants of the occupied territories] can negotiate the details of settlements and Jerusalem with the Israelis later." In other words, the attitude seems to have been that "we" would sign now, thereby giving up everything; thereafter "we" would hope that "you" would get something back later by being extremely clever.

Indeed, this quite bizarre notion seems to be at the core of the current flurry of Arab diplomatic activity concerning Jerusalem. Morocco, which heads the Arab League Jerusalem Committee, has made its peace with Israel; so too have the PLO, Jordan, and several other countries (unofficially), who have already welcomed or said they would welcome visits from Israeli leaders. While they have been so cordial with Israel, that country has continued its drive to increase the size of, and add new land to, annexed Jerusalem and the West Bank as well as Gaza settlements; the last now total about 40 percent of the "autonomous" area, and in the West Bank and Jerusalem, confiscated land amounts to 75 percent of the whole, all of it earmarked for Jewish use exclusively. Ninety-six incidences of such acts have been recorded by Israel between October 1993 and the end of January 1995.

Why then the sudden call for emergency UN sessions, the complaints, the uproar—most of it verbal, none of it revealing the slightest amount of coordination and strategy? How could the Arab leaders, plus the United States, and Israel have persuaded the Palestinian leadership to sign Oslo and its subsequent phases without a word about guarantees on settlements, Jerusalem, and self-determination, except that these central issues, the very core of the Palestinian claim to self-determination, would be "considered" at the final stage, when there would be nothing left to negotiate? Those are the questions that need to be answered now, as a matter of accountability and clear political and moral responsibility.

In the meantime, we would have to conclude that the great intellects that capitulated to Israeli pressure and were cajoled into believing that a big favor was being done them by "recognition" are, and will continue to be, incapable of leading the battle to recover Palestinian rights. A child can see that. What puzzles me is how so many Palestinian intellectuals, businessmen, academics, and officials persist in the illusion that the peace process is good for them and their people, and likewise persist in giving loyalty and deference to a Palestinian Authority that at best leads its people completely astray and at worst simply enforces the Israeli occupation at the behest of Israeli leaders who have persuaded themselves and their supporters that this is a genuine "peace process." Corruption? Venality? Incompetence? Or is it moral idiocy, that state of convincing yourself and others that your interests are being advanced, even as you continue to live as a prisoner? No matter what clever strategies are now planned for the Security Council and Arab League, and no matter how high the rhetorical level rises, there is no avoiding the issue of how such a leadership can continue to lead after having abandoned its people and its history to so fraudulent a set of promises.

The first step in liberating the occupied territories is to determine that they are to be liberated. Just because Israel and the United States have decided that annexation and the peace process are irreversible is no reason to accept injustice. The first step therefore is to admit that such a process is indeed reversible and that in order to achieve it there has to be real mobilization and preparation. As for relying on Rabin and Clinton—"trusting them" in the words of Arafat—would it now *not* be apparent after the U.S. Security Council veto, that far from being trustworthy, they have nothing but contempt for the Arabs? It is obvious to me, even though I must also say that I am quite certain that every Arab leader will now send the U.S. a private letter of apology, asking to be excused for having had the ill-grace to complain in the first place!

Al-Ahram Weekly, May 25, 1995

Chapter Two

How Much and For How Long?

D URING THE PAST few weeks there has been a quite remarkable series of confessions and revelations delivered by leaders and public figures in the West and in Japan. On July 14 Jacques Chirac used the Bastille Day celebrations in France to apologize for the Vichy government's behavior during World War II in turning over French Jews to the Nazis for deportation and extermination. Various Japanese officials, including the prime minister, have made public apologies—many of them rather cautious and not very far-reaching ones—to victims of Japanese imperialism before and during the world war. For the last few days in early August several Japanese intellectuals and writers, including Kenzaburo Oe, the 1994 Nobel Prize–winner in literature, have spoken commemoratively and regretfully about the results of the U.S. atomic bombs dropped on Hiroshima and Nagasaki fifty years ago. In the United States, there has been an ongoing debate about the wisdom and morality of the atomic bomb having been used for the first and only time in history; the official position of Bill Clinton's government characteristically has been to maintain a stony silence, as if issues of retrospective morality and guilt bore no relationship to the behavior of a government believed by many of its citizens to have acted criminally.

In addition, two sets of revelations have been of particular interest: first an article by Richard Rhodes in the June 19th issue of *The*

New Yorker magazine that details the life and ideas of the late General Curtis Le May, once the most influential and powerful of American Air Force generals, who was responsible for the firebombing of Tokyo, plus the destruction by air of North Korea and North Vietnam, both of which resulted in the deaths of about eight million people; and second, an essay by the Israeli historian Benny Morris that appeared in the spring 1995 issue of the *Journal of Palestine Studies* and describes the contents of recently released Israeli cabinet meetings for 1948, as well as private papers of Joseph Weitz (among others), a man who was responsible for the Israeli land authority, that have just become available.

Although surprisingly, he was a favorite of John F. Kennedy, and a man of great prestige, Le May emerges in his own words as a war criminal, a bloodthirsty man who was quite eager to start World War III with the Russians, even though both sides would have experienced losses of several dozen millions of human lives. Coming on the heels of Robert McNamara's maudlin revelations about himself during Vietnam—in a memoir that excuses himself and his colleagues as being well-intentioned—Le May's confessions at least have the virtue of brutal honesty. At one point, for example, he admits that had his country not won World War II he would certainly have been tried as a war criminal. Benny Morris reveals that contrary to the official Israeli government position from 1948 on (which maintained that Israel bore no responsibility whatever for the flight of almost 70 percent of the Arab Palestinian population, who left Palestine because "they were told to"), top leaders of the Zionist movement like Ben Gurion and Weitz made it very clear to their subordinates that the Arabs should be made to leave. Most Israeli historians and propagandists thereafter falsified the record, removing from it those traces of incriminating evidence.

What both Rhodes and Morris try to do therefore is of course to restore the record, but also to take a step as individual Americans and Israelis to try to right the wrong done by their governments against a relatively innocent people. Public apologies or expressions of atonement such as those of Chirac have greater symbolic significance; not only do such statements constitute recognitions of wrongdoing that give victim and victimizer a sense of satisfaction in the present; these statements usually come after a great deal of debate and analysis of the past on the part of public officials, as well as historians, philosophers, and descendants of the victims. In the United States, where crimes against black citizens have been legion, there has been some attempt to make official restitution, largely through the efforts of leaders such as Martin Luther King, Jr., and Jesse Jackson, as well as their mobilized grassroots constituency. Thus the doctrine of affirmative action was enacted as law specially to benefit blacks whose current social status was seen as the direct result of slavery and segregation. Legislation now actively favors minority students and job applicants, gives them an advantage as a way of compensating for what their community suffered in the past. The United States has also built the Holocaust Museum, as a memorial to the Jewish victims of the Nazi genocide, even though the Holocaust took place in Europe. To some degree this form of public memorial and restitution testifies to the effectiveness with which Americans of Jewish origin were able to make the Holocaust a universally relevant symbol for the moral consideration not just of Europeans but of all peoples.

In the non-Western world the first stirrings of the need for acknowledgment of evils historically suffered occurred during the immediate post–World War II period, when decolonization on a world scale began to occur. Three Caribbean writers of major significance take the lead first in demonstrating that Europe bears responsibility for what it did, then in articulating the need for some kind of reparation from Europe for the many years of colonial exploitation. Aimé Césaire's powerful *Discourse on Colonialism* (1955) is a full-scale indictment of Europe's imperialist ideology, which was by no means restricted only to bloody-minded soldiers and administrators. Césaire's point is that even respectable European scholars and philosophers contributed directly to the idea that colored people actually deserved punishment and oppression just because they were less civilized than Europeans. In Frantz Fanon's last work, *The Wretched of the Earth* (1961), he makes the point that for years Europeans acted in the Third World without scruple or conscience; this of course raises the question of how Europe is to pay back the colonized peoples for what was taken from them, and for what they endured. Building on the work of Césaire and Fanon, the Guyanan economist Walter Rodney argues in *How Europe Underdeveloped Africa* (1972) that Africa's current destitution and backwardness can be traced directly to the nineteenth-century Western practice of entering a wealthy region in Africa, enslaving the natives, stripping it bare of its natural resources, then either abandoning or directly colonizing it.

Neither Césaire, nor Fanon, nor Rodney is very explicit about what Europe needs to do now for what it did then; what seemed to be most important for them was to affirm the principle that, as Fanon put it, European responsibility for colonialism should not be allowed to end when the last white official leaves the colony and it becomes independent. Beyond that, economic aid seems to have been one form of reparation; public acknowledgment, which usually occurred in the form of ceremonies of independence (Mountbatten conceding India to Gandhi and Nehru) was another. Yet to my knowledge there has never been the kind of open European acknowledgment of colonial sins that one would like. There are still far too many British, French, Belgian, or Dutch citizens who believe that *they* were wronged when the natives gained independence, though they are offset to some extent by compatriots who struggled against colonialism, people like Sartre in France, who adopted the cause of Algerian independence.

Underlying all these examples is a pair of almost mathematical questions for which of course no simple formula exists. How long after a collective injustice was committed does it need to be atoned for? And how much atonement is required? In the case of perhaps the most wronged people during the past five hundred years—the native American Indians—a steady outpouring of films and books has enlivened the public consciousness about how shamefully their buffaloes were killed, huge numbers of their people exterminated, their land stolen, all in the name of American progress. The only proper restitution would be to restore their land to the Indians, but since that is an impossibility, there is considerable justification for believing that *all* Indians are entitled to a great deal of public compensation. Again the questions no one can answer are for how long and how much?

Of one thing we can be certain, however: None of these questions

would have ever been raised, much less answered, had there not been
a serious discussion of the issues themselves. It is the role of intellectuals, scholars, philosophers, as well as politicians and advocates
of a particular cause, to make matters of collective historical responsibility and accountability into questions of present awareness. The past has to be uncovered if it has been hidden; responsibility
for wrongdoing has to be assigned and volunteered, denied or affirmed; proposals for atonement, reparation, or restitution have to
be brought forward, analyzed, debated if in the past silence has prevailed. An excellent example of modern success in placing a case on
the international public agenda is Israel's, which gathered international support for itself as the justified "state of the Holocaust survivors," even to the extent of acquiring billions of dollars from
Germany.

Many Arabs, I know, feel that the destruction of Palestine was
partly a result of Zionism's ability to make Palestinians also pay the
exorbitant human cost of the Holocaust. Even if there is some truth to
this, it is no reason at all for denying that the Holocaust ever took
place, or for asserting that Israel has exploited the Holocaust for its
own purposes. Many of us may wish to regard the Holocaust as none
of our business, even though I believe that all such outrages have to be
understood as affecting every human being. Surely there are connections to be made between the Nazi Holocaust and the genocide of the
Armenians, the massacres of Rwanda, and "ethnic cleansing" in
Bosnia.

But what we have concealed from ourselves as Arabs is a much
more serious thing: the fact that despite major wars, catastrophes, and
enormous human sacrifices we have spared ourselves a public debate
on accountability, historical responsibility, and collective guilt. Think
of the Lebanese Civil War, with its 150,000 fatalities, its mammoth
destructiveness, its untold social, environmental, psychological consequences. Today Lebanon goes on "miraculously" as if nothing happened, the same people more or less in charge. Or take the sudden
change between Palestinians and Israelis. Why were so many refugees
created, lives lost, property irrevocably gone, if with a stroke of the
pen they would all be forgiven Israel by Yasir Arafat on a sunny September day in Washington two years ago? Where are the Palestinian,

Lebanese, Egyptian, Jordanian, Iraqi, Moroccan, Syrian researchers and historians who have uncovered what was done in "the people's" name by way of unjust imprisonment, execution, confiscation of property? These are issues necessary for debate in healthy societies. They are stunningly absent in our Arab society, one of the many negative results that come from the absence of democracy.

Our collective memory seems to be blank, as if the past happened and will never return. Surely it is because of this chasm that there is an unhealthy quality to public discourse in the Arab world, and it also is why religious movements have found so many people willing to listen to them. For if examination of the past is forbidden by monopolistic public authorities, then the quality of historical, philosophical, and moral thought is devalued, acquiring a thinness and insincerity designed not to inform but to obscure. One of the most lamentable signs of Arab decadence is the irrelevance to our present lives of archives (which are mostly nonexistent) and historians, who are likely to be antiquarians at best, and apologists for party or state at worst. To care about oneself is to care about one's past: alone of most contemporary civilizations, we Arabs risk the loss of our history almost entirely. And with that we lose any capacity we might have had to discuss present realities and past responsibilities.

Al-Ahram Weekly, August 24, 1995
Al-Hayat, August 26, 1995

Chapter Three

Where Negotiations Have Led

RECENTLY A HIGH U.S. State Department official met in Beirut with a small group of Lebanese cabinet ministers and senior journalists. He was reported to have encouraged them to start preparing their files for an eventual face-to-face negotiation with the Israelis. "And whatever you do," he was quoted as saying, "do *not* do what the Palestinians have been doing." When asked to be more specific about Palestinian negotiating behavior he told a story of tragicomic blundering and unforgivable carelessness. For in effect without maps of their own, without the requisite detailed knowledge of facts and figures possessed by the Israelis, without a firm commitment to principle and justice, the Palestinian negotiators—acting in all things under the instructions of Yasir Arafat—have yielded to Israeli and American pressures. What Palestinians have gotten is a series of municipal responsibilities in Bantustans controlled from the outside by Israel. What Israel has secured is official Palestinian consent to Israeli occupation, which continues in a streamlined and more economical form than before.

These facts dismiss any claim made by the Palestinian Authority and its apologists that the real battle with Israel has now crystallized at the bargaining table. After Oslo, Arafat and his delegates have in fact *not* negotiated with the Israelis: they have simply surrendered, accepting Israeli *diktats* as a servant accepts the orders of his or her superior, without preparation, or principle, or seriousness of any kind. This is a dispiritingly prevalent Arab pattern in dealing with Israel.

Take as a case in point the much-heralded agreement on West Bank re-deployment that the Palestinian Authority has just accepted (1995) from the Israelis. Let us leave aside the fact that it is months late according to the schedule of dates laid down in Oslo; Israel has strung the Palestinians along just as a way of keeping Mr. Arafat and his unimpressive teams under the Israeli collective thumb, revealing them for the weak and dependent village league subordinates that Israel has always wanted as its Palestinian partners. The Taba interim agreement, which immediately followed the September 1993 signature and took up the implementation of what was agreed on at Oslo, postpones still further the dates for army re-deployment, which is now to be done in six-month intervals; this will not end for at least two years. Sixty-two new Israeli military bases are to be established on the West Bank. Moreover, Israel will withdraw its troops from the center of the main West Bank towns (excluding Hebron), but it will retain control of exits and entries to them, and it will control all roads on the West Bank. It will be relieved of responsibility for about four hundred villages, but will hold fifty or sixty, many of which, near the Green Line, in the Jordan valley, and heights, will later be incorporated into Israel. Not one inch of East Jerusalem will be given up, and at the same time that Israel is "negotiating" with the PLO it has begun systematically to threaten Palestinian institutions in Jerusalem. The new system of roads on the West Bank will connect all the settlements to each other, thus making it impossible for Palestinians to rule their own territory continuously; the West Bank will be divided therefore into a series of cantons, which I prefer to call reservations or Bantustans, separated by Israeli roads and settlements except in the north. And, finally, Israel will retain control of all territory on the West Bank which it has designated as military or state or public lands: this amounts to over 50 (closer to 60 or 65) percent of the whole. In effect then, through the Palestinian negotiating tactics we have ironically fulfilled the Zionist dream of giving Palestinians rule over and municipal services for their own people but not land. Israel reserves the rights to the land, the total amount of which under Palestinian Authority self-rule for one million

Palestinians (Israel retains sovereignty) equals about 4 percent of the total land surface (the West Bank settlements with 140,000 Israelis account for 8 percent of the land); with Gaza (40 percent of which Israel still controls) it adds up to 18 percent. This is supposed at an unspecified later date to be augmented by 22 percent of jointly controlled land with Israel.

Politically and economically this patchwork agreement is disastrous, and it is absolutely legitimate to suggest that no negotiations at all, and no agreement, are better than what has so far been determined. The main effect for Palestinians seems to be that Oslo Two gives the Palestinian Authority the trappings and appurtenances of rule without the reality. Arafat and his people rule over a kingdom of illusions, with Israel firmly in command. Any West Bank town, under the new agreement, can be closed at will, as Jericho was during the last days of August and Gaza in September. All commercial traffic between Gaza and the West Bank autonomy zones is in Israel's hands, even though safe passage is supposed to be given later. Thus a truck carrying tomatoes from Gaza to Nablus must stop at the border, unload onto an Israeli truck, then reload the produce onto a Palestinian truck upon entering Nablus. This takes three days, with the fruit rotting in the meantime, and the costs going so high as to make such transactions prohibitive (it is cheaper to import tomatoes from Spain than from Gaza). The main idea of course is that Israel controls the Palestinian economy in as humiliating a way as possible. There is also now disagreement about the number of members that is to be elected to the Legislative Council at some point next year: eighty-two (Arafat wants eighty-eight members), although Israel and the Authority can decide who may or may not be a candidate. But what is certain is that Israel retains the power to veto any piece of legislation enacted by this body, which has no jurisdiction over or presence in East Jerusalem. Arafat has won for himself the privilege not only of a separate election to consolidate his autocracy, but also of being called Chairman-President. Although the Israelis have insisted that he also name a vice-president-chairman, he seems to have refused, at the same time insisting that anyone inferior to him must only be known as *mutahaddith* (spokesman).

When, during a typically theatrical moment on Sunday, September 25, Arafat stormed out of the Taba meetings, he claimed he was responding to pressures from the people of Hebron. "You want to make us your slaves," he told the Israelis. As the entire process was thus suspended, he received a call from Dennis Ross, the American "consultant" to the State Department responsible for "the Middle East peace process." He told Arafat that unless he signed the agreement immediately he would forfeit $100 million in U.S. aid. Arafat forgot his objections, came back sheepishly to Shimon Peres, and signed the offending agreement unchanged.

The major issues, however, remain unresolved. This includes the fate of the town of Hebron, which, for the misfortune of having been the site of a massacre carried out by Baruch Goldstein, an Israeli settler, has been punished systematically since February 1994. There are curfews, house demolitions, imprisonments, killings, in Hebron, and naturally the settlers remain where they have been, as provocative and as aggressive as ever with the army to guard them and their exploits. There are more land expropriations, and the settlements continue to grow. Reparations have never been raised as an issue. Arafat cooperates with the Shin Bet and the settlers in rounding up "opponents of the peace process," while the occupation of his people's land proceeds. Israel still holds over six thousand Palestinian political prisoners and still controls unilaterally the water supply (although it has conceded in principle that Palestinians will be given a small additional amount of water), and of course the military occupation continues. Rabin's plan is to substitute direct control, i.e., Israeli troops in the main West Bank centers, for indirect control, i.e., Israeli troops outside the towns. Shimon Peres, who continues to be described by some leading Palestinians as their best hope, is unregenerate when it comes to Israeli rule and Israeli settlers. In an interview he gave to *Der Spiegel* on March 5 this year, he refused to accept his questioner's premise that settlements were an obstacle to peace. The main issue with regard to peace, he said, categorically, was "how settlers and Palestinians get on with each other." A moment later the interviewer said that he found it "inconceivable that all the settlers should remain in the West Bank following the conclusion of peace," to which Peres replied, "That is your opinion, I find it conceivable."

If this is the kind of peace that the Palestinian Authority under

Arafat is able to achieve, then we should call it by its real name: a protracted, disorderly, hypocritical, and undignified surrender. Even if we
accept the premise that there was no alternative to Oslo, what has
occurred subsequently can only be described as a disgrace, a complete
abasement on the part of of Arafat and his handful of sycophants and
apparatchiks before the Israelis, without even the dignity of trying to
do some hard work. The other side of this is the abysmal situation
which the PA's rule has created. When Arafat met his Executive Committee in Tunis a few weeks ago to discuss the interim agreement,
there was no real discussion, and there was no quorum. One would
have thought that the occasion would have called for a serious discussion of where as a community we were, and where we are going. No
such discussion occurred, precisely because Mr. Chairman-President
wants the perpetuation of his one-man rule and the continuation of
his methods.

What I find unforgivable is that in all this he has appealed not
to his people's best instincts, but to their worst. On the one hand, people are made to feel that their interests can be personally served
by attaching themselves to the Authority's large, corrupt, bureaucratic, and repressive apparatus; on the other, people are cowed into
silence and apathy. The various beatings, tortures, closures of newspapers, and summary arrests have induced an atmosphere of fear and
indifference: everyone now looks out for himself. At times I find it
hard to believe that this is happening to a people who fought stubbornly against the British and the Zionists for so long, but who seem
to have given up all hope and all will to resist the extraordinary disasters visited on them by their leadership, which cares not a whit for anything except its own survival. The cynicism of the Authority, with its
thugs, its crooked dealmakers, and its huge army of incompetent
bureaucrats, is worse, I think, than its collaboration with the Israelis.

The only responses that I get to my criticisms are those that draw
attention to the fact that I live in New York, not in Gaza, plus the
haughty comment that "we," i.e., the Authority and its minions, know
what the problems are. Most of the Palestinian people do not live in
Palestine; they are languishing in the refugee camps of Jordan,
Lebanon, Syria, and elsewhere, with little to expect from the "peace
process" or from their own leadership, which has simply abandoned

them. As if being in Gaza is any guarantee of telling the truth, or of acknowledging the reality: it simply is not. As Palestinians we have now produced a propaganda and enforcement apparatus that in its poverty and bumbling rivals any in the Arab world; after years of being the victims of Arab and Israeli repression, Palestinians have finally earned the right to a repressive system of their own. There is no real law under the Authority, there is no due process, there are no real freedoms and democratic rights. Look, for example, at how badly Palestinian women—the real core of the Intifada—have been treated. They have been given no positions to speak of in the Authority, their needs and their aspirations are not part of Mr. Arafat's agenda, and their situation has become worse. There are more child marriages, more killings for "honor," more forcing of women back into the kitchen or field, than ever before.

What is symptomatic of the Palestinian Authority's mentality is its total inability to answer criticism, or seriously engage with its critics, whose number is growing as the situation deteriorates. I am not speaking here of Hamas or of Islamic Jihad, who in my opinion are not an alternative to the Authority, even though of course they express resistance to the Israeli occupation. Arafat and his advisers have closed themselves off to their own people. They have no conception at all either of accountability or of democratic and free debate. The worst thing of all is that in his disastrous policy of capitulating to the Israelis and then signing all sorts of crippling limits on his people into agreements with his occupiers, Arafat has mortgaged the future of his people to their oppressors. It is as if in his haste to get things for himself and a few symbols for his Authority, Arafat has thrown away his people's future, leaving it for later generations to try to extricate themselves from the mess he has now created. What immorality, what short-sighted irresponsibility! And to those of his supporters who keep saying that we have no choice but to do this, we should say that Syria's method is a real alternative: to accept the idea of peace and negotiations, but also not to discard principle and national priorities.

Al-Hayat, October 1, 1995

Chapter Four

Where Do We Go from Here?

WE ARE SUPPOSED now to move from the interim stage of negotiations between Palestinians and Israelis into final-status discussions. These are scheduled to begin during 1996 and will at last bring into focus what Israel and Yasir Arafat—who alone makes decisions and disposes of his people's future unilaterally—have for different sets of reasons preferred to leave undiscussed. The main subjects here will be sovereignty (or the lack thereof) over the land, resources and security of Palestine, and the fate of the refugees who constitute well over 50 percent of the extant Palestinian population. Based on what Israel has done, Jerusalem's fate is largely predetermined in the short run. Leaving that aside, however, the Palestinian Authority will enter into negotiations whose purpose is to decide the exact land surface, borders, and security for Israel and for the Palestinians; in addition, considerable attention will have to be paid as to whether approximately 3.5 million refugees (I speak here only of those Palestinians and their descendants who were forced out by Israeli forces in 1948 and now live outside the land of historical Palestine) will be permitted return or compensation. Since 1948 the United Nations has annually affirmed that they are entitled to one or the other. In my opinion the fate of the refugees is the core of the Palestinian issue, and it is plain to see that from the early part of this century until now the Zionist movement has done everything in its power to ensure that the majority of Palestinians remain outside their native land. For those who have remained inside, the idea has been to reduce and limit their political existence to a bare minimum in what is considered to be a state for all the Jewish people.

The immediate problem is of course that final-status negotiations will not be beginning from point zero: the interim agreements have already limited, as well as prejudiced, the likely outcome of the next phase. The presence of 450 settlers in Hebron, which was agreed to in Taba, becomes a bargaining chip in Israel's hand; it is easy to predict that getting them out (as they must be made to leave) will require a Palestinian concession. The increased size of confiscated land in Jerusalem and elsewhere might lead to some Israeli withdrawals here and there, but the settlements alone—their needs and "security" already accepted by Arafat—not only place huge limitations on territory to be ceded to the PA, but will also furnish Israel and the United States with strong arguments as to why more Palestinians should not be repatriated. The Palestinian territory, divided up, crisscrossed by Israeli roads, settlements, and military posts, will be considered too small for the 1948 refugees. Finally, and most important, a Palestinian negotiating style that has been neither well organized nor well stocked with both real experts and hard facts (including reliable maps, statistics, and minute knowledge of the changes instituted by Israel on the ground since 1948 and 1967) is simply going to repeat the mistakes— a euphemism under the circumstances—and passivity of the past. Whatever any of us may personally feel about Yasir Arafat and his tight circle of politically appointed loyalists, we should be able to admit that they are simply not capable of comprehending and dealing with the immense complexities of the real Palestinian situation. There is too much at stake, too many people who can be affected, too much of the future to be given away for that fatal yet characteristic mix of incompetence and authoritarianism to be given a free hand.

Part of the general mood of capitulation and despondency that prevails among most sensible Palestinians is due to a feeling of helplessness. One of its symptoms are the two sentences "There is no alternative" and "Let the PA do the work: after all they are there at the negotiating table, engaging the Israelis, while individuals like you who sit in New York or London are just critics, with no serious contribution to make." There *are* alternatives, however, as there always are to incompetence and dictatorship. But the second statement is at once more pernicious and more subtly flawed. The very fact that supporters of the status quo and of the PA, both of whom of course are entirely beholden to Israel, now feel the need to reply to my articles and admit incompetence and autocracy, proves that criticism does in fact make a contribution. When a situation occurs in which one person rules according to his own ideas, there is always room for someone to say out loud that that is dictatorship; and the fact that more people now publicly admit this proves the correctness of, and the need for, the criticism. There can be no such thing as solidarity before, or without, criticism; everyone is fallible, even Yasir Arafat, and where there is no fully articulated legal or constitutional order the need for criticism and reminder is still more crucial. This is true not only in Gaza and the West Bank, but everywhere in the Arab world, and elsewhere for that matter. The point is that criticism heightens awareness and recalls leaders to their constituency. Above all, I believe, criticism of authority is a moral duty. Silence or indifference, or compliance, in such a situation is immoral.

What has made matters worse now is that the Palestinian Authority seems to have subdued or compelled the majority of its secular critics into going along without complaint or organization. Certainly the configuration of power in the self-rule area suggests that Arafat has either bought off or frightened most of his opponents; even those who a few months ago appeared to stand independently of him now reappear as petitioners at his office or they sit in the front row and applaud loudly for him. He is of course a genius at manipulating self-interest and the power of his security forces (well stocked and supported by Israel and the United States) in order to make it seem that everyone is with him. I fear that even the much-touted elections will effectively self-select his supporters, thus assuring him of a free hand with the Legislative Council. No one dares to say that the Authority is at bottom a kind of mafia, operating all kinds of special deals on, for example, oil, cement, tobacco, wood, etc., that profit the inner circle of Arafat appointees and "experts," thereby alienating both the competent and the honest. Of course it becomes very easy to say that only by being an insider can you get anything done, since critics in New York or Beirut are too far away and too uninformed to be of much use.

This is nonsense of course, especially where it concerns the final-status negotiations, which are of central concern precisely to these Palestinians *not* under the combined Israeli and PA thumb. As for the celebrated notions of "pragmatism" and "realism" argued in support of the peace process by heavyweight Arab thinkers and strategists in Amman or Cairo, they amount to little more than a debased parroting of the ideology by which tyrants everywhere use middle-class intellectuals to formulate "expert" advice that allows them to rule their countries by force and corruption, assuring themselves of the 99.9 percent consent that these "experts" tell them they enjoy. That is all that appeals to pragmatism and realism in our circumstances really amount to: let the leadership do what it wishes, and our job as strategists and intellectuals is to make sure that authority remains untouched by accountability or any sense that most people are now poorer and more discontented.

For these strategists and the status quo that they serve to advise us as Palestinians on the final-status negotiations is the equivalent of dooming these negotiations entirely. What is now needed is that the diaspora Palestinians should finally rouse themselves into action. The Palestinian Authority is simply incapable of conducting *our* business while trying to cope with administering self-rule as well as the Israeli occupation. Besides, an Authority confined to the parts of the West Bank and Gaza is not, and never can be, representative of Palestinians in Beirut, Amman, Damascus, Europe, and North America. It is imperative that a substantial, serious meeting be held in Europe of diaspora Palestinians who will set the agenda for final-status negotiations. Arafat of course will try to ignore them, or to suggest that they are incompetent and "rejectionist." But there is enough clout—intellectual, political, economic, and moral clout—in the diaspora to give such a meeting its real due.

First of all we need an accurate and credible account of numbers: how many Palestinians live outside Palestine, how many have property lost to Israel, how many want to be repatriated? There is still the Palestine National Council (ignored by Arafat) and its authority: it needs to be revived, with a new membership based on true demographic representation and competence. This body will be designated to represent Palestinian interests beyond those supposedly embodied

in the Legislative Council, whose powers are severely curtailed by
Israel. Second, we need a combined technical brain trust, a think
tank, an office of strategic services; on issues having to do with land
and geography, water, borders, property, economic development—
now either undiscussed or monopolized by Israel—this group of
genuinely expert experts must be commissioned to produce files that
will be of immediate use in negotiations with the Israelis, who of
course have already done all of their preparation.

The main thing is that a set of unbendable and unnegotiable principles should be articulated to which negotiators must be held.
Arafat's style necessarily rules this out. Since 1990 he has made a total
shambles of all the central political principles of Palestinian political
life, including UN Resolutions 181, 242, and 338. No one gave him the
right to do that, although he is too shrewd and calculating a politician
not to go through the motions of rounding up his tame colleagues on
the Executive Committee, and on one occasion in late 1993, his broth-
ers on the Central Council, in order to rubber stamp his deal with the
Israelis. He seems totally unaccountable to the Palestinian people,
simply taking for granted the sense of passivity and defeat in them
that he has done so much to create. It (theoretically) might not be
so bad were he truly capable of understanding every detail of the immensely complicated and crippling Oslo Two agreements he signed on
September 28, but since no one person at all can possibly master over
four hundred pages of legal entanglements, it is correct to assume that
he has tied himself and, alas, his people into an agreement with Israel
the full implications of which no one can fully grasp. It is an ominous
sign that a "peace" agreement is so long, and more ominous yet that it
has not been released for general scrutiny.

Another matter Arafat and his people have not bothered to look at
carefully is reparations. Iraq illegally occupied Kuwait for seven
months, and is still paying reparations. Israel has mysteriously been
released from any such reckoning. But this question cannot be
handled unless a Palestinian body has the facts and figures from
1948, to 1967, to 1995, during which time Israel not only stole and
destroyed property, but deliberately planned Palestinian developmen-
tal backwardness. Sara Roy's new book, *The Gaza Strip: The Political
Economy of De-development*, makes it clear that even after Oslo,

Israel continues to impede Palestinian development; only the vigilance and discipline of political economists who are accountable to a body of representative Palestinians can deal effectively with the apparently endless hemorrhaging of our assets, a process which, far from stopping, the Palestinian Authority has done a lot to increase.

No final-status negotiating team can represent national (as opposed to municipal) Palestinian interests unless there are to be no further compromises on settlements, on sovereignty, water, and other natural resources, on entrances and exits, and on Jerusalem. This does not preclude a step-by-step approach with a firm timetable, along with constraints against lawless Israeli behavior built into it. I have said before and will repeat here that no negotiations are better than endless concessions that simply prolong the Israeli occupation. Israel is certainly pleased that it can take the credit for having made peace, and at the same time continue the occupation with Palestinian consent. It even went so far as to publish an extremely misleading "summary" of Oslo Two which was picked up by Arab as well as international journalists who, lazy as ever, simply repeated the misinformation. Salient details such as the invention by Israel of Zones A, B, and C, or the fact that the total land area from which Israel is to re-deploy amounts only to 25 percent of the West Bank, or the fact that sixty-two new military bases are being established, were excluded from the "summary," thereby rendering it useless as an accurate picture of the new situation. In short, the fundamental law of the negotiations must, for Palestinians, be the unconditional end of the occupation. There can be no compromise on that.

As I implied above, Israel cannot even claim peace with us unless someone like Arafat signs a document saying that there is peace. If what he has negotiated and signed is acceptable to him and to the residents of the West Bank and Gaza, then I must say so much the worse for them. But such agreements cannot be allowed to continue if diaspora Palestinians expect to have any rights or restitution at all. I am firmly convinced that unless we take the initiative in Beirut or New York or Amman or elsewhere, Arafat will give away the little that is left. I would say finally that we must enter final-status negotiations as a people, not as a collection of tribes, and that necessitates preparation and principle, as well as a firm commitment not only to stop negotiations dramatically, but also to make as loud and as effective a noise as possible. Arafat has cajoled or blackmailed many in the occupied territories and, it must be said, elsewhere, into believing that he is the only alternative and must therefore be supported more or less unconditionally. Unseemly displays of reverence and fealty to him now appear to be the norm everywhere he goes these days, including New York. We do not, luckily, have a monarchical tradition, but you would not know it from the excesses of veneration and supplicancy directed at Arafat these days. I refuse to believe that this is what we now need, and the sooner it is stopped, the sooner we can survey the damage his negotiations and his autocracy have done us.

Until then, however, being "outside" and being able to think clearly and without ridiculous illusions seems to me, and to perhaps a few of my readers, a better thing. It only takes a few bold spirits to speak out and start challenging a status quo that gets worse and more dissembling each day. I ask those of you who feel that Palestinians deserve better than this to organize, speak up, and refuse to march in this degrading and really quite ridiculous procession.

Al-Hayat, November 8, 1995

Chapter Five

Reflections on the Role
of the Private Sector

As I understand it, the Amman economic "summit" was convened at the end of November 1995 in order to bring economic development into the peace process, thereby guaranteeing a change for the better in the lives of people (principally the Palestinians) whose deprivations and generally low quality of life have to be addressed. Thus political arrangements alone are regarded as insufficient, whether because they have to do only with changes in administration and jurisdiction, or because, as I believe, they do not really improve the lives of most Palestinians, except superficially. So if people could experience actual economic prosperity, then perhaps the current peace process might stand a better chance of long-range acceptance. No less important an issue in Amman was Israel's role as a newly powerful entrepreneurial force in the Arab world. To this end, a large number of Israeli businessmen appeared as part of the Israeli delegation, in effect looking for Arab business partners in enterprises that ran the full gamut from big industrial ventures to the manufacture of consumer products and the marketing of services.

The word "private" in such a context is somewhat misleading, since every independent businessman, Arab or Israeli, was there by virtue of a massive change in governmental policy. This change made it possible for the first time since 1948 for individual Palestinians and Israelis to cooperate in joint business ventures. So in effect the private sector followed the government's lead, acting within an area of economic activity for which prior protection and approval had been granted by politicians, not by businessmen acting on their own. But whether it admitted it or not, the delegation of Palestinian businessmen was acting to consolidate the asymmetries and discrepancies in power and advantage that now exist between Palestinians and Israelis as a result of Oslo, Cairo, Taba, plus of course a whole series of economic agreements that disadvantage Palestinians vis-à-vis Israelis.

Two arguments have been put forward by the business community to justify its sudden rush to investment and development—either alone or with Israeli business partners—in the autonomous zones. Both arguments depend on appeals to progress and development. The first argument takes as its point of departure the undoubted fact that the peace process has become a reality within which Palestinians now live on less than a quarter of the occupied territories, if not in an improved, then certainly in a different status; there they have some control over civil affairs, municipal functions, and internal security. Why not then use this different status to begin to establish businesses that would employ Palestinians, build a few institutions, and give them a chance at "trickle-down" prosperity? The second argument is more sophisticated, and even a little cynical. Since the Palestinian Authority can never be capable of fully controlling the economy, given that all it seems to be interested in is civil control and security, why not let it concentrate on those matters, and leave everything else to the private sector, which is supposedly made up of loyal, nationalistic Palestinians who want to help their people develop and have proved their ability in the Gulf, Europe, and elsewhere to do so efficiently and effectively? I have even heard a few Palestinian businessmen suggest that since Israelis want to come in on some of this activity, why not use their money and expertise in *our* favor?

Just before the big Amman meeting last May between Palestinian businessmen, Yasir Arafat, and King Hussein, I spoke to one of the prime movers, an extremely prosperous and influential Palestinian businessman behind all of this. I expressed my discomfort with various aspects of what the private sector was proposing, and I said that I found it difficult to accept the notion that what moved businessmen to invest in Gaza or the West Bank was altruistic nationalism. I pointed out that a probably temporary real estate and building boom had already begun, and that on its own it scarcely suggested a general improvement in the lives of all Palestinians. And when it came to large projects of national scope—electricity, telephones, roads, water—those had to be administered not by the private but by the public sector. I was told in response that this kind of thinking is now outdated, since with the demise of the Soviet Union, "socialist ideas were dead" and the economy was to be delivered back to private investors and private organizations. Gone are the days when a national authority was responsible for the infrastructure: even in the United States, I was reminded, electric companies and prisons in some states have been privatized. I responded with two arguments. No one has proved that privatization and "free" enterprise have actually improved services like electricity, transportation, and the penal system. The indications are in fact that rates have gone up, service has gotten worse, and in many instances the less advantaged citizen is not treated as well as a wealthy one. Second, and more important, deregulation in the United States exists in an environment and society of laws: there are federal commissions that oversee the stock market, the airline industry, power, transportation, and the media. In Gaza and the West Bank, there are no such provisions made for private sector investments. If a "public" electricity company is about to be established, the stockholders are going to be wealthy businessmen who can buy up and control all the shares, and can thereafter operate without regulatory or oversight committees who represent the interests of the consumer and indeed of the population at large. Besides, in an autocracy of the sort that now obtains in the Palestinian autonomy zones, the main requirement is that Mr. Arafat give his approval (as he has to so many dealmakers); there are no provisions for anything like public sector supervision, since the Chairman rules by personal fiat, not by constitution or by law.

Israel has a highly developed, aggressive economy; it has a relatively efficient public sector and, so far as its governmental strategy for the surrounding region is concerned, it has a definite plan to penetrate and enter markets, using its competitive edge plus its superior organization and economic as well as technological skills. The crucial thing is not just Israel's power, but its system of accountability, for which no

equivalent at all exists in the Arab world, and certainly not in Palestine. Contracts in Palestine are awarded by the ruler—as Mr. Arafat
has done—and a compact is set and maintained between the individual entrepreneur and the ruler. There is very little to inhibit or to
call to account the investor, except for the ruler's goodwill and short-
term interests. In the Palestinian context this vacuum is particularly
debilitating since, in the absence of independent institutions (courts,
citizens' groups, a relatively free media, etc.), it is the private sector
made up of individual, or groups of, businessmen which has the power
to control economic and commercial activity. And this sector, no matter how much its members say otherwise, is guided not by altruism or
nationalism, but by interests, profits, and the vagaries of the globalized economy. Very few of them have ever lived under a rigorously
administered tax code—indeed, one of the anomalous things about
the Arab world is that, to all intents and purposes, its business community is largely free of the burden of taxes of the kind paid by its
Japanese, European, and North American counterparts—and very
few of them are likely to do so in the new Palestine.

Finally, there are two serious misapprehensions on the part of
Arab businessmen who extol the virtues of the free market and an
unregulated private sector. One is that they wrongly compare themselves with Western businessmen who live and work in countries that
have a very vigorous civil society, with institutions like universities, the
media, an independent judiciary, a functioning parliament, and a
whole host of private citizens' groups (unions, associations, clubs,
etc.); there is no equivalent of this in the Arab world, and certainly
not in Palestine. Second, the middle class from which European and
American businessmen eventually emerged grew out of a long battle
with the feudal aristocracy; one of the results of this struggle was the
French Revolution, the bourgeois revolution as it has been called, that
was later to produce an internal social dynamic involving the new
class and remnants of the old. The new class not only produced
wealth and industrialization, but also culture, including the great realistic novel, scientific and philosophic societies, operas and concert
halls, philanthropies. All this constantly challenged or restricted the
power of the monarch or the executive. Such a development has not
occurred in the Arab world. Thus the Palestinian business community,

for example, has very little social advantage to its side, except for its alliance with the ruler and its money. Bound to and restrained neither by an active civil society nor by a flourishing culture, the private sector cannot, and indeed should not, be expected to provide the kind of moral and truly nationalist leadership which it claims it has the right to exercise. It is no wonder, then, that the Palestinian Authority—like other such bodies in the Third World—has decided that its allies are businessmen and its enemies are nongovernmental institutions, i.e., the institutions that make possible a genuine civil society. It is in opposing this situation that efforts should be placed, and not in unrestrained private investment. In other words, the real requirement for development is not simply capital but an awakened social consciousness and a serious interest in national *civil* institutions.

Al-Ahram Weekly, December 7, 1995
Al-Hayat, December 12, 1995

Chapter Six

Elections, Institutions, Democracy

I AM EXTRAORDINARILY GLAD that Samiha Khalil is running against Yasir Arafat in the upcoming Palestinian elections. A separate election is to be held for the position of *Ra'ees*. (Among its many ungenerous provisions, the Taba treaty doesn't allow the word President, only the ambiguous Arabic word for Chairman and President.) She is Arafat's only competitor, a tough, smart, energetic woman who has openly espoused the cause of the majority of Palestinians, those whose voices have not been heard, and who have been forgotten in the vulgar celebrations over "self-rule": women and children, the disinherited, prisoners, and all those whose lives have become worse as a result of the peace process. She seems particularly interested in righting the wrongs of the interim agreements which, she says with admirable clarity to the British journalist Graham Usher, do "not provide a just solution to the Palestinian question. The Israelis are still expropriating our lands . . . forcing us to live in isolated cantons. The so-called by-pass roads are separating one Palestinian area from another. Students in Gaza cannot travel freely to their universities in Bir Zeit, Hebron, Bethlehem, and Jerusalem. The prisoners are still in jail despite promises from the Israelis that they are going to be released. For these reasons, I am standing for election." When asked how her program differs from that of Yasir Arafat she responds with cool irony: "I am unaware of Chairman Arafat's program." This is perfectly true, since Arafat is running without any real program, in order simply to be confirmed as the head of everything.

Yet just because she has spoken out against autocracy and occupation—in both of which of course the Palestinian Authority has already acquiesced—Ms. Khalil has opened a small window in the elections. Arafat will (and did) surely win, although thanks to his opponent's courage he will not get 99.6 percent of the votes; he will of course gain a sizeable majority, and this will allow him to say that he now represents all Palestinians democratically. This is pure nonsense. The election law agreed upon with the Israelis suits him and them: it is by no means an instance of real democracy, however. Through a joint Israeli-Palestinian Liaison Committee (controlled by the Israelis, who have veto power) every voter is registered according to his or her Israeli identification number; this also means that every voter has been cleared by the Israelis. Every candidate of the seven hundred now running for the Legislative Council must also be approved by Israel. No racists, terrorists, or opponents of the peace process are allowed to run; on the other hand, Israel is not reciprocally obligated to exclude Israelis who hold racist or anti-peace views from running in Knesset elections. It is the Israelis and Yasir Arafat who alone and unilaterally can decide who is excluded, who is included.

On January 1 Eric Lidbom, chair of the Electoral Unit of the European Union, issued a statement from Ramallah entitled "Enough is Enough." In it he accused the Authority (in effect Mr. Arafat) of tampering with the elections so as to undermine their credibility internationally as well as domestically. Arafat increased the number of candidates from eighty-two to eighty-eight (most of them from Gaza, whose population did not suddenly increase). He shortened the three-week campaign period by almost two weeks, then suddenly restored it. He did not name the supposedly independent Central Electoral Commission until late in December. The group was supposed to be appointed three months ago to take charge of regulating the elections, making sure that fairness prevailed, looking into complaints about abuses and infractions. It was also supposed to be composed of distinguished jurists and, more important, well-known independents, men and women whose credentials were above party or commercial interests. Not only did Arafat name the Commission several weeks late, but he put at its head Abu Mazen (Mahmoud Abbas), his second-in-command, a man with no known experience in law or elections or impartiality. No complaints have been dealt with. Almost without exception the members of the Commission are either employees or have some direct connection with the Palestinian Authority. This is hardly a guarantee of fairness.

To make matters worse, Abu Mazen refused to meet with the European Unit. Thus Abu Mazen's unavailability made it impossible for Lidbom's people to find out more about all the irregularities whose purpose, it is obvious, was to give Arafat more control over the result of the elections. It is worth quoting Lidbom directly:

> *At such a meeting [had Mr. Abbas made it possible] [I] would have listened with interest to an explanation of why the Central Election Commission was not set up much earlier and why none of the allocations of seats was issued in the name of the Central Election Commission, the supreme body organizing the elections, which was given that specific task in the Election Law. The first allocations of seats was done instead by Presidential Decree, and the number of seats has subsequently changed twice also by Presidential Decree. [I] would also have welcomed reassurances from Mr. Abbas about the political independence of the Central Elections Committee.*

The sarcasm in these lines is plainly evident. To people who know Arafat and Abu Mazen, and have had direct experience of their contempt for democratic procedure and for citizens who are genuinely concerned about it, their actions come as no surprise. For them, Palestinian leaders do what they wish, without any regard for accountability or democracy. Ever since the Oslo process began, this has been their practice, which no one has been able to change. Why should they now do otherwise? Besides, neither one nor the other has ever participated in a free election, so it is quite clear that for them the January 20 elections are simply a public display of going through the motions, without any risk for them. Most of the candidates are either linked to Fateh (Arafat's party) or to leading families, groups that Mr. Arafat finds it easier to deal with. In addition, the very fact that there are elections—no matter how flawed and unfair they may be—guarantees his Authority some international prestige. Jimmy Carter will be there to say predictably (as he did in Haiti) that democracy has finally come to Palestine. And perhaps the international donors will pay out a little more money.

In the meantime Arafat continues to run things as a personal fiefdom. The imprisonments of Maher al-Alami and Bassam Eid were grossly unfair and brutal, but they were also almost comic (not to the prisoners of course) indications of how far the Chairman will go to reinforce his personal will against his own people. The idea that a journalist like Alami was punished for putting praise of Arafat on page three instead of page one of *al-Quds* is grotesque, and shows a further degeneration in Arafat's rule. There is no freedom of the press under Arafat, who clearly wants to reduce the media to his personal mouthpieces. That so many decent journalists nevertheless go along with this is a sad commentary on Palestinian ideas of independence and free speech.

But the worst thing, which the elections will not help, is that economically the condition of most Palestinians (especially in Gaza) has deteriorated steadily since Oslo. Twenty percent of the population there lives below the poverty line (about $650 per capita per year); Sara Roy, the American researcher at Harvard's Center for Middle East Studies, who knows more about Gaza's economy than anyone else, says that 33 percent of the Palestinian poor were forced into poverty *after* the Oslo accord was finalized. Unemployment is sometimes over 50 percent and, Roy says, the number of poor exceeds by 74 percent the number now being helped by the Authority's Ministry of Social Affairs and UNRWA (United Nations Relief and Works Agency). Each Gaza family now spends 58 percent of its income on food, and the overall Gaza economy loses $3 million a day because of Israeli strictures.

One of the main reasons for so terrible an economic deterioration is the sheer cost of Arafat's rule through his police force, plus his seven, eight, or nine security apparatuses (no one is quite sure how many he has established for himself) and his over four thousand secret agents throughout the West Bank and Gaza, who spy on the population. Raji Sourani, the Gaza human rights lawyer who was imprisoned

by Arafat last year, estimates that there are now twenty thousand security men for the 1 million residents of Gaza; at one policeman per fifty
people, this is the highest police per capita ratio in the world. The
total number of police throughout the self-rule areas is close to thirty
thousand (and still rising), which costs the Palestinian economy about
$500 million a year. This is a totally unproductive, albeit by far
the largest, economic sector, which is already $150 million in debt.
Because Arafat spends so much money on police he has nothing left to
spend on housing, education, health, and welfare. It is difficult to
imagine how the Palestinian elections can change this situation, since
Arafat and his candidates are running on a purely "Palestinian" platform that simply does not address the basic control of the self-rule
areas by Arafat. He would like to go on doing so after the elections,
and of course will claim that he has "the people's" support for what
he does. In effect, however, he will be fulfilling Israel's program for
keeping order—and Israel's security—in the occupied territories.

Nevertheless, the *idea* of elections introduces something new in
Palestinian life. I think we should remember first of all that the Arab
and Third Worlds are full of elections that have consolidated more
undemocratic regimes than one would care to mention. Even so, this
does not invalidate the idea of elections, which at least promise the
likelihood and even desirability of democratic change. The problem
with elections in Palestine and the Arab world now is that they have
the status of a ritual that takes place once in a while, without resulting
in democratic change. How many rulers or ruling parties have been
seriously affected by elections? Most institutions in our societies operate as immense, glacier-like structures, with one person (or a small
group) more or less permanently in charge; this is why our universities
are substandard and why no important work of real consequence has
emerged from them in the social and natural sciences. Scientific and
humanistic research require a relatively open environment in which to
flourish, an environment in which researchers can say things without
fear that doing so might endanger their lives or jobs.

Second, for elections to work they must be part of a continuing
dynamic in which the government is entirely accountable to citizens
who have the right to vote and thereby directly affect the government's
performance. For this we need a functioning civil society, with trade

and professional associations, an independent judiciary, a relatively free press, and a well-endowed education system. None of these of course exists in Palestine today, and it is one of the greatest drawbacks in Mr. Arafat's style of authority that he has neither the capacity nor the vision to understand that Palestine must aspire to be a society, not simply the reflection of his personal will.

I wish I could participate in the upcoming Palestinian elections, if only to vote for Samiha Khalil and her program of social and economic change. But being unable to do so, I can at least hope that the idea of elections at the very least promises the possibility of change. And this idea is going to make things slightly harder for the present Palestinian Authority to go on exactly as before. Perhaps people will ask more questions, issue more challenges, demand more answers. But my real hope is that the elections might also make it slightly more difficult for Yasir Arafat and his trusted men to govern as they please, with no respect for the people they supposedly serve.

Al-Ahram Weekly, January 18, 1996
Al-Hayat, January 19, 1996

Chapter Seven

Post-Election Realities

For two or three days around January 20, 1996, the Western media had a picnic discussing, celebrating, and echoing one another over the Palestinian elections. At most there was an admission that the elections were part of a "complex" reality, although the very fact that they took place seemed to be quite enough of a good thing, without anyone's bothering too much about the actual circumstances (i.e., the Israeli occupation and the Arafatian autocracy) that seriously flawed them. At least, there was an underlying journalistic assumption that, as a lesser people, the Palestinians could expect nothing more; the presence of a few foreign celebrities like Jimmy Carter added a little polish to the otherwise depressing occasion, and the disingenuousness of Arab-American "expert" James Zogby heaped more tinsel on the forced gaiety of the occasion. Zogby, who claimed that for thirty years he has observed elections in Chicago, New York, Detroit, and Philadelphia, said expansively that there were hardly any irregularities, and that the elections were free and fair. Zogby knows no Arabic, is a defender of Arafat and his peace process, and could hardly have been exposed—despite his thirty years experience—to what really went on at all the voting stations all over the self-rule areas.

That there was a dramatic level of participation is undeniable, and reflects a deep-seated, indeed urgent, wish on the part of Palestinians for a change to take hold of their fate. That was the main positive thing about the elections. That there were no political parties or real platforms, that Arafat—like every other dictator—made himself and his minions into the inevitable winners, that undeserving candidates (like Marwan Kanafani, with no real constituency—what would his constituency be in any case?) emerged, that fraud was practiced, and that the Legislative Council still had no really defined duties: all these were the negatives, which effectively buttressed the Israeli plan for the occupied territories. Arafat was to continue to be their enforcer; the Israeli army and settlers remained in charge and would demonstrate their authority and brutality at will. Shimon Peres reminded Arafat that his talk of a Palestinian state was a dream, with no basis in fact. And then he asked sarcastically what more the Palestinians wanted, since he had given them a small autonomous area (with Israeli sovereignty); how could they want more? he added.

After three days of international attention, the Palestinian story disappeared. Undeterred, Arafat, who takes himself very seriously indeed, had himself sworn in on February 12, as a way of preempting the Council, which has still not met; this added more fantasy to the pathos of the occasion. The egregious Mahmoud Abbas (Abu Mazen) declared that the newly elected council would soon declare an independent Palestinian state, as if everyone had forgotten that in November 1988 an independent state had, in fact, been declared by the National Council in Algiers. How many declarations of a state are required before the state—like the genie—finally appears, and why must Aladdin frantically rubbing his lamp be our model for everything we do?

That the Israelis are not readers of the *Thousand and One Nights* became clear both during and after the elections. They prevented all but four thousand of the sixty thousand registered Jerusalem voters from actually voting. In the month since the elections they have closed Ramallah, Bir Zeit, and Bethlehem for all sorts of "security" reasons, the net effect of which was to show Palestinians that, despite elections and Yasir Arafat's eloquent declarations, they were the masters. Nearly every day since January 20 a Palestinian has been killed by the Israelis; land confiscations and settlement building continue; and repeated violations of the Oslo agreements have occurred. All of this, by the way, and the West Bank gets chopped up further; in mid-February, for example, a security fence was built between Qalqilya and Tul Karem. Gaza is more depressed economically than it has ever been; unemployment is higher than a year ago; speculators and real estate sharks have used the land for their own benefit while thousands of refugees inhabit the appalling hovels of Shatti and Jabalya camps. Not for want of money, though. Roughly forty to fifty million dollars flows in every month, but nobody except the Boss of Bosses knows where the money goes, or is entitled to make any inquiries about it. Most of it goes for his eight or nine security forces. In addition, he now has formed a commercial company with Khalid Slam, and this has become an instrument for skimming money off local enterprises. In short, the autonomy areas are like a Mafia territory, run by a party at the expense of the entire population. Force, beatings, imprisonments, and threats rule, not law. And this, we are asked to believe, is the foundation of a Palestinian state.

Not to be outdone, "dovish" Israelis like that visionary of peace Peres, and his smooth-talking deputy Yossi Beilin, are beginning to campaign on the basis of a platform that takes the Oslo accords as the final settlement. I can do no better than to quote the respected Israeli commentator Haim Baram:

> Most Israelis, Likud supporters included, treat the Oslo accords agreements as a fait accompli, and brace themselves for the final phase. Yossi Beilin, Peres' main ally in the cabinet, is consolidating the new consensus. Most settlers will stay put; Israel will continue to deal with Yasir Arafat, expecting him to erase the Palestinian Charter and to fight "Islamic terrorism" on Israel's behalf; Israel will maintain the River Jordan as a line of defence, and no settlement in the Jordan Valley is to be dismantled; the huge settlement of Ma'aleh Edumim is to be annexed; united Jerusalem [which constitutes twenty-five percent of the West Bank] will be the "eternal capital" of Israel.

As against these harsh realities backed up by Israeli power and resolve, Arafat's strutting and posturing and declarations amount to very little indeed. Even if Israel were to be deterred or stopped from going through with the current Labor plan, a real Palestinian state cannot emerge from so rotten, so hopelessly corrupt and incompetent a start as this. At this point I do not think it is even enough if Arafat were to resign (which he should have done several years ago). The disease infecting our society is very deep, since most of us by now have lost the ability to discriminate between fact and fantasy. Thus language has lost its meaning: when you have a leadership that has led the Palestinian people from one disaster to another, from Amman, to Beirut, to Tunis, to Baghdad, to Gaza, all the time proclaiming its new victories, something has very seriously gone wrong in the Palestinian psyche, which seems to have an almost unlimited toleration for the follies of our great leaders. At what point does stupid loyalty end and serious questioning begin?

Israel can never want anything better than a leader like Arafat who concedes everything to them just to save his own skin; who since 1982 has rarely had the stomach to fight and even suffer for his people's rights, but rather gives in at the slightest offer of a token symbol of his continued autocracy; and who will never be able to convert himself into a serious opponent of the nation, Israel, which had dispossessed his people, occupied its territory, and oppressed Palestinians and treated them with contempt for half a century. As with most things in politics, the issue between them and us is a moral one, not strictly a matter of how many tanks or planes they have. Our leaders never behave with the conviction of their own right: indeed, Arafat shamelessly used the White House platform offered him in 1993 to utter a cringing, whimpering speech, full of apologies and half truths offered up to Israel and the United States, who continue to oppress his people to this day. I should like to remind my readers that Nelson Mandela, whose organization had been completely defeated by the South African regime, whose colleagues were either in exile or killed, and who himself was a state security prisoner for twenty-seven years, never compromised on the truth of his struggle, which was to hold out without change in the original political goal of one person, one vote. It was that, and neither an air force nor secret decisions made with Beilin or Sarid, that brought about the defeat of apartheid, which was morally confounded and compelled in the end to submit to the greater truth of the *human* power of Mandela's courage and principle.

We have no sense of that at all. Language no longer means anything to a tyrant who boasts about building airports and insists that
he be compared with Omar Ibn el Khattab and surrounds himself
with sycophants, and outright crooks, all in the name of an "independent" Palestine. Unfortunately I cannot understand why our intellectuals and people of conscience, with a few exceptions like Haidar
Abdel Shafi, go along with this comedy, pretending to believe in a
peace process that with the passing of every day indicts itself for the
unjust situation that it really is. When I first met Professor Israel Shahak years ago, he told me, from the standpoint of a fearless critic of
Israeli policies against Palestinians, that the PLO never understood
Israeli society. Recently he told me that the reason Israel respects and
fears Hizballah and Hafez el Assad is that Israelis respect strength,
especially if their opponents are courageous enough to hurt them,
militarily or morally. The PLO mentality, he said quite correctly, wants
favors from Israel, does not confront it (except for the intifada, which
Arafat conveniently enough finished off for Israel). Of course that
attitude of supine servility, which always accompanies the feelings of
someone whose main concern is not the good of his people but of his
own survival and profit, communicates itself to our Israeli enemies
(whom Arafat persists in calling his "friends" even as those "friends"
continue to take his people's land and occupy their territories without
respite), and the net result is the Oslo peace process, one of whose
main components is humiliation, letting Palestinians feel that Israel
can do what it wants, when it wants, however it wants.

I have been criticized for being too pessimistic and for not present-
ing alternatives. Well, let me be very plain: the only alternative to what
we have now is a serious attention to the meaning of words, a proper
belief in the right of our cause, and an end to the rule of the present
leadership.

We have never learned how to build our power as a people, to build
and to accumulate. Our leaders historically have only been interested
in their authority over us, not in self-sacrifice nor in a winning strategy
that puts the good of the whole over the wishes of the few. In effect
this has meant that we are still without institutions—since despots
think of institutions as a threat to their power—and we have done
very little to construct a functioning society that can grow and

develop. One would have to be a fool to deny the unimaginably difficult circumstances in which we find ourselves as a people—divided,
scattered, without real independence anywhere. But we must first have
a serious and collective critique of the policies and the leaders that
brought us to this pass, and we must be able to assign considerable
responsibility to ourselves and our failings, not just to our enemies
and their conspiracies. As I said, this cannot be done unless we use
language and reason to address the reality, responsibly and seriously. It
is no use saying that we have a "state" when in reality we are about as
far from one as we have ever been. Arafat and his partners use words
as if they lived in a dream of their own making; Peres was not wrong.
When will we wake up?

Al-Hayat, March 1, 1996

Chapter Eight

The Campaign Against "Islamic Terror"

AT A MOMENT of considerable Anglo-Indian tension in 1926, the British missionary and intellectual Edward Thompson (father of E. P. Thompson, the great historian of the British working-class movement) published *The Other Side of the Medal*, a small book that dealt very critically with British colonial policy in India. One of the points he made in his eloquently anti-imperialist tract is that writings about India in English—even in so authoritative a source as the *Oxford History of India*—simply left out the Indian side of things; this, Thompson says, further deepens the irreconcilability between Indians and the British and makes unlikely any hope of reconciliation and understanding between the two sides. Most British historians of India, for example, described the famous "Mutiny" of 1857 as a barbarous, terroristic attack on defenseless women and children, thereby converting the Indian into a savage barbarian to whom the only response was force. Thompson points out that for Indians the "Mutiny" was in fact a rebellion in their struggle against the British, provoked by generations of punishing colonization, racist discrimination, and savage imperial repression of Indian independence.

What was unusual about Thompson's book, however, is that he was one of the first to grasp that when great political and military power is translated into language that misrepresents the weak and the oppressed—as in "official" histories or declarations—even so relatively innocuous a thing as language can have a tremendously wound-

44

ing effect on the object of that description. "Our misrepresentation of Indian history and character is one of the things that have so alienated the educated classes of India that even their moderate elements have refused to help the Reforms [of colonial policy]. Those measures, because of this sullenness, have failed, when they deserved a better fate."

Change Thompson's context and time, substitute "peace process" for "Reforms," Palestinians and Arabs for Indians, and Israelis for British, and you have an accurate account of the present impasse. Great, deliberately bloody and indiscriminately violent actions like the 1857 Mutiny or the recent bombings in Jerusalem and Tel Aviv are ugly, indefensible things; they sacrifice the lives of Israelis and Palestinians as they did Indians and Europeans; they induce more hatred and feelings of revenge; and, for the stronger party, they inevitably produce savage retaliation against the whole population of Palestinians. "Kill the Arabs" was a frequently heard refrain among ordinary Israelis, much as "Kill the Indians" was the chorus of 1857.

The bombs that killed sixty Israeli civilians were morally unacceptable, quite aside from the fact that they were strategically unproductive. Cynical manipulations of religion are appalling: to kill children or bus passengers in the name of God is a horror to be unconditionally condemned, as much as one should also condemn leaders who send young people on suicide missions. But there has been little more obdurate and arrogant than the Israeli and American response, with its sanctimonious choruses against terrorism, Hamas, Islamic fundamentalism, and its equally odious hymns to peacemaking, the peace process, and the peace of the brave. The grotesque display of bad faith, graceless posturing, and for Clinton and Peres, brazen electioneering that was the Sharm el Sheikh summit simply made the contradictions even more glaring. Here were Israel and the United States, whose military record of imperialist behavior in the postwar world is virtually unrivaled for its lawlessness, wrapping themselves in the mantle of moralism and self-congratulation, even as lumbering figures like Boris Yeltsin—who has been terrorizing Muslim Chechnyans for several years—were allowed to draw down some of the event's counterfeit aura for themselves.

The fact is that the peace process has been an offense to the

Palestinian spirit. Each declaration of its virtue, each resounding compliment paid to it, each parade and celebratory event, has reminded
Palestinians of how their history as the native inhabitants of Palestine who were deliberately kicked off their own land, their society
destroyed, the West Bank and Gaza kept under military occupation
for twenty-nine years, has been ignored, violated, misrepresented. Terrorism is bred out of poverty, desperation, a sense of powerlessness
and utter misery: it signals the failure of politics and vision.

On the other hand, Israel has behaved with no understanding or
magnanimity at all. It has conducted open war against the very same
people it now appears to be making peace with; it has violated even
the niggling provisions of the Oslo accords; and it has shown its open
contempt for Palestinian society and its leaders, not only by pretending that the Palestinian presence in Palestine never existed, but by continuing to intervene in Palestinian life, assassinating leaders at will,
using its military might to destroy homes, shut schools, arrest and
deport anyone it feels is a "threat" to its "security." It is simply extraordinary and without precedent that Israel's history, its record—from
the fact that it introduced terrorism against civilians to the Middle
East, that it is a state built on conquest, that it has invaded surrounding countries, bombed and destroyed at will, to the fact that it currently occupies Lebanese, Syrian, and Palestinian territory against
international law—is simply never cited, never subjected to scrutiny in
the U.S. media or in official discourse (by Clinton and Warren Chris-
topher most notably), never addressed as playing any role at all in
provoking "Islamic terror."

What has made the events of the past few weeks even more dreadful is that Israel and the United States, deliberately using the weapons
of mass media, psychological warfare, and political pressure, have
also been leading a campaign against Islam (with Iran as its main
agent) as the origin of terror and "fundamentalism." Consider the
background. Ever since the collapse of the Soviet Union there has been
an active search in the United States for new official enemies, a search
which has now come to settle on "Islam" as a manufactured opponent. True, there are ancient rivalries between the West and Islam, and
there has been a massive amount of rhetoric in the Islamic, especially
Arab, world against the West, plus a whole array of parties, leaders,

and ideological trends for whom the Great Satan is the United States as the West's repulsive embodiment. In addition, recent bloodshed in Algeria, Sudan, Egypt, Syria, Iraq, and elsewhere, in which one source of conflict is a brutalizing manipulation of religion, has totally corrupted the Arab world's civil life.

But this has to be seen along with the long history of imperial Western intervention in the Islamic world, the continued assault upon its culture and traditions as a standard feature of academic and popular discourse, and (perhaps most important) the frank disdain with which the wishes and aspirations of Muslims, but particularly Arabs, are treated. There are now American and Israeli armies settled on Arab soil, but no Arab or Muslim armies in the West; few Arabs or Muslims in the West feel like anything except hated terrorists. Official Israeli discourse has taken advantage of all this. During the 1970s it was a staple of Israeli foreign affairs jargon that Palestinians were always to be identified with terrorism. Now, in the same cynical and calculated manner, both Israel and the United States identify fundamentalist Islam—a label that is often compressed into the one word "Islam"—with opposition to the peace process, to Western interests, to democracy, and to Western civilization.

I do not want to be understood as saying that all this amounts to a conspiracy, although I do think that there is active collusion between Israel and the United States in terms of planning, conceptualization, and now, since Sharm el Sheikh, grand strategy. What they both want is compliance, in effect, an Islamic and Arab world that has simply resigned itself (as many of its leaders already have) to the dictates of the Pax Americana-Israelica. In my opinion one can only *obey* such dictates as these; one cannot have a dialogue with them, since according to their most basic underlying premise, the grand strategy regards Muslims and Arabs as fundamentally delinquent. Only when Muslims totally fall into line, speak the same language, take the same measures as Israel and the United States do, can they be expected to be "normal," at which point of course they are no longer really Arab and Muslim. They have simply become "peacemakers." What a pity that so noble an idea as "peace" has become a corrupted embellishment of power masquerading as reconciliation.

The evidence for the existence of such a grand strategy is

compelling. In 1991 the *Washington Post* leaked news of a continuing
study in the U.S. defense and intelligence establishment of the need to
find a new common enemy: Islam was the candidate. Many of the
authoritative foreign policy journals, seminars, newspapers of record
have held symposia, published articles and studies proclaiming the
threat of Islam. In addition, feature films as well as television documentaries have also trumpeted the threat. Judith Miller among several
others is one of the leaders of the journalistic effort; Bernard Lewis
and his students, many of them Israeli, lead the so-called scholarly
effort. Samuel Huntington's famous article on the clash of civilizations put forward the much-debated thesis that certain civilizations
are incompatible with the West, Islamic civilization (sometimes in
alliance with Confucian culture, an extremely quaint idea) being the
central instance. What hasn't been noted about Huntington's article is
that its title came from Bernard Lewis, and that most of its pages are
in fact devoted to Islam as a Western enemy. Finally, the Fundamentalism Project of the American Academy of Arts and Sciences has made
Islam the preferred candidate for demon status in that study; neither
Jewish nor Christian, not to mention Slavic or Hindu, fundamentalism gets much comparative attention. By now the media equates Islam
with terror and fundamentalism, so that no matter where a bomb goes
off in the world, the first suspects are always Muslim and/or Arabs.

What I have described is only part of the phenomenon. Not
only are there newsletters, clubs, continuing seminars in the most
unlikely places devoted exclusively to Islamic—the word itself has
acquired the bristling status of a frightening, irrational monster—
politics and activities. Every article published about Hamas or Islamic
fundamentalism or Iran—about which it is now nearly impossible to
speak rationally—describes an ahistorical world of pure despotism,
pure rage, pure violence, all of it in some way targeting "us," a group
of innocent victims who happen to ride buses or go about some harm-
less daily business, as unconnected with the decades of suffering
imposed on an entire people. There is never an indication at all that
for centuries there has been one form or another of Western infringe-
ment directed against the land and peoples of Islam. Long articles by
instant experts create the impression that Hamas flourishes gratu-
itously or because of Iran for no other ascertainable reason at all,

except to attack Jews and the West. Few of those who fulminate against terrorism mention the occupation or the constant attacks on Arabs and Muslims.

A few days ago the veteran French journalist Eric Rouleau appeared on a national discussion TV program with the former head of the CIA, James Wolsey, and Geoffrey Kemp, a so-called "terrorism expert." Kemp and Wolsey were asked by the moderator about the Sharm el Sheikh summit and both spoke with great effusiveness and enthusiasm about its value; Rouleau tried three times to explain the "context" that produced Hamas, but the moderator never gave him a chance to say a word. All anyone wanted was proof that "we" were opposing Islamic terrorism and feeling good about it. Moreover, no one bothered to point out that Hamas's quarrel with the "peace process" has from the beginning been advanced on nationalist, rarely on Islamic, principles. Thus Huntington's thesis, which in my opinion amounts to a blanket declaration of war against all civilizations that do not conform to Western values, is now being put into effect.

The worst aspect of all this is that the United States–Israeli strategy risks turning Arab governments into collaborators in the effort against an ever-increasing number of their own people. I am not sure how many are conscious of what is happening, but I am certain it is happening. On a popular level, the policy threatens to rob us of our memory and of our past, so that we will be faced with the choice of either coming into the American fold, which humanly offers very little (the terribly compromised peace process is an excellent instance of one reward), or remaining outside, stripped of everything except the terrorist-fundamentalist identity and therefore subject to intimidation, boycott, and perhaps even extermination. In my opinion this is what makes the efforts of groups like Hamas so futile, since they offer no real resistance to the whole plan I have been describing, although they do in effect cause the collective punishment that jeopardizes the interests of the majority of the people.

Peace and dialogue can occur only between equals. The general condition of the Arab world has never been weaker and more mediocre: we have no institutions, no science, no coordination, no counterstrategy. Most people are now indifferent or despondent. The rise of Islamic militancy is a symptom of how deplorable things are. Yet there is no short road, no easy fix for our present predicament. It falls once again to intellectuals and men and women of conscience to speak rationally of what is really before us as a people. We must avoid easy formulas, and misleading displays like the recent summit, which make hypocrites of all of us. Analysis, dedication, and a decent, realizable vision: that is what we need to build ourselves up to a position where we can truly engage in dialogue, where we can really show those who speak for the West and Israel that we cannot tolerate our present status either as angry religious terrorists or as compliant Red Indians.

Al-Ahram Weekly, March 21, 1996
Al-Hayat, March 24, 1996
Dagens Nyheter, April 13, 1996
The Progressive, May 1996

Chapter Nine

Modernity, Information, and Governance

FOR WEEKS THE American press has been full of articles about the Israeli elections. A few days ago half of New York was shut down because of an immense Fifth Avenue parade in support of Israel, although it was meant to be a routine celebration of the country's Independence Day. The most recent issue of the weekly *New Yorker* magazine carried an admiring profile of Ehud Barak, whose exploits as a commando killing Palestinian leaders in Beirut and Tunis are described with the kind of innocent zeal that I had last encountered in Kipling's *Jungle Books*. Wherever one turns there is a reminder that Israel now occupies a place in American imaginative and political life that has no equal; even Europe and the Orient seem to have lost their aura of importance when compared with Israel's. I vividly recall a few phone conversations I had some years ago with Seymour Hersh, the former *New York Times* correspondent who was celebrated for his courage in taking on Henry Kissinger, the My Lai massacre, and other "difficult" subjects that he tackled without regard for consequences. He was beginning a piece on the United States–Israel relationship, which, he told me in typical Hersh style, would deal with a lot of intelligence material (including the U.S.S. *Liberty* case in 1967) that had defied every other reporter. "I've already done a lot of research," he said to me in one conversation, "and it is absolutely staggering how deep the relationship is. What you already know is less than 10 percent of what there is. Most of the rest is so secret and so profound that even I am surprised."

What he subsequently published was a watered-down version of some of the things he told me, since his book turned out to be about Israel's nuclear option, unfortunately not a very surprising topic. He had obviously thought better of his earlier plan, since the consequences of exposing the Israeli–United States relationship in too much detail would have been prohibited. I found myself echoing Hersh's hushed accents of awe, as I started to reflect on the extent to which Israel is now so interlocked with the United States on every level: military, political, economic, cultural, scientific, and ideological. I certainly do not have the information he suggested he had, but it is a fact that when it comes to thinking about the Middle East today, Israel's concerns, perspectives, views, and purposes set the tone, determine the agenda, dominate the discussion, no matter whether the Israeli Right or Left is in power. The United States simply accommodates.

As a small example of what I mean, there was a series of recent articles on the West Bank and Gaza published in the *New York Times* by Anthony Lewis, a famous liberal columnist, who has had the courage over the years to be critical of Israel's Palestinian policies. I do not think it is important that Lewis happens to be Jewish, since his views correspond with those of many liberal Americans who are non-Jews. In any event, he has been writing about his experiences with moderate Palestinians in Gaza and Ramallah, who have reported to Lewis the horrors of the closures instituted by Israel, as well as the land confiscations, humiliations, and general misery all around that have resulted from the peace process as administered by the famous "dove," Shimon Peres. Now none of these views is particularly unusual; anyone coming from Gaza or the West Bank would have voiced them routinely. Lewis, on the other hand, is deeply impressed since, he says, he had not thought that way before. What he does not explicitly say is that the Israeli Labor Party view of the peace process is the authorized one, because of which it has been impossible even to think about Oslo *except* as a good thing. Thus Israel speaks for and in a sense represents Palestinians in what Israel has considered to be a decently advantageous peace process.

An ironic result of Lewis's reporting has been that Iyad al-Serraj, the prominent Gaza physician and human rights activist, was imprisoned and tortured by Arafat. This is a perfect example of why it is that today Arab societies and their rulers—we must not detach them from each other, as one in effect produces and is a mirror image of the other—have given backwardness and underdevelopment a new sort of clarity. Arafat's model of rule is based entirely on coercion and personal gain: what he does not like or he thinks opposes him must be blotted out, made to disappear, put behind bars. It has not occurred to him, as an erstwhile disciple of Saddam Hussein, that people and societies do not work that simply, and that the only way to deal with something you don't like is to put it away is an assumption that cannot forever be maintained. Such is the power of human thought and resourcefulness that Serraj's courage and arrest may in fact create more courage, protest, and resistance among Palestinians, not less, as Arafat believes. To the Palestinian Authority everything—including human rights—must be sacrificed to a willful image of "the peace process." Only thus will Arafat survive, he believes, and in this way he will be carried along with his Israeli mirror-image, the elusive Peres.

In the overall media context shaped by the United States, Shimon Peres has been seen as the man who must win the elections, if the country is going to remain a bastion of democracy and progress. In the short run, therefore, U.S. foreign policy in the Middle East was based almost exclusively on helping Peres to win. In effect this meant that whatever he did, he received unconditional U.S. support. A Likud victory (always, in my opinion, more likely) was considered to be a catastrophe that would threaten the peace process, undermine U.S. influence, produce a ruinous instability in the region. The paradox is of course that with a Netanyahu victory U.S. policy would most probably take on his agenda (as it did Shamir's for years), and continue an extremely high level of support for Israel. The odd thing is that all the Arab leaders have believed the same thing about the importance of a Peres victory; they have accordingly done everything in their power *not* to make it hard for him. This was shamefully evident when more than one hundred refugees were killed in a UN tent during the bombing of Southern Lebanon in "Operation Grapes of Wrath" in April 1996. At that time, except for a few popular demonstrations in Arab capitals, the official response to Israel's criminality and ruthlessness was, to put it mildly, muted. Even Yasir Arafat, under whose authority Palestinians have continued to lose land, essential economic power, and social progress to Israel's "peace" policy under Peres, thinks his main priority as Palestinian leader is to support Peres in the elections.

In all this, Israeli propaganda has achieved an important success. It has made opposition to its policies (including the closures, and military operations) seem tantamount to opposing peace; it has convinced the world that it is striving for peace, although of course it wages war; it has elevated itself and its four million citizens to the central focal point of the Arab and Muslim world, which comprise two hundred million and one billion respectively; it has compelled the Palestinian leadership to believe that any unnecessary resistance on its part will upset Peres, and weaken his appeal to the electorate, as if the Israeli electorate were the only one that counted. A report in *Davar* by the respected Israeli journalist Daniel Ben-Simon on May 10 states that at Taba the Israeli negotiators not only insisted on seeing Abu Mazen's speech before he gave it, but also changed and rewrote most of it the night before he delivered it. All this was supposed to be about helping Peres to help the peace process.

Such excesses give a new meaning to preserving the status quo, which used to signify holding on to what one has, but which now means aggressively robbing your peace partner (with his help) in order to secure more gains for yourself at his expense. In the meantime even a semblance of Arab solidarity has been dissipated, with the result that innocent Lebanese civilians are murdered wantonly while their leaders in the leading capitals either look the other way or press on with business as usual.

Were this lamentable state of affairs simply the result of Israeli military power and the ascendancy of Likud, it would be possible to say that Arab defeatism was perhaps inevitable. But it is not that. The real issues are human and moral. These *are* capable of being addressed if we retain and are willing to employ our rudimentary capacities of rationality and will. Israel's pre-eminence is first of all the result of work and organization dedicated to one main task, over time giving Israel assent in the minds not only of its citizens, but over many Americans and Arabs. For this task Israel's supporters understood something essential to modern politics which has so far escaped the Arabs: namely, that a policy of persuasion and consent where information and communication are concerned is much more effective in the long run than insistent propaganda based on falsehood and exaggeration. This is not to say that the Western media, for example, are totally free and independent; they are not, of course, since they operate according to the economic and ideological constraints of the giant corporations (owned by people like Rupert Murdoch) that run them. But their methods are to try to seduce consumers of the news by employing simplified, appealing images actually based on reality which win approval with minimum resistance on the part of American newspaper readers and TV viewers. In five decades Israel has solidified its position as a peace-loving state surrounded by vicious enemies who want to exterminate the Jews. Israel never attacks; it "retaliates" in "self-defense." Israel values human life; Israel is a Western country; Israel is necessary for the defense of Western values against fundamentalist, terrorist Islam.

There is a further effectiveness to this information policy. The global economy is undergoing a massive shift in the northern countries away from industrial production toward knowledge production. By the last part of this century 60 percent of the GNP in the United States was based not on steel, coal, and automobile manufacture but on the goods and services offered by computers, high-speed electronic communication, media, management, and consultancies. It became possible to use labor-intensive Third World countries like Nicaragua, Mexico, Malaysia, and China to produce the consumer goods (clothing, furniture, TV sets, automobile parts, etc.) which were planned for and managed in the West. And governments themselves relied more on the media and the distribution of images than they did on direct coercion and police forces, although in the United States there is now a political reaction to this insofar as it has become necessary to regulate the permanent underclass in Black or Hispanic urban ghettoes by brutal police violence.

The revolution according to Ronald Reagan entirely finished the mainstream media as a really independent force in society; they were turned into extensions of power, never more evident than during the Gulf War, when they fought Operation Desert Storm as a department of the U.S. military. The collusion between most U.S. journalists and corporate or governmental authority is now almost complete. Alternative views are marginalized as "minority" or "extreme" while powerful white male pundits and Washington "insiders" play golf with the President. News has become a branch of entertainment in which celebrities like Dan Rather or Peter Jennings, indistinguishable from each other as to content, compete for the title of most reliable newsman, as if reading the news from a prepared script had anything to do with journalism or truth.

In this situation Israel has again managed to maintain its public image. (Israel has benefited from every change in the international system and it does the same thing with changes in the media systems.) A mere three weeks after its murderous attack on Lebanon, Israel is now at the center of things, as the elections have seized world attention (largely through the help of CNN). Whether Netanyahu won or not, the style of "peace" was and is going to be dictated by Israel, with the other Arabs, especially the weak Palestinians, completely under its thumb. Our tragedy is that as a people and culture we have not liberated ourselves from a crude model of power, forgetting that knowledge, information, and consent are more important than brute force and policemen.

The only way to begin the change is to do what Serraj and others have done: change the battlefield from the street to the mind. Speak out, tell the truth, refuse to accept clichés and ideological constructions, examine and reflect concretely on the nonsense produced by the media. The struggle is not only *against* Israeli and Arab tyranny and injustice: it is *for* our right as a people to move into the modern world, away from fear, the ignorance and superstition of backward-looking religion, and the basic injustice of dispossession and disenfranchisement. For those of us who speak and write, our fundamental issue is the right of free expression (and not who won the Israeli elections), which no appeals to security, military emergency, or national unity can continue to abrogate. There is no other way of achieving the minimum goals of a decent life without also translating ourselves from a primitive to a modern condition in which for the first time in our modern history leaders are directly accountable for their policies to the people. We should stop waiting for "things to improve" or for "better leaders." The Arabs as a whole have created their own weakness and the incompetent leaders that have been tolerated for so long. Surely we must do better than that now.

Al-Hayat, July 3, 1996

Chapter Ten

Total Rejection and Total Acceptance Are Equivalent

I T IS AN IRONY of recent Arab political analysis that we went suddenly from a style of considering *everything* about Israel as being always the same, to one in which we saw differences everywhere inside Israel, differences that were total. Just twenty years ago, for example, Zionism was considered as coloring all Israeli political parties, personalities, discussions, and actions. Everyone was a Zionist enemy, from the bus driver to the army chief of staff. A few intellectual attempts were made here and there to moderate this quite rigid picture, but until Anwar Sadat went to Jerusalem in 1977 the unanimity and uniformity of Arab views of Israel were nearly complete. After Camp David, a greater sophistication set in, but certainly after the Gulf War and the Madrid Conference, Israel became a subject for all kinds of Arab experts to pronounce on. I recall that in June 1992 I was in Amman, having just arrived there from the occupied territories; it was my first visit to Palestine since my family and I left there in late 1947. By coincidence Yasir Arafat was in Amman, convalescing in one of the royal palaces from a recent operation. So my family and I paid him a social visit on the very day of the Israeli elections that brought Yitzhak Rabin's Labor Party to power. What struck me at the time was how Arafat and about fifteen of his closest advisers were watching the results on television with extraordinary precision and discrimination; they seemed to have precise knowledge of each parliamentary district and its candidates that distinguished each one from the other, something that would have been impossible five years before.

Of course the change from rigidity and blindness to analysis and considered reflection is a good one. But that is not what I am talking about. The worrisome factor is when in becoming more sophisticated you begin to believe that differences between Labor and Likud, for instance, are absolute instead of relative, and you begin to forget or overlook the abiding continuities within Israeli, or for that matter, all national politics. Now that the Israeli elections are over, it is perhaps useful to confirm that there are important differences between Peres and Netanyahu. The former is a cultured man, a European-style politician, raised in an international atmosphere of socialist politics, on which the first generation of Israeli politicians—like Ben-Gurion, who was Peres's mentor—thrived. Netanyahu is an American-style technician, a manager as well as an ideological soldier whose ideas about Israel and the world are extremely simple, even crude. He represents a reaction against the inbred, clubby world that produced Peres, and therefore thrives on the notion that he is a brash outsider. I vividly recall my impression of him when he was UN Representative in New York and we would occasionally appear together on TV programs. First of all, he always categorically refused to be in the same room with me, requiring a separate studio for himself, even though we were debating each other. Once, on Ted Koppel's *Nightline,* a widely watched late-night program, Koppel himself felt called upon to explain that Netanyahu had specified the extremely bizarre arrangements, otherwise he would not appear with me; I used the oddness of the man's behavior to make a comment on Zionist ideology as being premised on the absence, if not total effacement, of the Palestinian.

Second, it was impossible to engage Netanyahu in any kind of discussion. This was during the intifada, when issues like human rights, resistance, and the struggle for justice were our watchwords. Netanyahu always resorted to the numbing repetition of a few phrases about Israeli security, the need to resist terrorism, and, over and over again, the importance of defeating terrorism. He gave me the impression of addressing everyone and no one at the same time. I never had the sense of him as anything but a programmed voice in a suit, unwilling to open out one inch beyond his extremely circumscribed ideological vision. He was glib, never at a loss for words, and utterly committed to what he said. The last time I saw him was in April 1988; I was sitting in my airline seat bound for Europe, when he rushed on board and was shown to the seat in front of me. At first he did not see me, and spent the first hour of our flight nervously leafing through old issues of *Time* and *Newsweek*. When he came back to his seat after going to the bathroom he saw me sitting just behind him, and his face froze. He immediately called the attendant and asked to be transferred to another seat, which of course he promptly was. A senior UN official who happened to be on the plane came up to me after witnessing the odd incident. "Mr. Ambassador seems to be frightened of you," he said with a chuckle. I never saw Netanyahu after he moved seats, not even when we arrived at our destination. In a similar situation, I suppose, Peres might have engaged me in polite conversation.

Those are the differences: background, generation, style. Yet both are bound to each other in the most important ways. Neither man would seriously entertain the possibility of conceding sovereignty to Palestinians, even though Peres is a master at using the language of conciliation and "peace" to seduce Westerners and Arab leaders and experts into believing that he really meant what the world wanted him to mean. Both men are radically committed to the superiority of Israeli Jews over Palestinian Arabs, or all Arabs for that matter. Both men are unshakably convinced that for Israel to survive as it has survived it must have, and be willing to use, devastating power over the Arabs. Whatever mode of coexistence would be settled on, for both Peres and Netanyahu the Arabs are seen as required to satisfy Israeli demands in politics, economics, and military terms. Peres seemed to make concessions, but if one looks back at his record the pattern is quite clear. He took advantage of Arab disunity and Palestinian gullibility to open up Asian and African (and of course Arab) markets to Israeli economic advantage; he and Rabin manipulated the United States and the peace process so as to keep Israel in a position of superiority whereby it dictated the terms, the agenda, and every possible outcome; and all this without giving up a single strategic objective. He bombed Lebanon without real restraint; he gave up nothing—except a few verbal hints—to Syria; in Gaza and the West Bank he continued land expropriations, increased the settler population, closed off area

A from areas B and C, strangled the economy, and imposed horrendous security conditions on Yasir Arafat, turning the autonomous areas into zones of oppression that were subject not to the norms of civilized life but to the harsh imperatives, both real and imagined, of security for every Israeli man, woman, and child.

Neither Peres nor Netanyahu cares in the final analysis what Israel's actions have cost the Palestinians as a people. The difference is that Peres wants moral approval from Arabs and others, whereas Netanyahu is not interested in what anyone else thinks. Peres went out of his way to gain for Israel a retrospective forgiveness of any responsibility incurred toward Palestinians during the many years of occupation; in addition he wanted to continue the occupation indirectly, so that Israeli soldiers and settlers would not have to be seen. Netanyahu wants to rule directly, he wants everyone actually *to see* Israeli settlers and soldiers invading and occupying Palestinian areas. It is an interesting fact (unmentioned to my knowledge in any Arab or Western press report) that *Nekuda,* one of the leading settler weeklies, admitted one week before the elections that Peres and the Labor Party had done more for the settlements than the Likud.

Despite these facts, the leadership of the Arab world expresses regret and consternation at Netanyahu's victory. What we have been unable to see clearly in our search for symbolic change and difference in Israeli politics is that the basic core of Israeli attitudes to the Arabs generally, the Palestinians in particular, has not really been modified enough. We have accommodated to that core; we have changed; we have accepted it as a fact of nature, and as a result we have grasped at the cosmetic differences that a clever tactician like Peres has exploited. So long as the core is protected by Israeli power, and so long as there is no sustained, systematic Arab attempt to force the change, we shall remain as supplicants or as dependents.

There is a tragic parallel to the Palestinian situation in what has taken place between whites and blacks in American society over the past century. The recent outbreak of black church fires in a few Southern states (for which the word "terrorism" does not seem to be used) demonstrates that a vast gulf of resentment and racial prejudice still permits the white majority to treat blacks as a permanent underclass who can be kept in a state of permanent backwardness and oppression: it is this gulf of racial discrimination that produces the church burnings and the pauperization of the black race on a systematic basis. Whites are too powerful, blacks too weak to make the change. By the same token, Israelis can exist inside Israel, drive their cars, water their lawns, fill their pools, go to their schools and universities without having in any way to think of Palestinians except as a nuisance occasionally to be tolerated. Arabs can do the manual labor, they can serve as waiters, they can exist in their autonomous zones, but that is all. They do not in any serious way impinge on the consciousness or sense of identity of the average Israeli, any more than a middle-class white professional in America needs to spend too much time thinking about the tragedy and the waste that define African-American life. On *that* level, there has been no integration to speak of, neither in Israel nor in the United States. In this respect the Labor Party and the Likud are more or less the same.

We cannot say a great deal that is better about our own societies, which remain extremely closed in on themselves. Take as an example the large number of non-Westerners that live and function today inside Europe and the United States: Japanese, Koreans, Indians, and Pakistanis, Africans, Arabs, among many others. I think it is not unfair to say that of them all Arabs have contributed the least to the changing of Western culture, politics, societies. In our own countries, we have the latest in consumer goods, we enjoy great creature comforts that have been imported from abroad, and when it comes to know-how and technical expertise, we are peerless in our knowledge of the latest Mercedes or the best TV programs. Yet I know of no systematic effort in Arab universities, in our civil institutions, to deepen our awareness of the Other, of the different societies, languages, and histories that make up the world we live in. We are stuck, subject to the call of the past and the weight of our history, unable to get beyond ourselves, or to seek others. Most of our literature is devoid of any attempt to portray, much less to understand, the Other. How many recent novels seriously attempt to represent an American or an Israeli? Hardly any.

And because of our alternation between subservience and total rejection, we have made very little effort to get inside the Israeli consciousness in order to force our cultural presence on our neighbors as a people worth taking seriously. The signs are discouraging. Over the years I have noticed that Arab university students know fewer and fewer foreign languages. I was struck by this when I visited Arab universities for the first time in the mid-1980s. Yes, more young people knew English than before, in the sense that more of them could work for a bank or an airline; but being able to carry on a literate conversation in English or French (much less Hebrew or Japanese) is beyond the capacities of most intelligent Arab college graduates today. We tend to rush toward the past, to earlier, less complicated periods, rather than to confront the difficulties and the challenges of the present. There can be no change in our status as Arabs unless we engage others through debate, dialogue, free exchange. Rejectionism does absolutely nothing to advance our cause.

I detect the emergence of a new rejectionism in the argument now being put forward by precisely those same Arab intellectuals and leaders who were once so enthusiastic about the peace process. Suddenly they have discovered that Oslo was full of difficulties and inequalities. Peres is now revealed in their minds for the scoundrel he, along with all other mainstream Israeli leaders, always was. I am convinced that this new sweeping rejectionism is just as foolish now as it was in the past, when we used to refer only to "the Zionist entity." Netanyahu's election will surely give us the opportunity first of all to see how many and how seriously Israelis object to his policies, and how many are willing to oppose him on behalf of a just peace with Palestinians and the other Arabs. When four years ago we fell into the arms of Labor we had already been infiltrated by their intellectuals and policy elites, who persuaded us that if we made the accommodations they requested from us we could get something. That turned out to be mostly a chimera. Now, I think, we should decide what *exactly* we believe in and are willing to stick to. Only then can we begin to make a change in ourselves, and in Israel.

The Gulf Today, July 5, 1996
Al-Hayat, July 3, 1996
Al-Khaleej, July 5, 1996

Chapter Eleven

Mandela, Netanyahu, and Arafat

At roughly the same time, Nelson Mandela was visiting Great Britain, and Benjamin Netanyahu was on his first official trip to the United States. A greater contrast between two political leaders could not be imagined. Mandela came to London representing not only the new South Africa, but also the victory of political principle and moral reconciliation as no other leader on earth today does. This is not a matter of idealizing or sentimentalizing the African National Congress, the liberation organization that Mandela has headed for over thirty years, most of them spent in solitary confinement well away from the political spotlight. The ANC was certainly guilty of corruption, cronyism, political murder, and a whole host of other unseemly crimes. Yet what it always stood for, the single goal for which it was created, and what Mandela himself embodied, never changed: the end of apartheid, and the institution of legal equality— one person, one vote—between blacks and whites. It is important to remember that by the 1980s the ANC had been defeated militarily by the South African government; most of its leaders, like Mandela and Walter Sisulu, were in jail, the rest either killed or in exile, like Oliver Tambo. Only the force of unyielding principle held on to from the position of moral strength, again represented by Mandela, was capable of delegitimizing apartheid all over the world; this gradually compelled the white government to begin negotiations with the ANC not on its terms, but on Mandela's.

Nor was this all. Throughout the negotiations Mandela's policy was to attract to himself an important segment of the white business and intellectual community in his country, on the grounds that there would be reconciliation between the races, and not revenge, once apartheid was abolished. So great was the moral force of Mandela's promise to bring the black and white communities together after apartheid that his presence alone seemed to guarantee the future. It was felt that only Mandela could bring the country together, heal the wounds; and because his people had been the victims of white oppression, he was the man who could forgive—but not forget—the past. One of the things Mandela did after the South African elections was to set up a continuing committee whose role it was to keep before the public the evils of apartheid; this was done not in the spirit of recrimination, but so that no one would forget the evils of a system that condemned millions of people to servitude and perpetual subordination. When he appeared in Great Britain, therefore, Mandela was recognized for his two great achievements, which he accomplished with dignity and amazing persistence. The only person he refused to meet— justly, in my opinion—was Margaret Thatcher, a crude and unregenerately reactionary politician who had always refused to recognize the ANC except as a terrorist organization. It is a measure of Mandela's stature that he was able to maintain his refusal in Thatcher's own country despite the fact that she is after all a former prime minister and a peer of the realm.

On the other hand, Netanyahu's visit was a parade of bigotry and falsehood. He was given several standing ovations when he addressed a joint session of Congress, and to all intents and purposes his unyielding positions on Jerusalem, the settlements and his opposition to a Palestinian state were supported by President Clinton. Netanyahu's presence in the United States represented the triumph not of reconciliation and peace but—despite all the choruses since 1993 about the immense successes of the peace process—of power and injustice. Like all other Israeli leaders, he denied the past and the reality of the Palestinians; he was a man insensitive to the heavy human toll caused by Israel to literally millions of Arabs. And once again, the Arab states were condemned to silence or to impotent hand-wringing from the sidelines. A few short years ago, when Menachem Begin came to America bearing the Likud message, a number of Arab-American groups mounted demonstrations against him, and in fact were heard as they raised their voices in protest. For Netanyahu this time, it is extremely likely that a few Arab-Americans tried to meet with him behind the scenes. In this way have we lost the moral strength of our position on Palestine, which today represents nothing more than a few tattered symbols in the Bantustans of the self-rule areas. Palestine used to represent an ideal—very much like anti-apartheid—of justice and a struggle for equality; today it is scarcely remembered except as it is applied derisively to the corruptions and injustices of Yasir Arafat's Palestinian Authority.

I have just returned from a short trip to the West Bank and Jerusalem. What struck me—aside from the forlorn hopelessness expressed by most people—is that conversations between Palestinians are confined almost entirely to everyday worries and anxieties, most of which reflect the frustration of a people whose struggle has been demoted, passed by, reduced to a simple matter of minimum survival. All the newspapers run advertisements praising Mr. Arafat as a great man, and they express gratitude for the things he has done. Yet no one has any illusions at all that his rule is anything but corrupt, that his police and prisons (there are thirty-five prisons in Gaza alone) are cruel, torture is rife, due process is suspended most of the time, and if you need to get anything done you have to have a connection with someone in the Authority. An index of this is that elected members of the Legislative Council express frustration at the fact that despite their attempts to pass reform bills, Arafat simply refuses to implement them: he wants to rule in his own way, unilaterally and without any significant civil interference. A lawyer friend told me that the most recent version of the Basic Law—or Constitution—being studied by the legal experts that Arafat appointed has produced a draft which is a good deal worse (in terms of democratic freedoms) than earlier drafts. For one, Arafat no longer promises to limit his time in office to two terms; for another "the president" has the power on his own to pass laws; for still another, the powers of the Legislative Council are greatly reduced relative to the Presidency; and finally, there are severely curtailed possibilities for citizens to have recourse to the law should their rights be diminished or threatened. The whole idea is that the

Palestine envisioned by Arafat is one that leaves him entirely alone to
rule at his pleasure, which in turn is dependent on what Israel allows
him to get away with.

The tragedy is that Palestinians who view Netanyahu's ascendancy with trepidation and alarm have very little to fall back on. And
in the world's eyes it is difficult to say that Arafat and what he represents constitute a genuine alternative to the unacceptable vision of
things offered by the Likud. Is Arafat's vision really any better? Here
is an Authority, whose major figure he is, that has accepted the unacceptable, that has effectively given away most Palestinian rights
just to be able to rule a series of tiny non-contiguous enclaves more or
less as it wishes, collaborating with Israel in the suppression of real
Palestinian self-determination.

While on the West Bank I paid a visit to Hebron, whose present
sorry state is due to a combination of settler fanaticism and Palestinian negotiating ignorance (or villainy, the difference is unimportant).
The Ibrahimi mosque today is totally surrounded by the Israeli
army: Arafat agreed to this *after* the February 1994 massacre by settler
Baruch Goldstein. The whole Arab center of town is now deserted,
commercial life has been stifled, and wherever you look you see crazed
Jewish fanatics protected by the Israeli army—legally there because
Arafat and his negotiators simply accepted their demands—making
life impossible for the one hundred twenty thousand Palestinian residents of Hebron who are forced to submit to curfews, searches, and
prohibitions on movement, *after* the massacre. Mr. Natshe, the mayor
of Hebron, told me that he had pleaded with Arafat and his men not
to sign those clauses in the Taba agreement that gave Israel such unre-
stricted power over Hebron, but those requests were turned down. The
same thing happened in Bethlehem, a town entirely within the Palestinian zone, where Israel has now opened a road for itself to gain independent access to Rachel's Tomb; this too was agreed to by Palestinian
negotiators, who had no concrete idea at the time what they were giving up to Israel.

Because of this depressing background, then, the vision of Palestinian struggle that had mobilized people all over the world, before the
various changes instituted by Arafat and the PLO had begun, has now
collapsed totally. Arafat's pronouncements are viewed by most Pales-

tinians as empty talk, whereas of course the cruelty of his security apparatus is much more seriously believed. Unlike Mandela, who never abandoned the principles and the goal of his struggle, Arafat and the people who follow him have trampled on principle, sold out on commitment, and emptied language of any connection with political truth. This, alas, reflects the current situation of the Arab world as well. Which leader is looked up to, admired, held up as a role model? The number is extremely small. With half the Arab population now made up of extremely young (below age sixteen) people, the vacuum in moral leadership is very grave. This, I believe, is why so many well-educated Arabs are turning back to the certainties of religion; what enrages them is not, as the Western Orientalists and Islamic "experts" allege, their fear of modernity, but rather the usurpation of political discourse and social space by a particularly mean-spirited, uninspiring brand of "realism."

This is especially true where Palestine is concerned. For the first time that I can remember, non-Palestinian Arabs in Egypt, Lebanon, Syria, Jordan, and elsewhere have underlined the need for restoring political idealism and principle to their proper place in the struggle for Palestine. And also for the first time, Palestinians on the West Bank and Gaza no longer play a prominent role in this movement, so taken up have they become with competing for ministerial posts, as well of course as the struggle for daily survival. These are difficult truths—no one can be blamed for being preoccupied with the problems of survival under the double occupation of the Israelis and the Palestinian Authority—and they must be faced, at least so far as their results in Palestinian and Arab political life are concerned.

I have been criticized by respected friends like Dr. Haidar Abdel Shafi and others for not being concerned enough with the problems of what needs to be done now in a practical sense. Oslo, they say, is a reality, and we must learn how to live and deal with it. To me this simply evades the main point, which is that "reality" must be improved and changed, not accommodated to. Netanyahu and, to all intents and purposes, the United States have made no secret of the fact that their conception of the peace process grants the Palestinians extremely limited rights, no sovereignty, and little self-determination. Why are we supposed to accept that? Every careful reading of the Oslo and Taba agreements has shown that they were designed to defuse Palestinian energies, maintain overall Israeli control, and keep Arafat in power. It seems quite clear to me that we should begin—practically speaking—by simply refusing all three stipulations, substituting instead a policy of noncooperation with Oslo's specific injustices while at the same time building up our civil and cultural institutions. We need more coordination between Palestinians inside and outside Palestine, more coordination between us and other Arabs, more coordination between us and our worldwide constituency. I have been advocating an active information policy by which we not only inform the world of our peaceful intentions but also of our unshakable commitment to equality, self-determination, independence. We must address Israelis plainly and openly. The point is that there are many practical steps to be taken which I have been speaking about for three years, and I am now tired of the uninteresting chorus of requests for "practical proposals" that leave Oslo and the present Palestinian power structure in place as a "reality" with which we must "deal." The sooner Arafat is made to understand that his route via Oslo and Tel Aviv will take us further and further away from our national goals, the better. But what I see is nearly everyone trying to come to terms with the impossible situation as it is now, and that will just as certainly take us absolutely nowhere.

The history of Palestine in the Arab and non-aligned worlds is that it represented a cause whose idealism and vision inspired people to a better understanding of both past and present. Oslo put an end to that as, I believe, Israel and the United States had intended. The time has come to put Palestine back in the center as an ideal for individual action and individual commitment to principle in the same way that Mandela's actions and principles inspired the anti-apartheid movement. This does not mean a return to the bombast of aggression and threat, nor to the glorification of one person, but rather to the establishment of a new movement for peace, in which the goal is that all peoples should live together as equals. Only the vision of a multicultural and democratic Palestine can inspire such a movement. The time for a new politics—and indeed for a new human being—has come.

Al-Hayat, July 27, 1996

Chapter Twelve

The Theory and Practice of
Banning Books and Ideas

I RECALL QUITE VIVIDLY that when I was about fourteen or fifteen and living in Egypt, the films of Elizabeth Taylor—whom I've always considered one of the world's worst actresses—were banned. The reasons given at the time were not aesthetic but that she was considered to be a Zionist supporter, and therefore somehow unfit to grace Egyptian cinema screens. What I also recall was that during the fifties and early sixties, well after the Revolution had been established, copies of various foreign magazines like *Time* and *The Economist* would often arrive in Cairo with passages about Egypt or Israel (at that time in Arab discourse Israel was referred to only as "the Zionist entity") that were deemed offensive to the censor carefully inked out on the page; that government employees should spend hours going through magazines removing politically incorrect passages seemed like a lot of work at the time, but was accepted as an aspect of national security.

I also remember that during the sixties while I was working on my Ph.D. in literature, I would often spend the summer in Lebanon at my family's house reading and writing; because I had three months, I would regularly air freight a large parcel of books to Beirut via Pan Am, and then would reclaim them at Beirut airport two days later. Each time I did that, however, I would have to carry the heavy bundle over to a censorship office where my books and I were examined—the operation took about ten minutes—for possible evidence or traces

of Zionism. On one occasion I was asked by a burly employee of
the *Sûreté generale* whether there was anything in my books (the
poems of Keats and Wordsworth, novels by Fielding, Sterne, Stendhal,
and Thackeray) about Israel, as with one hand he held one of them
upside down.

All this changed somewhat as a result of the Palestinian Revolution, as we then called it, after 1967, when not only did the movement
make possible a whole new self-critical style and rhetoric in politics,
but also research articles on Israel and the Arabs were published complete with footnotes (a new thing at the time), frankness was permitted, and for the first time, the articulation of criticism about the past
and various leaders was openly practiced in Beirut. I do not mean to
suggest that everything became liberal and open: indeed, I recall how
Yasir Arafat during the early seventies sent an armored car to the
home of Elias Khoury, then working as an editor of *Shu'un Filas-
tiniyya,* because of something he had written which had offended
Arafat. But Lebanon was not the whole Arab world. Censorship continued to exist elsewhere, although perhaps on not so ridiculous a
scale as in the pre-1967 years. The point I am trying to make is that
after 1948 at least two generations of Arabs were gradually inoculated
with the idea that part of our struggle as a people required the suppression not only of certain unwelcome and unpleasant actualities by
our rulers who disapproved of them but were otherwise powerless to
do much about them, but also that we ourselves as a people should
accept the principle that our duty as citizens was to acquiesce in the
abrogation of our right to freedom of thought and expression. This
was a miserable legacy to pass on.

No society is entirely free of control over thought and expression,
though not all such control is instituted and maintained by the government. I think it is quite true in the United States that certain things
cannot be easily said or written—for years it was impossible to say
anything critical about Israel, and even today it is virtually impossible
to publish material from a Palestinian point of view in major American journals of opinion—but there is no American Ministry of Information or government office of censorship. People and organizations
can be banned (as the PLO was for many years) but there was always
popular, outspoken resistance to the prohibition. Freedom of expres-

sion is therefore relative, but it must, in my opinion, be protected by law and by constitution. Otherwise what can be said or written—and finally, thought—is subject to the whims, opinions, moods, personal interests, of the ruler.

In the West relative freedom of expression was won over a long period of time, the result of a contest first between the landowning aristocracy and the monarchy, then as the result of a contest between that aristocracy and the middle classes. This has not been the case in most, if not all, Arab countries, where executive authority dominates even the constitution and the state's written laws, and the middle class remains at best a commercial and professional, but not really a political, class. When it comes to the regulation of expression, whether for civil or religious reasons, the prevailing situation in the Arab world is almost comic, since electronic communication, travel, and reality itself defy the ridiculous strictures imposed by the religious and secular authorities. But the practice of censorship still exists, and is often maintained with violence at far too great an expense in our societies. I have yet to hear or read a real defense of censorship, even though large numbers of journalists languish in Arab prisons, and an estimable number of artists and intellectuals pay the price through exile, torture, or an imposed silence. No Arab constitution countenances censorship, but the ban on certain statements is still severely enforced. No ruler really ever wants to get into a debate about censorship, because censorship cannot withstand the clear light of reason or the rigors of debate. My books have been banned in Palestine for almost a month, yet no one has taken responsibility for the order to confiscate and remove them from bookstores.

There are two especially troubling aspects of the practice of censorship as it exists today in Arab societies. One is that it does not work. It has not made one regime better, one ruler more loved, one army more efficient, one newspaper or university more up-to-date, one society more secure and modern. Its damage even to the regimes that enforce it is incalculable. It has made Arab societies as a whole among the least democratic on earth. It has dispirited and discouraged every Arab who today is ashamed even to be an Arab. Untold riches have been lost to us in spirits broken, in talents exiled, in research, exploration, thought left untried, all because of censorship and the prohibition on free debate and discussion. Censorship has turned people away from their governments and individuals away from other individuals. The question is then why, since it does not work, censorship is still there.

This is the second and more disquieting aspect of censorship in Arab societies today. The fact is that as individuals we can no longer evade responsibility for our own social evils, or for the governments and rulers that are either unjust or unresponsive to the real needs of the majority. Censorship exists because many individuals collaborate with it: individuals who censor themselves, who say it is better to be inside a regime trying to do good than to be outside and marginal, individuals who say what difference does it make if I allow myself to be censored since after all the world goes on. Everyone complains privately, but few, very few like Nasr Hamid Abu Zeid in Egypt or Laith Shubailat in Jordan, take the next step and say what no one else is willing to say in public. Above all, we accept censorship as we do nearly everything else that has been forced on us in this miserable, damp, gloomy period of mediocrity and defeat, because we say that we are powerless, the world is against us, Zionism and imperialism have won. We are told that we must be realistic and *pragmatic*—a nauseating word as it is used by our leading policy intellectuals to justify their own compromises, Baathists or Marxists one day, advisers to presidents and princes the next—we have been told, we must realize that we have no alternative, etc., etc.

There can be no meaningful compromise on censorship, on the banning of books and ideas, on the imprisonment and torture of critics or opponents of the regime. The time has come to hold the practice and the theory up to the scrutiny of reason and light, and to ask publicly why censorship is still necessary and whether it would be better for all Arabs to do away with it entirely, and to say that as prospective citizens of the twenty-first century we are entitled to say what we want to say and read what is available to be read, and enough of all this nonsense about security and danger and protecting ourselves against some imagined outside enemy. After all, Elizabeth Taylor is still before the public despite being banned in Egypt, and *Time* and *The Economist* still publish their opinions forty years after they were censored. But look at us.

Yasir Arafat and his Authority use censorship not just to silence and threaten opponents of his policy, but also to hide his past mistakes from discussion and accountability. He accepted an agreement with Israel that said nothing about Palestinian self-determination on the one hand, and tacitly accepted occupation and the settlements on the other. For the past three years his partners Rabin and Peres have been building and expanding settlements; they have sealed the doom of Arab Jerusalem; they have destroyed the Palestinian economy and corrupted its political class; they have imposed military rule on areas B and C, and have simply walked away with over 90 percent of the land. All of this with Mr. Arafat's cooperation. After Netanyahu came to power and exposed the peace process for the fraud it always was, Arafat is pleading without dignity or credibility with anyone who will listen that he needs help. All the while his security forces torture and kill anyone who objects to his colossal failures as leader. He announces a four-hour general strike, which will hurt no one except his people (Israelis don't do their shopping in Ramallah and Nablus), and he urges people to go to Jerusalem on their own to pray. This man has learned nothing from any of the nonviolent struggles against imperialism, has taken nothing from Gandhi or from Martin Luther King, and he has never understood the meaning of armed struggle as practiced by the Vietnamese or the Algerians. The South African experience means little to Arafat. What he should be doing now—instead of strengthening his power inside Palestine like the incompetent general that he is—is to lead a series of nonviolent demonstrations against the settlements, announce publicly that he does not want to fight Israelis but rather the bricks and stones of their settlements and that he will do so unarmed, leading his people in large numbers, instead of sitting behind his guards and his palaces in Ramallah and Gaza. We should all speak out against a policy that will cost us the rest of Palestine unless it is changed, and unless the leadership is forced to change or be gone.

Al-Hayat, September 4, 1996
Al-Khaleej, September 4, 1996
The Gulf Today, September 6, 1996
The Nation, September 23, 1996
Courier International, October 17, 1996

Chapter Thirteen

On Visiting Wadie

T HE PRINCIPAL PALESTINIAN city on the West Bank is
Ramallah, about ten miles north of Jerusalem. My parents and I
spent the summer of 1942 there. I recall it as a leafy, slow-paced, and
prosperous town of freestanding villas, largely Christian in population, served by a well-known Friends High School. Today it is the West
Bank capital of the Palestinian Authority set up under Yasir Arafat as
a direct result of the Israeli-PLO negotiations; most of its Christian
residents have been replaced by Muslims; it has considerably increased
in size and is now full of office buildings, shops, restaurants, schools,
institutes, and taxis, all catering to "al-Dafeh" or "The Bank" as the
West Bank is known. But there are very few hotels in Ramallah, nor is
it any longer a resort, as I remembered it. While I was there during the
second half of March, Mr. Arafat's office in Gaza announced that the
West Bank was to be renamed the Northern District [of Palestine]. No
one I spoke to understood what that particular change really meant.
But it is true that more than in most places, and despite their long history, the Palestinian territories seem to spawn new names, jargons,
initials, and shorthands. They are a feature of the unstable circumstances in which Palestinians now live.

My twenty-four-year-old son, Wadie, works as a volunteer in
Ramallah, at an NGO (nongovernmental organization) called the
Democracy and Workers' Rights Center (DWRC) which is headed by
an activist lawyer, Hassan al-Barghouti. (The Barghoutis are probably

74

the single largest family-clan of Palestinians that exists anywhere; estimates of their uncounted number range from seven to twenty thousand, many of whom live in the United States as well as other Arab countries.) Wadie discovered DWRC on his own when he visited Palestine from Cairo during the winter of 1995. He is the older of my two children; his sister, Najla (twenty-two), is now a senior in college. Although they both were born in the United States and grew up as New York City kids, only Wadie has developed a consuming interest in the Arab world, the Arabic language, and of course Palestine. At age fourteen he asked us if he could be tutored in Arabic, and he was. As they were growing up, both children heard the Arabic that my wife, Mariam, and I normally communicate in; both came to understand it to some degree, but neither was able to speak, read, or write it with any fluency. Until 1982 we would visit our families in Lebanon, but we stopped going there regularly after that year: the civil war and Israeli invasion finished off Lebanon for us as a summertime destination and as an Arab-speaking environment for the children to enjoy and learn from.

Still, Wadie persisted in his solitary efforts to acquire a working knowledge of his parents' language: in college he took eight semesters of Arabic and made heroic efforts to speak to relatives and friends, despite the fact that he was inordinately sensitive to their natural wish to correct his mispronunciation or grammatical errors. Arabic is a difficult language for at least three reasons, all of them applicable in Wadie's case. It is made up of a spoken version that varies dramatically from country to country; a Moroccan cannot readily be understood by a Lebanese, for example, though Palestinians, Syrians, and Egyptians—each with a distinctive accent—can communicate with each other. Which dialect does one learn? The written version, on the other hand, is common to all Arabic readers and writers, but it is an almost completely different language from the spoken dialects; its relationship to demotic Arabic is rather like Latin's to French, Italian, and Spanish. The rich vocabulary, grammatical complexity, and rhetorical structures of written or classical Arabic are difficult, but necessary to master. Linguistic knowledge and fluent literacy are an almost obsessive concern for most educated Arabs. Third, there is a cultural barrier against Arabic in the United States. Arabic is associated with violence and terrorism and, of course, anti-Israel rhetoric; Arabic literature is scanted and the Arab contribution to civilization is usually ignored or downgraded in universities. For a young person growing up in New York, the challenge to press on and actually get hold of the language is formidable: learning Arabic was the hardest way for a young Arab-American like Wadie to understand his heritage, but it is also the most serious.

Wadie majored in history in college and wrote a senior thesis on the Bandung Conference of 1955; meanwhile, his Arabic kept getting better and better, almost unbeknownst to us. We should not have been surprised that the kid who surmounted an early learning disability, who suffered osteomyelitis and a shattered elbow from hockey and bike-riding respectively and, despite both, was an honors student and a member of the tennis team, turned out to be as persistent in his resolve as he was. He graduated in 1994, Wadie then won a Fulbright award to study intensive Arab language and culture in Cairo. During that year he steeped himself in novelists from Mahfouz to Ghitany, the films of Rihani, Shahine, Adil Imam, television and radio serials like *Layali Hilmiyia*, Koranic studies, as well as the dubious pleasures (afforded by seedy cafés) of the hookah. He applied to and was accepted to law school in the United States but, he informed us last spring, decided to defer it for another year. His exploratory visits from Cairo to the occupied territories convinced him that he wanted the experience of living in the new, post-Oslo Palestine now, and having settled on DWRC as the place to work, he moved to Ramallah last September. Barghouti gave Wadie and Rudiger, a German volunteer, a tiny unfurnished house rent-free, plus $100 a month.

In December the house was broken into. Wadie's glasses, his Heavy Metal CDs, the CD player, and a mobile telephone's battery charger were stolen; his plane tickets and money were not. Though he dismissed it as "a typical Third World crime," the robbery seemed to wound him, and he resolved to find a new place, which he did in Ar-Ram, a small outlying town near the Jerusalem–West Bank border. He moved in there in January, this time with his girlfriend, who works as a freelance photographer. It is a matter of considerable wonder to his parents that throughout his stay Wadie has taken no money from them. He is very spartan in his lifestyle but has also managed to supplement his DWRC pittance by producing English translations for academics, researchers, and journalists; this has financed trips he's taken to Jordan and Upper Egypt.

In the meantime the peace process has continued to unfold. I was an early dissenter from what I interpreted as a poor deal for Palestinians; for the past two decades I had had few doubts that a negotiated political settlement was the only valid option for our struggle with Israel, but, after the Gulf War and his disastrous alliance with Saddam Hussein, I had lost confidence in Arafat's abilities to lead or truly represent our national interests. The Oslo accords were the result of his crippled, but still potent, position as Palestinian leader of which the Israelis took full advantage. Coincidentally I was diagnosed with leukemia, which made my exit from Palestinian politics (I was a member of the Palestine National Council since 1977) seem imperative to me in 1991, although I continued to write (mainly in the Arabic press) and speak.

For my children, their father's involvement, plus the enormous hoopla of White House ceremony and media celebration, made Palestine even more of an inevitability in their lives. We had gone as a family to Israel and the territories in 1992 (my first trip since leaving West Jerusalem as a boy in late 1947). Wadie was stirred by what he saw—quite obviously this was the germ of his plans to return there—and this gave added charge to his Arabic studies. Ever the antipolitical skeptic, Najla rejected the whole thing as altogether too much, too involved, and confrontational for her as someone interested in literature, acting, fashion. Since 1992 I came to feel that the changing situation on the ground after Oslo warranted another look; besides, with Wadie there the notion of going as *his* visitor was attractive, and I could assess what was taking place through his eyes as someone participating in the life of the new post-intifada, post–peace accords generation. At this point, however, he could not acquire the permanent residency granted very sparingly to diaspora Palestinians by Israel: he therefore had to exit the country every three months and re-enter as a visitor.

He had had almost seven months of being there when I arrived during a sustained spell of unusually cold and wet weather; Mariam joined us several days later. The February and March bomb outrages had brought down on the territories the closures, arrests, and all-round discomforts that made life for everyone extremely hard. While we were there, Peter Hansen, the Danish Commissioner-General of UNRWA, which is the main aid organization serving Palestinians, spoke out strongly about the dangers—including starvation—to the West Bank and Gaza of Israeli policies. Ramallah itself had been free of Israeli soldiers since December, but what I hadn't quite bargained for was how isolated and cut off it (as well as the other six "liberated" Palestinian towns) had become.

The maddening complexities of the Oslo Two West Bank map provided for three types of area not including the Jerusalem area, which Israel considers entirely its own. Area A is now about 1 percent of the West Bank, and includes Ramallah and the five other main towns spread all over the West Bank, except for Hebron. Area A is under the PA's jurisdiction. Area B, a network of four hundred villages and adjoining rural areas that comprise 27 percent, is controlled by Israel with the PA as a very junior partner; Area C, which is made up of settlements and connecting and "by-passing" roads was entirely Israeli, accounting for the balance of almost 72 percent. Palestinians now speak of their land almost entirely in terms of the Arabic initials "Alif," "Beh," and "Jeem." One difficulty is that you cannot go from one part of Area A to another without going through Area B; this enabled the Israelis in early March to shut off exits and entries to towns like Ramallah in Zone A from Bir Zeit, which is where the leading West Bank university is, in Zone B. Moreover, since the expanded area of Jerusalem takes up almost a quarter of the West Bank and requires a special permit to enter, people from Ramallah find it impossible to enter the city, or even to get to Bethlehem, south of Jerusalem. Entrances and exits to Gaza are also controlled by the Israelis—even Arafat needed special permission to leave—so that negotiating the roads was for the average Palestinian both a costly and often discouraging business. During the time I was there I made repeated, but ultimately unsuccessful, efforts to enter Gaza. In 1992 and 1993, before the peace process Mariam and I did make it there; "peace" has made movement much, much harder for Palestinians.

Wadie was helped in his daily movements by his U.S. passport, although like everyone else he has to queue at all the Israeli barriers.

Most of the time he gets around by "service" taxi, which enables you to pay for one seat rather than the whole car. During my visit we rented a car with a Jerusalem (i.e., Israeli) license plate; this made it possible for us to go everywhere except Gaza. The change in road surface and width between Israeli and Palestinian areas is dramatic: roads in the former are wider, landscaped, and cared for, whereas in the latter they are extremely narrow, rutted, potholed, and unattended. It's as if one suddenly crossed over from Southern California into Bangladesh. As my driver, Wadie first drew attention to this with his comment that, unlike the Palestinians, the Israelis had a mania for building roads; he reminded me of Kipling's Kim in his knowledge of all the backways and shortcuts in the Ramallah area, as well as each building, road, and alley inside the city. He had the native's sense of known, familiar space. It was the first time in our lives that I felt that I was in his hands: I needed the feeling, since most of the time I felt disoriented and at a loss.

I stayed at the American Colony Hotel in East Jerusalem, a well-established albeit elegant and comfortable haunt of journalists, security men, and Israeli as well as Palestinian politicos. The Colony's staff, however, was halved while I was there because West Bank workers were prevented from coming to Jerusalem by the closures. Yet the alleys of the Old City, a short walk from the Colony (past St. George's Cathedral, where I was baptized, and St. George's School, attended by myself as well as the other male members of my family) were clogged with Christian tourists, transporting dreadful little brown crosses in their hands with a look of rapt vacancy, wandering all over, oblivious to the twentieth-century world of conflicting Palestinians and Israelis all around them. As the Holy Land's nerve center, and the likeliest source of future conflict, Jerusalem has never been especially attractive to me, although I was born there, as were my father, his father, and several generations before them. There is something ungenerous and unyielding about the place that encourages intolerance, given that all sorts of ultimate religious and cultural claims emanate from the city, most of them essentially denying or downgrading the others.

I discovered that the unbroken line of Said anti-Jerusalem feeling persisted in Wadie, who must come to the city in order to do translations for the Jerusalem Media and Communication Center (JMCC), an enterprisingly conceived and run Palestinian outfit that produces daily press digests, reports, and translations for the benefit of journalists and diplomats in the East Jerusalem area. Wadie works two days a week there, using his fluency in English and Arabic to maximum advantage. Like Wadie, the other JMCC workers have comparatively little trouble getting around, since their Jerusalem IDs and license plates allow them access to the city as well as the West Bank. Still, he finds the city tense and stifling at the same time, he told me. On the other hand, West Jerusalem is a more interesting place, but after a few visits there in November and December, he now goes there infrequently. "Uncomfortable for me," he explained, "and anyway, Jerusalem is still divided."

So even though the Arab and Israeli parts of Jerusalem were pulled together by Israel in 1967, East Jerusalem and its people lead essentially segregated lives, hemmed in by the increasing number of Israeli Jews who have taken up residence there. The disparity in power, the differences in culture, language, and tradition, the accumulated hostilities of the past century: all these keep Jews and Arabs apart. In addition, the hassle of simply getting around and keeping alive for ordinary Palestinians makes it nearly impossible for them to interact with Israeli Jews. "I belong to *this* world because of where I work and live. There's no way for me to see or talk to many Israelis who live inside their world, as I do in Ramallah and East Jerusalem," Wadie said on one of our first drives into Ramallah. The closures were designed to enforce the separation anyway, he added, and the sight of Israeli soldiers impassively stopping, then waving cars in (or out) hardly added to the likelihood of fraternization. Wadie uniformly spoke English to them, but only if he was addressed by them. "What should I say?" I asked him. "Don't say anything until they speak to you. Don't even show your passport until they ask," he responded. The experienced child instructing the confused and apprehensive father. I let him be the guide in this, except for the one time that a soldier appeared on my side of the car. "Passport," he said to me. When I showed it to him, he asked, "Where are you from?" to which I almost replied "from here" but prudently settled for "New York" instead. "OK," he said noncommittally, and nodded us through.

But entering "Area A" through the mud and rain, and driving along the main street of el-Bireh, the town just before Ramallah, you do feel as if you're being forced to accept all the unpleasantness, inefficiencies, and general feeling of disorganization and dilapidation so common in the Third World. Wadie, however, had come to feel at home there. "This is al-Manarah," he said, as we drove into a crowded bustling square with a handful of indifferent-looking Palestinian policemen listlessly signalling one impetuous car after another to stop or go through. "You remember it, don't you?" he asked. I certainly did not, since what had once been a small quasi-rustic space had metastasized into a noisy cauldron of zinging cars, bicycles, and motorbikes swooshing and swerving to miss an assortment of stationary peddlers' carts, spritely pedestrians, and gigantic potholes. We were heading for Ibrahim Abu-Lughod's office, a research center (there are dozens of them now in the West Bank) for curriculum development. It was Wadie's idea that we check in with Ibrahim, my oldest friend, a charismatic and brilliant political scientist from Jaffa who after forty years living and teaching in the United States had pulled up and returned to Palestine, first to teach and be academic vice president at Bir Zeit, then to launch his center under the auspices of UNESCO and the PA's Education Department.

To Wadie, Ibrahim is (in the Arabic popular tradition) an "uncle"; he stayed with my old friend, now in his mid-sixties, a lively, witty man who has an engaging way with youngsters, for the first couple of weeks before he moved into his little ill-starred house with Rudiger. My son and my friend have a joshing, affectionate relationship which is conducted (this never fails to surprise me) in Arabic. Wadie used to be extremely skinny; he is still very lean, but has filled out, is now solidly muscular, and at six-three, towers over Ibrahim and me. He has a gentle, open manner that especially endears him to very young children, and to older people, who find him unusually reflective and serious. Unlike most of us who use English words inside Arabic speech, he has disciplined himself not to do that. Thus his deliberate, routinely understated, even taciturn manner ("It's OK" is almost a term of high praise for Wadie) appears reinforced as he concentrates on producing perfectly idiomatic Palestinian sentences. As this is the first time I see him in a situation created *by him,* I find the exchange between him and Ibrahim about the plan for my visit slightly irritating as I am spoken

about in the third person. "Where do you plan to take him?" asks
Abu-Lughod. "I want him to see the *shabab* first," answers Wadie,
"but we'll have to wait till the afternoon."

The *shabab* (young men) are Wadie's wards, a group of six young
Gaza men, most of them Ibrahim's former students at Bir Zeit, now
illegally on the West Bank. This is one of the many ironies of the
peace process, that Palestinians are more restricted legally in their
movements and possibilities for work than before. By a stroke of the
pen Arafat agreed to the cantonization of his people under his
jurisdiction, while Israel retained control of who could go where. As
a result of the closure, all Gazans have been confined to Gaza, even
students who were in the middle of the semester. Wadie's friends
attended class surreptitiously during the day (not every day, not every
week) but imprisoned themselves more and more in a small Ramallah
apartment, unable to circulate freely, dodging the PA police, whose job
it was in Area A to reinforce Israel's closure by arresting and sending
them back to Gaza.

"Who else does he want to see?" Ibrahim asks again; there is no
question of sightseeing in Palestine; it is understood that I am here to
meet with people, and they with me, since this is the life blood of our
political life at present. "At some point," I interrupted, "I'd like to see
a member of the PA. I've been criticizing them publicly for two years.
Perhaps they wouldn't want to see me, but I'm interested in what they
have to say." Both Wadie and Ibrahim chuckle. "You must be kidding,
Dad. Of course they'll see you." I later glean from this that no one at
all on the West Bank feels impelled to defend Arafat so categorically
against any of his critics: this has less to do with my popularity than it
does with the problems of Arafat's regime, which to everyone I meet
represents autocracy, corruption, and especially now, an unpopular
alliance with the Israelis in their obsession with Hamas, their security,
and holding on to as much Palestinian territory with Arafat's help as
possible.

The visible signs of discontent are there to see. As Wadie drove me
back toward Jerusalem on that very first day, we passed the former
headquarters of the Israeli Civil Administration in Ramallah, now
the PA's headquarters, with detention centers, interrogation rooms,
barbed wire enclosures intact. Standing in the grey drizzle across the

road was a group of about 250 young people holding up signs saying "Let the students go," "Detention for how long?" etc. As we drove past Wadie said, "There's Esam, let's talk to him," and quickly pulled over about twenty yards up from the group. We said hello to Esam— the obvious leader—and to a young colleague of Wadie's at JMCC, Imad Saleh; I had met him in January when he had interviewed me in my Columbia office. A moment later we greeted a friend, Yusif Nasir, who hurried by; a teacher at Bir Zeit, he said he had come to show solidarity with his students.

I was struck by the bleak pathos of the scene. During the intifada the same students were demonstrating against the Israelis; now they were making claims against the Palestinian Authority, which was using a cruder version of Israeli techniques in picking up dozens of students under emergency military procedures recommended by Israel and the United States to Arafat in the war against Hamas terrorism. Esam told me—more irony—that the group was a coalition of Hamas and Fateh students who were protesting the absence of democracy and "the state apparatus" practice of "political arrests." One of their flyers asked the Authority to remember that "law is supposed to protect citizens," and further demanded a critical reassessment of all those measures now taken that have been imposed on it by "circumstances." Polite, sorrowful, firm, idealistic—but, I thought, ineffective against an obdurate dictatorship. One of the students said that an official had come across to talk to them. "We haven't really arrested or detained your friends," he was reported to have said. "They're our guests." Everyone laughed.

"By the way, Professor Said," Imad chipped in. "They've welcomed you to Palestine officially. You heard the broadcast, didn't you?" When I asked what he meant he said that at nine-thirty that very morning on Arafat's "Voice of Palestine," one Yusif al-Qazzaz had attacked me vehemently for fifteen minutes. "He called you an Orientalist who is against the Palestinian people. He also said that your criticisms of how they torture and imprison journalists are simply lies. It was all pretty angry and aggressive." During the next ten days I tried to get a tape of the broadcast but failed. Several friends—among them Hanan Ashrawi and Ghassan al-Khatib (Wadie's boss at JMCC)—gave me more details about the broadcast. I did not feel threatened by it;

rather, I told myself that the attack was a compliment that at least took me seriously enough to warrant attack. At first Wadie seemed alarmed at the broadcast, but not for long. "What incredible jokers they are," he said.

He stopped the car (with me in it) at a grocery store to pick up an oversized bag stuffed with cookies and chocolate on the way to his six Gaza friends in their hideaway house somewhere in the bowels of Ramallah. I had no idea where it was, since we reached it by an exceptionally circuitous route, but the young men were vociferously welcoming. Their apartment had filthy yellow walls, run-down furniture, and naked bulbs hanging from the ceilings. It was colder indoors than out. This was the first time I saw Wadie among Arab peers with whom he had formed a relationship based neither on school nor on family. Most of them were a fraction older than he was; all but one had been in solitary for periods of one to three months in Israeli jails; all were paralyzed by the present situation in which the valid options—return to Gaza, go back openly to school, look for work—were closed to them. Two of them had once been supporters of Hamas and Islamic Jihad, but were now neither. There was one cherubic-looking young man—Ahmad—whose story seemed to summarize the current political situation for Palestinians with all its absurdities and Kafkaesque conundrums. A Fateh student activist during the intifada, Ahmad was jailed, tortured, and interrogated; in the process he lost his left ear. "They shook and slapped me with my head in a paper bag, for hours," he said. The others told of similar stories of *tahqiq,* although at first I could not grasp what it was that the Israelis wanted since everyone "confessed" to what was demanded in order to get off. Later I gathered that these measures were designed more to break the victim's will than to extract information.

After Oslo Ahmad sought work with *al-amn,* i.e., Palestinian security forces, now the territories' chief employer, and Arafat's instrument of patronage and control. "Do you know that he has thirteen separate security forces," Ahmad carolled, and proceeded to itemize such outfits as police, preventive intelligence, Force 17, Presidential Security, State Security, foreign intelligence, regional security, military intelligence (I've forgotten a few), and then in triumphant conclusion "naval security." When I mentioned something about there being no navy (logically, since the Israelis control the sea around Gaza) Ahmad produced the magnificent non sequitur "that's why he (Arafat) has sixty of them stationed in Nablus." The young men roared at the absurdity of the sixty sailors in Nablus, which is many miles from the sea. Ahmad continued with a look of almost sublime delight. He had been assigned the job of spying and informing on students at Bir Zeit. "Then what?" I asked. "Then we bring them in for *tahqiq*. Just as I used to be interrogated in the past, I now do the interrogating. It's my turn." When I made a few disapproving comments his answer was to inform me that he hadn't been given a salary for two years, was going to resign or at least see an influential relative who would get him what was owed him. In any case, he was a Palestinian security man who according to the very security forces who employed him was illegally in Ramallah.

Wadie's face registered unhappiness with all this but I think he felt he had to appear supportive of his friends' general quandary. "Tell him about the appointments *(ta'yeenat)*," he said to Ahmad. The word was another one very much in currency. It signified Arafat's way of unilaterally giving his favorite supporters from Tunisia, Jordan, or the Gulf positions in ministries, security groups, and offices without regard for merit or for the sacrifices made by many competent West Bankers during the intifada. "Don't forget the army of one million colonels," Wadie added with a grin. "Every time I go into head-quarters," Ahmad continues, "I find a whole new set of officers with no assigned job, without even a desk—but they all get salaries, and they immediately out-rank all the rest of us." I realized that Ahmad was speaking about the very building outside of which the demonstration was taking place. "They're not only his people from Tunis," Ahmad went on complainingly, "but also cousins and nephews of rich families that Arafat needs. I have an uncle who's just been elected to the Legislative Council. I'm going to camp in his living room until I get my salary." It occurred to me that Ahmad's role as a police spy theoretically required him to inform on himself!

Mohammed Alwany, a dark, bespectacled youngster, came in with a tray packed with glasses of boiling tea. Wadie was specially fond of Alwany as a quieter, more intellectually serious man (a science major) than the others. The room was now filled with various neighbors and schoolmates who had heard Wadie and his father (Abu Wadie was what everyone called me!) were there. The overriding impression I got was of energetic, agile, and perceptive young men simply wasting their time and lives immured in the dingy flat, waiting for some change in the situation, hoping for a *deus ex machina* to get them living again. Wadie had given them some of my recent articles criticizing the results of the peace process to read: each of them expressed agreement, although one, the other Mohammed—an assertively cocky Islamist— begged to disagree with my too secular views. We didn't get to develop that argument at all, perhaps because too many Christians were in the room (besides Wadie and myself, an elderly neighbor, Mitry, whose brother was married to Natalia Makarova, had joined us), but we did get into how to solve their problem. All of them seemed to express a vehement desire—I could not gauge how really serious it was—to get married to an American woman, right away, and with no emotional or sacramental obligation on anyone's part. "It's the only way for us to get out of here," they said in chorus.

I started to explain my dismay at this to Wadie as he drove us back to Jerusalem; the line of cars at the *mahsoum* (the Hebrew word for "road block" that every Palestinian uses) stretched back a good half mile, close to where, with a nonchalant wave of his hand, Wadie pointed out his street. When I suggested that I go in to take a look he declined—"too messy. I'll show you later"—and abruptly U-turned, then sped off on a side road. "We'll take the Betunya detour; it's longer but the *mahsoum* there is always less crowded." I came back to the *shabab*'s plight, the dispiriting listlessness of their existence, their helplessness, and their lostness. "Everyone is like that," Wadie responded. "It's the indifference that kills me about my friends and myself. The mess is everywhere and the PA is laughable. Nobody wants to do anything to change it. There's no hope. And we can't get anything right." The *shabab* were his friends, but it was clear that besides being their link to the outside world, dropping in on them nearly every evening, buying them supplies and occasionally smoking a waterpipe with them, he was as stymied as they were. "You know," he said, "it's not that they're destitute. They're all from middle-class families. In fact, I visited one of them in Rafah (Gaza) and stayed over a few days. So it's not money, but the total absence of opportunity.

And the apathy of everything around." This prevailing apathy was the bane of his existence; more than anything else it kept coming up whenever we were alone.

When I asked him what he thought he was doing—the rain came down more heavily, it was very dark, and we seemed to be driving in an uninhabited area, the houses locked up and lightless—Wadie said he was trying to figure that out too. "When I was in Egypt last year they kept asking me where I was from, as if I didn't belong there. I liked being in Cairo a lot, in spite of the chaos, the dirt, the cars and eternal honking. But I *didn't* belong there. I *do* belong here. I'm Palestinian and this is it, for better or worse." He added with a cackle— "mostly for worse." Wadie is a gifted mimic with a marvelous gift for getting the essence of someone's verbal tics or accents. He suddenly became an Indian, "We are reading your books in Calcutta, Professor Said, and we are liking them too too much." Pause. Then he switched to the voice of a generic befuddled Arab professor speaking colloquially, "that man has a personality, I mean to say, he has a personality, really, I mean it, which is, how you say, a personality that is really, really, charming." I could feel Wadie slipping away. I remembered that as a child he'd lose his temper at us when my wife and I used the close quarters of a car to ask him questions about his schoolwork or— hated phrase—his future: to get him to concentrate in the way parents have of using the child's attention to focus on *them*, in the best Theobold Pontifex manner. Being a ventriloquist was his way of escaping now.

His sister says about Wadie that he does people's voices when he knows that they're acting a part. In addition to my being the aged parent, perhaps he felt that I was too much the interviewer. We slowed down for the soldiers. A flick of the wrist from one of them was all we got, and we sped on to West Jerusalem: it had stopped raining and the area vaguely resembled the hills around San Diego. Sure, we were able to drive around in our little rented car, but the sense of powerlessness we felt was insidious. At that moment, still aching through my jet lag and the incipient fatigue that is endemic to my illness, I felt that the dreariness of our collective situation as Palestinians was leading us absolutely nowhere. The peace process had become a new reality, but there were too many unaccounted for miseries left over from the past, too many inequities in the present and foreseeable future to help us round the corner into real peace and real independence. I think that Wadie experienced the same frustration as I. He confessed to me at the hotel that his single-minded assault upon Arabic was his way of getting over the taunts of his Lebanese cousins and the awful experience of being an Arab-American schoolboy in Manhattan during the Gulf War. "By forcing my way into Arabic I could be at home really. I didn't again feel as helpless as I did when they connected me with Saddam Hussein and terrorism. On the other hand," he added wistfully, "I can talk, listen, understand, but aside from my translations and work for Hassan, I don't do too much here."

WADIE IS NEVER disconsolate for long. He carries around some gaily colored juggling balls in his pocket, brings them out, and starts to juggle. "It's better than standing around," he says the next morning, as he brings me a rented *pele* phone, the Hebrew word for "magic phone," pronounced "belly-phone" in Arabic, which, despite its mispronounced name and provenance, is the major status symbol and indispensable instrument for being in Palestine: this is a cellular telephone which, since we spend so much time in delays on the road (a ten-mile trip can take an hour and a half), you must have with you at all times to make contact with anyone. Our routine was driving up and down the Jerusalem-Ramallah road, going to meet people whom Wadie and I thought of as *doing* something in the present morass. Unfortunately, there isn't much of a West Bank press to consult for orientation as you start the day. The two main papers are *al-Quds* and *al-Ayyam*, recently begun by an old friend, a former Fateh operative called Akram Haniyé who was deported by Israel in 1987, became a close adviser to Arafat in Tunis, is back in Ramallah, and having reportedly refused a political appointment, has been publishing his paper since the first of the year. It is better printed and put together than its rival, but I couldn't see the difference in content: replication and primitive imitation are everywhere in the new Palestine, a wilderness of mirrors. The striking thing about *al-Quds* the first day I look at it is that nearly every item on the front page is bad news: house demolitions, 70 percent unemployment because of the closure, food shortages, confiscations, and so forth.

   Otherwise, however, there is a tiny margin of press freedom, given that the Authority has routinely imprisoned and threatened journalists. Before Oslo my articles were run by *al-Quds;* now I appear only in Xerox copies passed around the West Bank, according to a cardiac surgeon I met in Nablus. But the really odd thing is that a couple of days after I was attacked on the radio, *al-Ayyam* ran a back-page guest column by Ghassan Zaqtan in which he defended me for opposition to Oslo and for my principled positions, political courage, and analyses. And a day after his column, I ran into Zaqtan, a poet and journalist who grew up in Beirut, at the Ministry of Culture where he works. Another irony—one part of the Authority attacks, the other answers.

   Hassan Barghouti, the DWRC's founder and director, is as tall and skinny as Wadie, but he has a serious back problem, the result of six years imprisonment and interrogation in Israeli jails. Despite an occasional wince, plus the awkward posture and stiff walk of the chronic back-sufferer, he communicated an attractive self-confidence. The Center occupies sixth-floor offices in the Bakri Building, downtown Ramallah's largest structure, which is filled with souvenir and shoe-shops on the ground floor. Wadie's relationship with Hassan is almost fraternal, though Wadie keeps the deferential silence appropriate for the very junior sibling who is his brother's assistant. Barghouti chronicled the rise of Palestinian working-class sentiment during the intifada, and its subsequent fall after Oslo, when Fateh operatives took over and converted the unions into nationalist organizations. "This is our bane," he says with considerable animus, "the use of nationalist discourse to cover over social inequities, real economic injustices, and the sorry state of our civil life generally. My idea [he sounds very much like the trained lawyer that he is] has been to go in and help laborers who because of incredible job shortages are either treated badly by their Palestinian employers or summarily fired. We [he nods at Wadie, who had told us about this in December] negotiated a settlement between the Ambassador Hotel and a dozen employees that they discharged unfairly. Wadie also helped us write up and translate a report on the unacceptable rate of child labor in the West Bank. He also must

have told you how we visited the tanning plant in Nablus where workers are given no protection against the chemicals they use or the fumes
they inhale." Agitatedly Wadie added, "I've never seen anything like
it, and what makes it worse is that the management tried to convince
me that the atmosphere was 'good for the workers.' "

The Center has about a dozen members, including a Palestinian
Israeli lawyer improbably named Castro and two or three Europeans
of Wadie's age. It is clear to me, the proud father, that Wadie is very
much liked by everyone: his remarkably unabrasive manner is envi-
able. That plus his sense of humor, his juggling, and his total lack of
affectation or pretentiousness make him extremely easy to be with.
Like his mother, he is also a very private person; unlike his loquacious
father and sister, he doesn't find it easy to reveal or articulate what he
feels, although it is clear that he takes things very seriously.

One of his colleagues gave me a handful of pamphlets about
workers' rights that Wadie had edited and translated. Hassan later
said about them that they were only a fraction of the real difficulty,
which was to prevent Arafat from grabbing hold of all the workers'
pension fund money now held by the Histadrut. "For all these years,"
he explained, "our people worked in Israel, sometimes at the rate
of 100,000 laborers a day. Now there are only three or four thousand who are allowed to work there, but Israel has been deduct-
ing money directly from their paychecks all along; that in addition
to the large sums they deducted before have accumulated into a considerable amount. Arafat is trying to convince the Israelis to give
him the money, claiming that he is the only national authority."
Another example of nationalism being used as an instrument of
blocking social justice for Palestinians.

Wadie was also eager for me to visit the JMCC where he worked as
a translator, occasional columnist, and editor to supplement his tiny
monthly stipend from DWRC. It's remarkable that "information" in
the form of news reports, speculation, official pronouncements, leaks,
constitute what seems to be about 90 percent of conversation and
activity. Aside from an occasional trip to Jordan or Europe, all of my
middle-class friends, most of them professionals, are condemned to
nightly social gatherings with each other. For the short time I was
there I found the hospitality and fellowship invigorating fun, but I

could also see that such a life diet could become claustrophobic. For the first time in our lives we find ourselves in a society with no certainty about, or prospects of, improving anything beyond a fairly narrow circle of friends or relatives. Arafat's office is in Gaza, as are many of his ministries, though some have branches in Ramallah and Jericho. This makes ordinary government, and a sense of continuity, order, stability impossible. There are three branches of the health ministry for example, one each in Gaza and Jericho; then there is Arafat's brother Fathi who directs the Red Crescent, the Palestine Red Cross.

A physician I met in Nablus spoke of the ensuing confusion. Medicines are in constant short supply, whereas fourth generation antibiotics suddenly proliferated even though they are useless in most cases of illness. Somebody made a killing on the super sophisticated drugs; in the meantime everything else is unavailable. He also told me that 70 percent of the serious illnesses on the West Bank are either cancer or heart related, yet there is neither a cardiac unit nor an oncological service anywhere in Palestine. In addition, Arafat throws his weight behind one health ministry, then another, keeping all three off balance and in need of his patronage.

I could discern two sets of functioning civil institutions in Palestine: one is the network of Islamic welfare organizations which is especially strong in Gaza; the other is the group of NGOs, most of which began during the intifada when the Israelis made life very difficult for Palestinians (closed schools, twenty-four-hour curfews, massive censorship, closures). Now Arafat's Authority is battling them in an attempt to reduce, and perhaps even dissolve, their influence. For someone like Wadie who came to Palestine as a volunteer the obvious choice to set down was the NGO network; not only are most of them run by gifted and in some cases charismatic people like Samiha Khalil, the seventy-year-old woman who was the only candidate to oppose Arafat in the January elections, but they were entirely staffed by natives of the West Bank or Gaza whose work began out of real and immediate needs.

The JMCC is a perfect example. Ghassan Khatib, who founded it and spoke with me and Wadie in his East Jerusalem office next to the Turkish Consulate, said that he got the idea when he saw wave after wave of foreign journalists who were in the territories to cover the intifada with no one on the Palestinian side able to give them systematic attention or information. So he started to contact them, arrange for interviews, take them into towns and villages, and generally supply them with a Palestinian view of the complicated uprising. A political science professor at Bir Zeit University, Khatib was naturally linked to many of the intifada committees; partly as a consequence of that fact, when the negotiations began shortly after the October 1991 Madrid Middle East Peace Conference, he was made a member of the Palestinian delegation in Washington.

He is a quiet-spoken, undemonstrative middle-aged man. "Most of the ministries are not really doing much," he said. "Health and education are at least managing to do something, but the overall level of services is extremely low. Mostly," and here he echoed everyone I spoke to, "mostly there are lots of director-generals, and under-secretaries—large numbers of them—who are there as a way for Arafat to appease his supporters. But they don't actually do anything. Except for the security apparatus, which is a going concern." I had recently read an article on this apparatus by Graham Usher, who does good foreign on-the-spot reporting from Palestine; his estimate is that Arafat annually spends $500 million on it, and still comes up short. I was curious to know what the overall legal situation was, since the Authority did not have sovereignty over Area A but only self-rule. Khatib told me that a draft set of Basic Laws was circulating around, but that it hadn't passed.

Another friend, a lawyer, told me later that he had been asked by Arafat to reconcile the commercial laws of the Gaza Strip (operating under Egyptian and Israeli jurisdiction) with those of the West Bank (formulated by the Jordanians and the Israelis). It was easy to do so and he turned in his report in early 1995, but until now nothing has been done. Merchants and investors therefore operate in a legal limbo, with Arafat's personal involvement necessary to conclude arrangements on any significant business. A fair amount of information in the Western press, including the *Wall Street Journal*, confirms this impression. For ordinary Palestinians, however, this reinforces their sense of being lost (*Diya'* is the Arabic word for it that I heard over and over again) and of powerlessness that goes with it. With the Israeli closures and house demolitions—there were at least two on my second day there—plus the Palestinian Authority since the February bombings picking up and holding what is now an estimated twelve thousand "suspects," the feeling is one of a bitter realization that this isn't peace. On the contrary, one woman told me, we're neither at war, nor are we peaceful and independent: frankly, she added, I'm lost.

A steady stream of publications comes out of JMCC, partly to inform foreign journalists of what is taking place in Palestine, partly also as a way of telling a story that is more truthful than the PA's. "Being in Jerusalem exempts us from Arafat's control," said Wadie's colleague Imad. "We publish the *Palestine Report* on a biweekly basis, plus we have a twenty-four-hour service that delivers bulletins to all the news agencies and correspondents on noteworthy events." One day last January, for instance, they carried a harshly critical interview with me that would never have made it into the West Bank papers. For its part Israel is far from careless about what information and discussion it tolerates. Yes, JMCC can send out its reports by fax and E-mail, but anything that seems to challenge Israel's real (as opposed to verbal) authority it definitely opposes. As they tell me about their work in trying to spread around real information, Wadie and Imad speak with the confidence and enthusiasm of people getting something done in a time and place where little was being done.

I heard those accents occasionally and they fired me up intermittently. Munir Fashie, for instance, heads another NGO called TAMER, an association for improving general literacy and intellectual awareness. "Two of the main problems are the absence of role models and the inability to write concretely about anything," Munir told Mariam, Wadie, and me in his spotless Ramallah office, which unlike all the others you visit is not dominated by a big director's desk; we sat around in a circle with members of TAMER, who speak freely and show no deference to the boss. "Young people who look out on our world see no one they can admire or emulate; our leaders are corrupt and autocratic failures. So there's a vacuum which we are trying to fill by encouraging ideas of self-development through reading. We've developed this notion of reading passports; you get one of these passports as a child, and as you take out library books or buy them from somewhere we certify that in the passports. Then you can move up and get a higher-level passport. As for lack of concreteness, we take out pages in *al-Quds,* for example, where we encourage people to express themselves about a given feeling or situation in which they find themselves. The idea is to focus attention on who one is, and to try to do that not in the abstract, fraudulent way that is promoted by our nationalistic discourse, but by expressing oneself simply and directly. Modest perhaps, but we think of ourselves as planting seeds." One of TAMER's associates is a handsome young woman, Safa, who has a U.S. graduate degree and has pioneered sex education classes, formerly an untaught subject, in Palestinian universities and schools. She now travels constantly throughout the territories, giving lectures, demonstrations, showing films about intercourse, hygiene, harassment, infectious disease, and the like. "What has been most fascinating," she said to us, "is that I have found most of my vocabulary readily available in the classical Islamic tradition. It's been there all along, buried under mounds of regressive prohibitions that actually misrepresent Islam for contemporary use."

But these are relatively isolated individual initiatives. The general climate is not hospitable. On Friday March 22 the Israeli police prevented a conference on Jerusalem from taking place in Arab East Jerusalem's Ambassador Hotel. We had been alerted to the conference when Wadie and I went to pay a call on the Alternative Information Center (AIC) in West Jerusalem; their publication *News From Within,* which I receive every month and on whose honorary board I serve, carries excellent coverage of the Israeli scene by dissenting Israeli Jews. Tikvah Honig-Parnass, the journal's editor, was particularly exercised by Israel's collective punishment of the Palestinians and quoted to me a leading writer, S. Yizaher, as saying that Palestinians were cannibals. Such racist emotions, she said, were never more prevalent than now. Anyway, she added, perhaps you could come to our conference tomorrow, although we've received information that it's going to be banned.

As indeed it was. What seemed like a small corps of Israeli soldiers in full battle dress stopped traffic fifty yards from the hotel, which perches on a hill in Sheikh Jarrah overlooking the Old City. We had to leave the car there and walk the rest of the way to the hotel. It was all I could do to restrain the usually unflappable Wadie from remonstrating. As we walked past he vented his spleen to me. "Here are these nineteen-year-olds with American rifles that they use to bully the

Palestinians who just simply take it. I don't know why I take it, but I do. The helplessness is awful, but so is their ignorance." He was to repeat this several times while I was there, each time making it harder for me to say something appropriate, or to explain the facts away.

I couldn't. This had been our condition all of my life. The basic difficulty is that when it came to being pushed around by young people with rifles, it did not finally matter whether the soldiers were Arabs in countries like Egypt, Syria, or Jordan, or Israeli Jews on the West Bank or in Gaza. As an individual one felt alienated and demeaned. The disconnection between oneself and a sullen, almost impersonal authority directed at one's personal freedom, in which the individual has no recourse except to acquiesce without complaint—this was a reality that endured all through the Middle East from my father's generation under Ottoman and British rule, to mine under Israeli and undemocratic Arab rule. Now my son was experiencing it. Each generation seemed to hand it on to the next without being able to do a great deal to change it. Israelis push us around because we are Palestinians; in Arab countries—even Egypt—we are routinely searched and detained at airports, despite our U.S. passports; and wherever one goes one senses that Arab authority is crude, directed mainly at civilians, unrestrained by laws or constitutions.

A small group of people was standing at the hotel's entrance. I greeted Tikvah, who introduced me to a chain-smoking, gray-haired man whom everyone addressed as Mikado. His name is Michael Warchavski, and he runs AIC. His wife is Leah Tsemel, whom I have known for a decade as an indefatigable Israeli lawyer stubbornly defending Palestinians in Israeli courts. Reminding me that Israel is an intensely legalistic country and that the only recourse was for Leah to be in court trying to get the ban lifted, Mikado explains that the police have the right to forbid any activity that conflicts with Knesset legislation passed a couple of years ago ruling "conformity with the Gaza-Jericho accords." "So in this case," he notes matter-of-factly, "the police have decided that a conference on Jerusalem in Jerusalem conflicts with the PLO-Israeli accords that ban any Palestinian political activity in the city." When I ask on what grounds an academic conference could be construed as political activity he says that Feisal Husseini's name on the program equals political activity. Husseini is close to Arafat, and has been designated PA minister in charge of Jerusalem affairs; he also belongs to one of the three "notable" Muslim families in Palestine (the others are the Nashashibis and the Nusseibehs). This adds to his status. "But AIC is an Israeli organization," I said. "It doesn't matter," Mikado responded. "It's the nature of the activity that is banned and of course the fact that West Bank and Jerusalem Palestinians are participating."

We hung around for about an hour without any change in the situation; even the announced press conference was disallowed. Then we went back to the car. Just as we were getting in the "belly-phone" rang: our appointment with the PA minister had come through. He was expecting us at his Ramallah office, and so we headed north again with some apprehension. I had no idea what our reception would be like. I had had a suspicion (which I was usually able to banish from my consciousness) that Arafat, or one of his over-zealous security people, might mean me some physical harm, or that they would try to detain me in some fashion. Dr. Haidar Abdel Shafi, the elderly Palestinian political leader who is universally admired throughout the territories, had sent me a message before I left the United States that I should not plan to come at all. I took that to mean that I should not come to Gaza where Arafat has his most effective and universal presence; on the West Bank he is far less in evidence, and—I found out later—he is much less interested in what goes on there than he is in Gaza, which after all is his power base. Although Wadie had been eager for me to visit, about a month before I left the United States he called and suggested that it might be better if I didn't give any lectures or make any public pronouncements. During two prior visits I had given lectures at Bir Zeit and been sought out by the local press. I decided to forgo lecturing and interviews this time since I didn't feel that I could muzzle myself and *not* be uncritical of Arafat and his people. I had never before succumbed to fear of threats or given much mind to physical violence against me. Now, because of my illness, I was a frailer person; because of Arafat's alliance with the Israelis and the volatility of Palestinian opinion, I felt myself to be more vulnerable.

All this weighed on my mind as we drove up to Ramallah in silence. The rain increased in intensity, the flooded roads and the ever more anarchic traffic in Ramallah adding to my sense of enervation. I had decided to seek out a meeting with Yasir Abd Rabbo, Minister of Information and Minister of Culture, for two reasons. One was that I've known him since the middle seventies. Well-educated, married to Liana Badr, also my friend and an accomplished novelist, he has long struck me as a cut above the other PLO regulars in intelligence and finesse. Once a leading member of the Democratic Front for the Liberation of Palestine (a Marxist-Leninist group headed by Naief Hawatmeh), he had broken off from that group because of Hawatmeh's post–Cold War dogmatic authoritarianism and had started a new party, Fida', of uncertain political status, which neither grew very much nor prevented him from becoming close to Arafat during the Tunis years. He was very much a part of Arafat's inner circle of advisers as the peace initiatives were being undertaken: given the changing political environment, this earned him a cachet of reasonableness that enhanced his prestige and visibility. The second reason is that because of his proximity to Arafat, Abd Rabbo would be the perfect insider for me to speak to. What he said, I thought, would directly reflect Arafat's thinking and the Authority's general climate.

In the case of the former this turned out to be very far from the truth. The elevator wasn't working in the Ministry building, a gaunt, unprepossessing hulk that squatted on the outskirts of Ramallah. We trudged up to the sixth floor and entered a poorly furnished anteroom, with a couple of coffee-stained plastic chairs and a ramshackle desk adding to the place's ill-kept appearance. Wadie's face was already registering disappointment and frustration. I perhaps added to his dismay by noting how the outer office replicated the PLO's office in Fakahani, the lower-middle-class area of Beirut whose name in the seventies had become a byword for the PLO's sloppiness and general heedlessness. Because male Palestinians are extremely heavy smokers, the collection of staff members and random visitors lounging about the landing and the waiting room had created a thick blue cloud which immediately had us coughing and sneezing. A young woman came out of the inner office, offered us coffee, and asked us to wait a few moments; these quickly stretched out to about forty. Then we were ushered in.

Abd Rabbo was very cordial. He is a good-looking, trim man in his early fifties, with (for Palestinians) unusually light brown hair and chiseled features. We kissed each other on both cheeks—Arab men do quite a lot of this—and both of us turned to embrace Liana, who came into the room just after Wadie and I entered. She is a striking black-haired woman with an open, animated face that radiates energy and enthusiasm. I was particularly glad to see the two of them take to Wadie, who is roughly the age of their two sons, both of them away in American universities. To their surprise, Wadie explained in his flaw-less Arabic that he has been on the West Bank for several months and that he only has a few more to go; he also exchanges phone numbers with them. (After I returned to the United States he had dinner at their home several times.) It sometimes surprises Arabs that I can still speak the language after so many years in the United States—but that my son, a patently American young man, can do so is almost a shock.

Abd Rabbo's office is handsomely appointed, in appealing con-trast to the other rooms that we saw. As he had just come back from one of his endless trips to Gaza, I asked him how "things were going," a very vague phrase that I hoped would draw him out. "There's a tremendous amount to be done," he said, "especially here"—he ges-tured out toward the window, through which the drenched gray land-scape could barely be discerned—"given that the man" (Arafat was never referred to by name) "is only interested in Gaza." I then asked what it was like to live through Arafat's leadership.

"Dreadful. You have to realize that all day long he goes through a mountain of papers that have accumulated on his desk overnight. Everything must be approved by him, from a request for vacation by a Commerce Ministry employee, to whether one of his cars should have its muffler repaired, to whether X or Y should attend the next meeting with the Israelis. There are two fixed points in his day around which his entire time revolves; both of them are night appointments. One is his daily eight o'clock meeting with the heads of all his security forces. He's absolutely fixated on his various security organizations; he doesn't take anything at all anywhere near as seriously. The other fixed time is when he directs the various newspaper editors about the next morning's headlines and front page items [In December Maher al-Alami of *al-Quds* was jailed for a week because he didn't put a Christian prelate's flattering comparison between Arafat and Omar ibn al-Khattab, the seventh-century conqueror of Jerusalem, on the front page]. Beyond that, the man has no vision, no idea of where we are going, no plan, no sense of direction. All he deals with are the details, and he loves those because they assure him of complete control. And they take up all his time. That's the way he stays on top: everything has to pass through him. It's a boon for me to be here, just a little beyond his immediate reach. On the other hand, no one can spend a penny without his approval and knowledge. He's now even into business through the monopolies he's set up that allow him to control petroleum products, tobacco, cement, building material, and a few others." I said that I'd heard about those and about the Palestinian Commercial Services Company he'd set up with Khalid Slam. Abd Rabbo nodded agreement.

"A few of us try to guide him through the horrors we're going through as a people. Let me tell you how he operates. He heard from someone that American presidents can declare suddenly stricken sections of the country to be disaster areas. So he came in to one of our meetings a few days ago and said that he planned to designate Gaza as a disaster area. One of us said to him that it wouldn't work here because we are so dependent on outside aid: if one of the donors heard that, despite the sums already pouring in and being used mostly to pay his security bills, Gaza was called a disaster area, there would be no further money. It took us several hours to dissuade him. The next day he came back with the same idea, and we had to go through the whole thing a second time."

"Or take the Sharm el Sheikh summit. Although Arafat didn't seem to be aware of it, Clinton had slotted him in for a half hour private meeting. We prepared a list of issues to bring up with Clinton that would try to get him beyond Israeli security and the fight against Hamas, which are the main concerns of American policy here; after all, we have very pressing needs that include getting some relief from the Israeli closures. Arafat put the list in his pocket, went into the meetings, and never looked at it or referred to what we had agreed on. I was there and from time to time I tried to prod him; it was no use. Clinton told him that his own re-election bid as well as Peres's in a sense depended on Arafat. Instead of using that fact as leverage to extract something for us from the Americans, Arafat went off at a tangent, boasting about how many Hamas members he's put away, how well he's doing against terrorism, and the like. He had no idea that to the Americans and the Israelis he is an asset that they need for the peace process, and for their success at the polls. He seems unaware of his own value to them. He finds it very difficult to concentrate for very long. And we are the worse for it."

This was profoundly depressing stuff. Abd Rabbo went on for almost ninety minutes in this vein. Liana then added that as someone working in the cultural field she and her colleagues were desperate to undertake programs in film, theater, photography; nothing was being done because in the nature of things most of the money went into "security" and besides, the sense of being completely alone, suspended between war and peace, was too much for Palestinians to handle. To this Wadie added that everyone's sense of stifling confinement was made worse by the absence of freely available papers and magazines, of movies and theaters, bookstores and public gathering-places. For the less disadvantaged, hotels like the American Colony drew them in on the chance of seeing foreigners, having coffee in a pleasant place, feeling that one was in contact with the outside world. Ironically, of course, even comfortably off professionals, like my friend, the urological surgeon Mamdouh el Acker, could only get passes to Jerusalem for a few hours; we met him at the Ramallah *mahsoum* rushing to recover his pass from the Israelis so that he could spend six hours in Jerusalem seeing patients.

All of a sudden the meeting was over: Abd Rabbo and Liana had to rush to another appointment, although we did promise to see them again. This never took place—the phone lines were down; I still berate myself for not asking Abd Rabbo, who is after all very much involved with Arafat, why he doesn't resign. This question has obsessed me since the beginning: why do all the people who lend Arafat considerable credibility continue to serve him, and why don't they quit in protest? A few days after I left Palestine Wadie sent me an interview that Abd Rabbo had published in *Dafatir* (*Notebooks*), a publication of the Culture Ministry. In the interview he said (I think for the first time publicly) that Oslo contained major mistakes, and that we are now in the worst fix we have ever been in. And this from one of Arafat's most prominent lieutenants, who participated in all the peace negotiations. Yet Arafat's astonishing powers of survival and domination—plus, alas, the unwillingness of so many good people to confront him with a serious, outspoken opposition to his single-minded ways—allow him to go on as before. During the meetings of the Legislative Council that took place while we were there he was reported to have disallowed any investigation or questioning of his authority over the money.

But there is a further, perhaps more serious problem, to which Wadie drew my attention. "Every organization here," he told me one afternoon, "is run by a boss who's like Arafat, who wants to do or to control everything. There are no other role models than the one he offers. So they all reign over their NGOs and don't even bother to have elections; most of them founded the NGOs and have remained president ever since." Maybe, I suggested, this is what a sense of insidious dislocation and insecurity breeds, this need to hold on to one's position of authority indefinitely, which also grows into a feeling that one is indispensable to the organization. I am torn about this, since quite a few groups have done crucial things (like Samiha Khalil's *In'ash al-Usra,* or Family Rehabilitation Project in Ramallah: it trains nurses and dressmakers, provides kindergarten and day care centers for working mothers, runs bakeries and crafts shops that sell their wares for profit. A formidable personality, "Um Khalil," as she is known, has been running the whole enterprise of about five thousand people for years and years; she has an able group of volunteers, but everyone knows that she is the boss. We were impressed with the three buildings where the organization is housed, which she took us through room by room; but you do have the feeling that if she didn't run it, it wouldn't exist: or perhaps that's what her commanding presence *makes* you feel. On the other hand, is that the only model for the new Palestine?)

Wadie and I put a lot of stock in what Raja Shehadeh, a diminutive middle-aged West Bank lawyer, has to say. As a prospective law student, my son is interested in how Raja managed at the same time to become a successful practicing attorney and, with little apparent prejudice to his practice, also establish al Haq, a celebrated Palestinian human rights organization that acquired prestige abroad during the seventies and eighties. "That sort of thing is what I would like to do," Wadie tells me, "since I'm not really interested in corporate law. But you [meaning me] want me to do law, earn enough money to be

able later to put my money and time to public service. Isn't that so?" I
demur at the thought of his becoming a Wall Street lawyer, although I
sheepishly confess to having said something of the sort. "Let's talk to
Raja," I say a little defensively.

Every time I have seen Raja for the twenty years I've known him I
come away impressed with his intellectual power: in the hasty, bustling
world of Palestinian life he stands out for his ability to analyze and
reflect with enormous precision. He's also someone who cares about
language, but not in the enthusiastic, frequently falsifying way that
many of our politicians have of using words to affirm illusions, or create a collective realm that is unfaithful to the people it describes. He
is therefore one of the few to have taken seriously the *texts* of the
accords, both as legal and linguistic documents. All the evidence I
have suggests that none of the Palestinian negotiators understood
exactly what was being put down, and what they subsequently agreed
to. It was not unexpected that we would find him in a somber mood
when we met him and his American wife, Penny Johnson, for dinner
that evening. But what I was unprepared for was how stubbornly he
defended his recent decision to withdraw completely from public life.
"It's no use at all," he told us with quiet finality. "I am very disillusioned, and I don't feel I can contribute anything positive to what's
happening. Our people are oblivious to what they're doing, and what
the Israelis are doing. The result is a worsening situation that is getting so disadvantageous to us that I am afraid nothing will reverse or
stop it." It was very difficult for either of us to tell him what he ought
to be doing; we didn't have any suggestions, and I think Wadie and I
agreed with his diagnosis. What struck me, though, was his ability to
separate his political disenchantment from his enjoyment of walking
in the pretty hills around Ramallah, plus reading, and writing, all of
which he has always done. He and Penny have no children; they give
the impression of a fulfilled and happy couple, quite a contrast with
the surrounding gloom.

In the middle of our last day Wadie drove me to Bethlehem to get a
look at the so-called bypassing road that the Israelis have been constructing near there: costing $42 million, it is known as the Gilo-Gush
Etzion highway, and it links Jerusalem with the settlements south of
Bethlehem. You see such roads all over the West Bank. Wide and

obtrusive, they are meant to go around the main Palestinian population centers, connect up with the settlements, and make it possible for
Israelis to punctuate West Bank life without having to see Palestinians.
They reminded me of the South African roads that skirted the black
townships; I recall driving in May 1991 from Cape Town to Stellen-
bosch on such a road without noticing those townships until—only
very momentarily glimpsed around a curve—they were pointed out to
me by an ANC friend. As Wadie and I entered Bethlehem itself a new
road and concrete barricade had been erected near the site of Rachel's
tomb; this totally slowed up traffic on the Palestinian side so that people could neither enter nor leave by the north road without great difficulty. On the Israeli side of the divided road I was struck by how its
powerful, almost arrogant calm was obviously meant as a contrast to
the crowded, harried appearance of the Palestinian side, narrower,
muddy, filled with potholes that were never going to be repaired.

To make matters more depressing, our last day was the one we had
appointed for touring the Jerusalem settlements with my oldest Israeli
friend, Dr. Israel Shahak. It was his idea that the three of us do this
and, being of a resolute temperament, he was not to be denied, although of course the upshot was that our mood turned sharply worse.
At dinner a few nights before he had already depressed us by detailing
the ways in which the present situation in the territories was the most
dreadful he had seen since 1967. Shahak is a great, albeit personally
eccentric, intellectual greatly admired and liked by the four of us, the
only Israeli Jew that I know personally who has been completely honest and outspoken in his criticisms of what he calls Israel's "Zionistic"
policies towards the Palestinians. A Polish Holocaust survivor, he
became Professor of Chemistry at the Hebrew University, and founder
of the Israeli League of Human Rights. Now retired, he continues to
supply me (as he has for over twenty years) with thousands of pages of
translation from the Hebrew press, plus his own commentaries, reports, books, and pamphlets that make the standard Western journalistic accounts of Israel look like a crude comic book. He's in frail
health but, sedentary in his ways, he is also as amazingly erudite as
ever. As we drove out toward the settlements, Wadie in the driver's seat
as usual, Shahak and I talked about music, which he listens to constantly. With almost childish glee, he told me about a radio program

he had just recorded about politics in music, in which for instance
he played extracts from works that illustrate the changing status of
women from the eighteenth to the end of the nineteenth century; he
ended with a passage from the *Missa Solemnis,* a piece he characterized over the air as "not peace, but the struggle for peace." I took this
to be a reminder to his Israeli audience that they were still very far
from peace.

"The reason I want you to see this is that you should have no illusions at all about what is being done in Jerusalem," he said as we daw-
dled in an appalling traffic jam leading us out of the city toward the
northwest. Soon we were on Shumel Hanavi Street, and that took us
directly into Ramot, a gigantic concentration of massive (extremely
unattractive) apartment blocks affixed to the gentle hills that ring the
city. Ramot is no hastily thrown up collection of housing units, however; it is a small city containing almost 40,000 Israeli Jews, who now
live on land that was acquired during the 1967 war, and annexed to
Israel. Ramot is served by regular buses that run between it and downtown Jerusalem. Though there isn't much street life or vegetation (in
fact Ramot struck me as unappealingly barren), it has stores, sports
clubs, restaurants. It was late afternoon and Wadie drew attention to
five or six Arab workers straggling home after a day's work. "I can't
get over that sight, even though I see it all the time," he said a little bitterly. "We are the coolies here."

"You can see," Shahak pronounced dramatically, "that nothing
will remove these settlements except for a natural cataclysm or a really
tremendous military operation. Otherwise they are permanent." Then
we drove out of Ramot (Shahak having lost his way until Wadie told
him that he knew the area pretty well, as indeed he did. I was impressed). We went on to another large settlement, Giv'at Zeev, that
abuts the Arab town of Beit Hanina. "You see," Shahak said simply.
Finally at Shahak's request Wadie drove us to a few hundred yards
from where he lived in Er-Ram (Area A) where the West Bank settlements of Neve Ya'acov (population almost 20,000) and Pisgat Ze'ev
(30,000) stand just beyond Central Jerusalem spreading into the
northeastern West Bank hinterland.

Neither Wadie nor I said anything to Shahak about our breakfast
meeting that day with Feisal Husseini, from whose Orient House

office in East Jerusalem the Palestinian effort to preserve (and perhaps even get back) East Jerusalem is run. In contrast to the sheer, overwhelming (if charmless) power of the settlements with their assertive presence making statements of Israeli strength, Husseini's soft-spoken, optimistic accents gave off a kind of unintended frivolity, even irrelevance. Husseini showed us lists of housing units that Palestinians were entitled to build in East Jerusalem. When I asked whether they were actually being built (the number seemed to fluctuate between 800 and 30,000) Husseini said no, but that once the money was raised they would be built forthwith. It sounded very much like Arafat's refrain, for which the Israelis mercilessly upbraided him, that there was *going to* be a *jihad* for Jerusalem. In the meantime more and more housing was being built around northern Jerusalem, thereby consolidating Israeli domination of the area from Ramallah in the north to Hebron in the south. "The best thing Palestinians should do for Palestinians who have not been here," Shahak asserted, "is to have someone take pictures of all these buildings to show the reality of the situation." And, I thought to myself, demoralize diaspora Palestinians still further.

Throughout my visit to the new Palestine I was haunted by an observation made to me over the phone about a year ago by my friend Ibrahim. "What you sense when you are here is that there is a mind working on *their* side; its effects are felt on all Palestinians. You don't feel that there is any mind on our side." I can confirm that and, when I brought it up to Wadie after we dropped off Shahak, he could too. "We can think," he said impetuously, "but the question is how to get past the apathy and self-hatred."

I was reminded of a visit to the University of Puerto Rico six years ago. One of the historians there told me that the tragedy of political life on the island is that people have been stuck in the status debate—should we remain a commonwealth, become independent, or are we really only a U.S. colony?—for almost the whole century. In the meantime, the general condition seems to deteriorate. In Palestine, I felt, it would be a good thing if we could have a status debate, but we are still not there yet. After three quarters of a year there Wadie now feels that he too is not moving forward; in addition, the daily tensions and uncertainties have accumulated to the point that his frustrations turn

into neck and head pains, sleeplessness, weight loss. My wife and I
think it is time for him to leave, and he is coming round to that view.
"But," he tells me on our way to the airport, "I will always come
back." At the airport we were put through a long period of intense
and, in my opinion, pointless questioning by a team of young Israeli
security personnel. "Why did you come? Who did you see? What did
you do? Give us names, people, and places. Where did you stay?" The
young American woman ahead of us was reduced to tears under the
grilling. When I asked an airline employee why the unpleasantness
when one was leaving, as opposed to arriving, he shrugged his shoul-
ders. "A mind at work," I muttered to myself as I rushed to the gate
with about two minutes to spare.

POSTSCRIPT, AUGUST 20, 1996: I write these lines from a New
York hospital bed. Wadie and I were again in Palestine for a few days
in early July, I to attend a meeting, he once again to accompany me
and take me around. Since I had left in March, Peres had invaded
Lebanon, created 300,000 refugees, killed about 200 civilians, and
wounded thousands more. Yet, as Israel Shahak had said to us in
March, he would lose the elections, which he did. In Palestine the
situation had deteriorated considerably. Arafat's security people
seemed everywhere on the West Bank. He had requisitioned the entire
six-story Ministry of Education for his personal "presidential" office
in Ramallah and in addition caused a demonstration in the city by
confiscating several acres for a new personal residence there. Mrs.
Arafat was spending the summer in Deauville.

A new spirit of resistance was apparent among the members of the
Legislative Council that I met, and that was clearly annoying to
Arafat, who was described to me as screaming the most obscene epi-
thets at members, including Abdel Shafi, who he thought had gone too
far. But there was also a sense that because of his still total control of
money and his security services, Arafat was getting away with murder.
Literally. A few days ago some spokesman of his admitted to having
killed seven Palestinians under torture. Hundreds are picked up
and detained, so much so that in late July Arafat's men were finding

themselves—like Israeli soldiers during the intifada—shooting at stone-throwing crowds in Nablus and Tulkarem.

His powers of cooptation are formidable. My friend and former student Hanan Ashrawi had (inexplicably to me) accepted a position as minister in his Authority. Through numerous phone messages, I was followed around by two members of his entourage whom I had known before Oslo, to get me to make up with him. I refused to speak to them or to see him. Two weeks ago security men appeared in all Gaza and West Bank bookshops (by order of the Minister of Information, Abd Rabbo) and confiscated every one of my books. I am now banned in Palestine for having dared to speak against our own Papa Doc.

London Review of Books, September 5, 1996

Chapter Fourteen

Uprising Against Oslo

OVER THE PAST few days there have been two battles between Palestinians and Israelis. One is over Jerusalem, and was most immediately provoked by Israeli Mayor Ehud Olmert's decision to reopen a tunnel beneath what some Jews call the Temple Mount, site of the second temple destroyed almost two millennia ago, and what Muslims call al-Haram al-Sharif, the noble sanctuary, where the Mosque of Omar and the Aqsa Mosque have stood for almost twelve hundred years. As both sides quite rightly see it, the issue is dominance over Jerusalem. Both Olmert and Netanyahu know perfectly well that the Israeli annexation of East Jerusalem after the 1967 war has been definitively consolidated by an enormous ring of settlements around the city, built on confiscated Palestinian land; in addition, Israel has steadily imported a large number of mostly orthodox Jews into the predominantly Arab old city in an unceasing attempt—abetted by house occupations, expropriations of land, deceptive property purchases from Arabs, and outright eviction of Palestinians—to "Judaize" what was formerly Palestinian about East Jerusalem.

As against all this there has been an inadequate, even pathetic, Palestinian and, generally, Arab and Muslim response. Conferences, ringing declarations, promises of money, have done nothing to counteract the Israeli juggernaut. Yet no country on earth recognizes the Israeli annexation. The fact remains, however, that, as Israel Shahak has said, it would take either a cataclysmic natural disaster to dislodge Israelis from settlements and newly Judaized quarters, or an unimaginably large military campaign. Since neither has been in the offing, the sudden, middle-of-the-night reopening of the tunnel seems the latest in a series of "created" facts, an act of arrogant triumphalism, a sort of rubbing of Palestinian and Muslim noses in the dirt. This had the added effect of pouring fuel on the smoldering sectarian competition that has been the city's long-standing bane. I do not think there is any doubt that this Likud assertion of what is unmistakably *Jewish* power over Muslim holy places was intended to show the world, especially the increasingly powerful right-wing Israeli religious factions, that Judaism can do what it wants. It is a profoundly ugly gesture planned also to dramatize Palestinian (Arab, Christian, Muslim) powerlessness.

The second battle is full of paradoxes and arises directly out of the Oslo peace process. Those of us who criticized it from the start were a tiny minority of Arabs and Jews who grasped its ungenerous, essentially humiliating implications for the Palestinian people. This view has since acquired considerable support. Sponsored by the United States, the peace process was built callously upon the sufferings of a people whose society had been destroyed in 1948 by an incoming Jewish population claiming biblical rights in Palestine. Two thirds of the land's inhabitants were driven from their homes. In 1967 Israel occupied the rest of historic Palestine. Yet Oslo neither ended Palestinian dispossession, nor genuinely alleviated the short-term miseries of an Israeli military occupation, during which the economy, infrastructure, human resources of the Palestinians had been programmatically damaged. It is true that Yasir Arafat, discredited and isolated after his ruinous pro-Saddam Gulf crisis policy, was allowed in 1994 to set up a truncated autonomy regime that was still controlled by the Israelis. But despite the rhetoric and some of the ceremonies and symbols of peace, Israeli West Bank settlements grew during the Rabin-Peres period that ended in May of this year. The newly redrawn areas of the West Bank and Gaza gave Palestinians limited autonomy (but no sovereignty) in 3 percent of the former and about 60 percent of the latter, which the Israelis were glad to get rid of anyway. Meanwhile Arafat built a Palestinian Authority that was corrupt, dictatorial, and, so far as generally improving conditions were concerned, a dismal failure.

The autonomy arrangements that Palestinians (excluding the four million refugees whose destiny was postponed to some nebulous "final status" situation) have to live with today are a bizarre amalgam of three historically discarded "solutions" devised by white colonialists to the problem of native peoples in nineteenth century Africa and the Americas. One was the concept that natives could be turned into irrelevant exotics, with their lands taken from them, and living conditions settled on them that reduced them to day laborers and premodern farmers. This is the American Indian model. Second is the division of lands (reservations) into non-continuous Bantustans, in which an apartheid policy gave special privileges to white (today's Israeli) settlers, while letting the natives live in their own run-down ghettos; there they would be responsible for their municipal affairs, yet subject to white (again, Israeli) security control. This is the South African model. Finally, the need to give these measures some degree of local acceptability required a native "chief" to sign on the dotted line. He temporarily gathered a little more status than before, the whites gave him some support, a title and a privilege or two, even a native police force so that everyone could rest easy that the right thing had been done for his people. This was the French and British model for nineteenth-century Africa. Arafat is the late-twentieth-century equivalent of the African "chief."

The problem of course is that as a nation the Palestinians were hardly likely to be content with ramshackle anachronisms of this sort. Arafat placed himself in an impossible situation. He kept promising things (like East Jerusalem) which he simply could not deliver, but he was also too jealous of his own power to allow anyone else any authority or breathing space. Most of the rewards he, as well as the Israelis and Americans, kept speaking about never materialized. Gaza has unemployment that has sometimes risen to 70 percent. Investments have not poured in. The clamp-down on expression and democratic practices is as severe as under direct Israeli rule. A vast police apparatus has transformed the barely discernible outlines of Palestinian self-determination into a premature replication of countries like Iraq. And still the Israelis clamor for security from Palestinian terrorists while their colons confiscate more land, build more houses, and bully more people such as the inhabitants of Hebron, whose current plight is a capsule version of the whole mess.

No human being can endure grotesque injustice and suffering of this kind for very long. Since Netanyahu came to power he has interminably made it clear that he is tough, and that peace with the terrorist Arafat is a negligible priority. But this was all icing on a cake already baked and partially eaten by the Labor Party. The terrible thing is how much some Palestinians trusted Israeli intentions, particularly at a time when the Arab governments were so supinely weak and villainous in their hypocrisy and mendacity.

A good deal of what has been happening in Jerusalem, Gaza, and the West Bank is therefore an explosion that could easily have been (and in some cases was) foreseen. It is an intifada against the very texts and maps of the Oslo accords, and against its planners and participants, Israeli as well as Palestinian. For several months Palestinian dissatisfaction with Arafat's regime has been expressed in mini-intifadas against his police in places like Nablus and Tulkarem. Polls have shown a marked increase in disaffection and anger. But when the die is cast and there seems to be a new Israeli push to hurt all Palestinians, the rage spills over, as it has during the past few days, with Arafat and Netanyahu having no real choice left except to try to bring things under control, to make Oslo work a little longer. Already Abu Mazen has been dispatched to Tel Aviv; Netanyahu returned abruptly from a European trip. My guess is that their efforts will win out, and an uneasy calm will prevail; each leader is imprisoned in a system that he does not fully control, despite the preponderance of power on the Israeli side.

The horror of so much Palestinian blood wantonly spilled is scarcely mitigated by a premonition of future eruptions. Israel is trying as much as possible now to preempt, perhaps even circumvent, the final-status negotiations. Palestinian options are not so clear, given the tremendous disadvantages under which we suffer as a people. The sight of Palestinians being beaten, shoved around, arrested, killed, and wounded is very painful and an occasion for deep sorrow and anger. It is perhaps possible that Arafat and his shaken Palestinian Authority may have begun to perceive that the final status is likely to be as dismal as the present one, thus egging on unarmed civilians to take on the Israeli army. But there is always the danger that such justified discontent cannot so easily be turned off and on, or manipulated whenever the going gets rough with the unregenerate Netanyahu. My hope is that Arafat will at last turn to his long-suffering people and tell them the bitter truth, which is that Israel has need only of a cosmetic peace now while we are so weak and undermobilized.

The present crisis is, I think, a glimmering of the end of the two-state solution, whose unworkability Oslo, perhaps unconsciously, embodies. Israelis and Palestinians are too intertwined with each other in history, experience, and actuality to separate, even though each proclaims the need for separate statehood and will in fact have it. The challenge is to find a peaceful way in which to coexist not as warring Jews, Muslims, and Christians, but as equal citizens in the same land.

The Observer, September 29, 1996
The Gulf Today, October 1, 1996
Al-Hayat, October 1, 1996
Al-Khaleej, October 1, 1996
Al-Ahram Weekly, October 3, 1996
El Pais, October 1, 1996

Chapter Fifteen

Responsibility and Accountability

Two principal themes in Arab and Palestinian discourse emerged during and after the recent crisis over the provocatively opened Jerusalem tunnel. One was the need to rally round the Authority in its time of crisis with Netanyahu. The second was the even greater urgency of returning to the signed peace documents between the PLO and Israel. Both are understandable reactions to a serious sense of great crisis and consternation. For without the Oslo accords, the Palestinian Authority would lose a great deal of its international legitimacy, as well as its internal coherence. Besides, it is natural in a time of what seems to have been a moment of extra arrogance by Israel, and after considerable Palestinian life had been lost, to speak passionately about laying down differences, setting aside inter-Palestinian quarrels, dropping all partisan politics, in the interest of the common welfare. A former Democratic Front military leader, now resident in Ramallah after prolonged residence in Tunis, ventured the thought that it was almost immoral of intellectuals at this time to say anything that went outside the accepted consensus, especially after Palestinian martyrs had fallen in the national cause.

While I understand and to some extent sympathize with some of this, I must also say that I remain unconvinced by this whole line of reasoning. Certainly unity is a good thing, as is maintaining pressure on the Israelis, whose shameless and contemptible attitudes to Arabs

and Palestinians have been the bane of the Middle East for five generations. But I cannot accept the thesis that we must all plunge ourselves
heedlessly into the seething emotional turbulence of the present, without a thought, or a bit of clarity about why we are in this terrible state
to begin with. The condition of Arab and Palestinian politics today is
desperate not because of an excess, but because of a poverty, of reason
and responsibility. Is it the intellectual's duty simply to become a
member of the chorus, or is it more valuable to stand aside (which
implies not detachment but, I think, a greater commitment to the common good) and reflect without undue emotion on why we are here,
and how we can move forward? The answer for me is clear: critical
thought is much more useful now than flag-waving, a rhetorical ploy
which I have always thought is one of the cheapest political tactics ever
invented.

In its October 14, 1996, issue, the influential American weekly
magazine *The New Yorker* published a very long account of the
Palestinian-Israeli negotiations in light of the impasse caused by
Netanyahu's policies. The author is Connie Bruck, someone who has
never before written about the Middle East, but whose work provided
readers with one of the most complete and intimate descriptions of
what has been taking place. Yet it is also perfectly clear that despite
her access to the substantial number of influential Palestinians whom
she quotes (Abu Mazen, Abu Alaa, who is her central source, Nabil
Shaath, Mahmoud Darwish, Nasir al-Qidwa, Hassan Asfour, among
others), some of whom were directly involved in the negotiations with
Israel, Bruck seems to be an ideological Labor Zionist. Throughout
her article she gives one example after another—some of which I shall
describe below—of how Peres literally cheated and bullied his Palestinian interlocutors, leaving them in the end with a pathetic patchwork of little autonomous regions that, she says, added up only to
about 3 percent of the land.

Yet she concludes her article by praising Rabin and Peres and Uri
Savir, with whom she reports Abu Alaa established a "mystical" bond
as men of principle and courage. The Labor leaders, she said, had a
"moral commitment" which nevertheless "extracted concession after
concession from the Palestinians, unquestionably overpowering them."
Then in total contradiction *with* her own account she adds that

the Israelis "did not see the Palestinians as a lesser order of being," whereas everything she talks about suggests that they did. "They did not see them as unruly subjects for whom some small, spotty parcel . . . of their homeland should suffice," which is exactly what the Israelis did give the Palestinians, and exactly how they did (and continue) to see them.

I mention all this about Bruck in order first of all to show that even when confronted with evidence of their own research and selection, supporters of Israel can override that evidence and conclude that some Zionists are fine people with a moral commitment. I recall feeling the same way when I first read Benny Morris's important book on the birth of the Palestinian refugee problem, in which Morris—also a liberal Israeli—gives example after example of the concerted Zionist plan to drive out the Palestinians in 1948. Yet he too concludes, inexplicably, that there was no real plan, only a series of incidents that were the result of a general war.

Be that as it may, Bruck's *New Yorker* article is important not because of its peculiar conclusions but because this is the first non-Arab and non-Palestinian account of the process from the American and Israeli point of view that confirms what I, and many other critics of the process, have been saying. The article deserves translation into Arabic for its details and accuracy; here I can only give two or three examples of how the future of Palestine was negotiated. Bruck tells us that according to Arafat's aides, the Palestinian leader probably never read the agreements, relying on his assistants (who gave him "a rosy picture" of its contents) or on a quick reading of the headings; Abu Mazen told Bruck that for several months after the Washington ceremonies Arafat did not realize that he was not getting a state, only autonomy. Furthermore, Arafat regularly intervened in the negotiations, making it easier for the Israelis to get concessions from him which his own people had already refused; the Norwegians were useful in this, and I must say, they emerge from Bruck's account as manipulative and slippery, as well as unreasonably pro-Israel in what they did.

The Israeli plan as formulated by Peres was to "remake" and "transform" Arafat into a partner for the Israelis, so that he could make historically unpalatable concessions to them and remain as an instrument for implementing their schemes. Before the negotiations began in earnest an Israeli-American lawyer with years of international experience had drafted the agreement *in sixteen drafts;* for their part, however, the Palestinians had done nothing. Bruck describes their woeful lack of preparation, their various cults of personality, the duplicity of which they were victims, at the expense of their people of course.

The worst deception by the Israelis was in Oslo Two. Both sides had agreed not only on a schedule of re-deployment, but also on what percentage of the land held by Israel would be conceded to the Palestinians. The coordination of timetables and percentages over a period of several months gave the process a semblance of success for the Palestinians; although they began by getting autonomy in the main cities—3 percent of the whole—according to the schedule-percentage plan they would be getting about 70 percent (some thought it was 80 percent) of the West Bank. When the documents were drafted and ready for signature, Bruck says that the percentages had been eliminated unilaterally. But the furious Palestinians were forced to sign anyway. This meant that if Netanyahu wants "to go back" to the implementation of Oslo he can withdraw six inches and say he had exchanged land for peace. The fact is therefore that Peres, Beilin, Savir, and company had bamboozled the Palestinians, all the while posturing as serious men of peace with real partners.

Bruck writes as someone in favor of the peace process, by no means as a critic or opponent. She too longs for the days of Peres and his group, which is to say that they were plausibly ripping off the Palestinians, while the ruffianly Netanyahu, who has more or less the same thing in mind, is less presentable, more embarrassing for supporters of Israel.

In view of the current crisis therefore it seems quite evident that a good deal of responsibility for the horrors of what the Palestinian people now endure at the hands of Israel is due to the negotiators, with Mr. Arafat at the top. This leadership produced the hideous map of many Bantustans, they agreed to the settlements, they did not prepare, they lied (Bruck says that Arafat "always lied"), they accepted the plan without real timetables and percentages, they made the concessions, they in effect connived with the Israelis to put forth what in reality was a travesty of peace, in which Palestinians got very little except the autonomy regime and the dubious privileges of running municipal affairs.

To return to Oslo, which has been the central plea in official Palestinian discourse, is therefore to go back to the very situation that produced the mess we are in right now. During the 1921 Anglo-Irish negotiations, when Britain was the most powerful country in the world, the Irish resistance leaders Michael Collins and Eamon de Valera always said that their ultimate strength in dealing with the British was their people and their power of refusal.

Is it not right at this juncture to refuse merely to reiterate the well-known formulas about national unity, while more of Palestine is conceded unwisely and without broad popular participation? I agree that we face a national emergency, but over four million Palestinians exist outside of Palestine: why are their needs and concerns never taken into account? Why are Palestinians in Lebanon, Syria, Jordan, and the Gulf never consulted? Inside Palestine there is a rule of autocracy in which people are afraid to speak, in which the press is controlled, and in which only authorized opinion is permitted. To say, as Mr. Ahmed Khalidi fatuously claims in a recent article, that it is irresponsible to ask for democracy in Palestine now, since we must wait for fifteen years before we can begin to think of democratic practices, is the rankest idiocy. As we give up more and more of ourselves to the Authority, letting Arafat do what he wishes without any check or accountability on his power to use his bloated security services, we are being as bad as any any Arab state. And we do not even have a state. How can we repeat the tragic course of the Arab countries, in which national unity and a state of permanent emergency have been used as a cover for sustained dictatorship, total corruption, and mediocrity, plus more and more losses to Israel?

Neither Israel nor the United States has the slightest desire to foster a peace process that guarantees Palestinian self-determination or independent statehood. Those are the plain facts, as even superficial scrutiny of the various peace arrangements between the PLO and Israel will immediately attest. The time for illusions and falsehoods is now over. Palestinian blood has been spilled in the fruitless cause of an agreement which is designed specifically to keep Palestinians under the perpetual domination of the Israelis. We have not hurt the Israelis, we have not defeated them in anything: why then do we expect that they will respect us or, as the official Palestinian mind keeps hoping, do we delude ourselves into believing that they will give us something? To depend on the United States for anything more than wresting further concessions out of us is, in my opinion, utter delusion. We must learn to live in a reality that we create by our own efforts, and we must stop waiting for some external savior to appear and fix everything for us.

I have been criticized for not offering alternatives, being too negative, etc. But everything I write is premised on the idea that what we have before us is a bad alternative, and that it needs changing. To expect me, or any single individual, to provide ready-made, easy solutions is part of the same ideological deformation that causes us at this late date to sit around waiting for a savior in the United States or France or Russia. The only way forward is *as a people,* with all of us challenging those who have given away Palestine in a fit of distraction. We must speak out, hold meetings, ask questions as loudly and as publicly as possible. Those are four alternatives already. And someone must finally be held to account for the loss via Oslo of what is left of Palestine: alternative number five.

Al-Hayat, October 29, 1996
Al-Khaleej, October 29, 1996
The Gulf Today, October 30, 1996
Al-Ahram Weekly, October 31, 1996

Chapter Sixteen

Intellectuals and the Crisis

D URING THE CONSTERNATION caused in Arab and Palestinian ranks by Benjamin Netanyahu's actions over the past several weeks there has been a tendency to emit bleats of regret over the Labor Party's disappearance from power. In addition, as I mentioned in my last article, the chorus has been that we should return to Oslo, as if Oslo with all the ambiguities and unfavorable clauses were not in fact the problem exploited by Netanyahu to squeeze, torment, and otherwise make life miserable for Palestinians. Far from being solutions for or escapes from the impasse, these two attempts to turn history back to some idyllic period when all things seemed rosy and invitingly possible strike me as dangerous illusions. We now know too much about Shimon Peres's actions since 1992 to accept the notion that as prime minister he was a man of peace in the real sense of the word. Everything he did vis-à-vis the Palestinians, and Yasir Arafat in particular, suggests that the continuity between the historical attitudes of Labor Zionism toward Palestinians, their rights, and permissible aspirations (Ben-Gurion referred to the Arabs as Red Indians) and Peres's policies was carefully maintained. True, Peres is a past master of *hasbara*—the art of disseminating information for the *goyim*—and he is a skillful manipulator of television, so that he can always appear statesmanlike and visionary: nevertheless most of what he did was to extract concessions from the Palestinians according to a rigorous ideological program whereby they would always remain a subordinate people, allowing them very little in return.

Given these realities it would seem to me inappropriate, to say the least, to consider the Israeli Labor Party and its leadership (even members of Meretz) to be the prime lobby for peace inside Israel. This of course has been Arab and PLO policy since 1991, and even before. In his recent article analyzing the discussion of normalization in Egypt and elsewhere the prominent Egyptian political analyst Gamil Mattar is absolutely right to say that all through the 1970s and 1980s Arab intellectuals were enjoined by their governments to enter discussions with Israeli and American intellectuals, functionaries, and politicians in the misguided hope that these meetings would convince Israel and its supporters that the Arabs were indeed ready for peace. All that happened was that Israeli positions hardened, and more demands were made on the Arabs. I recall that during the mid-eighties I was persuaded to meet a well-known Labor Party activist with a very famous name. "Give us your acceptance of Resolution 242 and the sky's the limit: we can do amazing things in return," I was told. "But we need to be assured that you are seriously interested in peace." In 1988 the PNC produced its recognition of 242, but the overall Israeli position remained unchanged. It struck me then as now that Arab, and especially Palestinian, positions were always guided by the prerogatives not of Palestinian dispossession but of Israeli psychology, as if having one of the most powerful armies in the world, a nuclear arsenal, and the full, unconditional backing of the United States was insufficient to allay Israeli anxieties. There was always another hurdle for us to jump, one more insecurity to address, still more fears to assuage—the list kept getting longer. Somehow it did not seem appropriate to think about *our* insecurities, or *our* fears.

This extraordinary self-forgetfulness on our part was, and remains, a legacy of the colonial era when it was assumed that natives were to be dictated to by the master, used, employed, exploited with scant regard for their concerns. There is also the added complication that our interlocutors were Jews who were at the same time survivors of the Nazi Holocaust, as well as colons who used the strategies and tactics of colonialists in other parts of Africa and Asia. No one to my knowledge has had to deal with such a complication anywhere else in the world, where white colonialists were wresting control of land and resources from native peoples. In addition, Zionism's authentically idealistic component so far as *only* Jews were concerned—which argued the world over that Jews were coming to Palestine in order to be reborn as a nation after centuries of unique ordeal—swayed public opinion, as well as the policies of Western governments whose guilt at doing very little to assist Jews during the Holocaust made them compensate (relatively inexpensively) in the present for their costly sins in the past. As a result Palestinian voices were simply unheard, and in very little time Israel became central to the ideology of European and American liberalism. The main beneficiary of this was of course the Labor Party, a full member of the Socialist International, and to all intents and purposes a representative of progressive causes in the Middle East and elsewhere. Little attention was paid to its aggressive wars, its disgracefully racist policies toward its Arab population or, since 1967, its brutal colonial policies, including the first massive settlements, collective punishments, annexation, and attacks against its neighbors. Labor was supposed to be tough, yes, but it was also believed to be rhetorically ready to be as forthcoming and as conciliatory as, inversely, the Arabs were not. Outside the Labor Party most Arab governments and their intellectuals perceived only the religious and political extremists associated with the Likud, Gush Emunim, Rabbi Kahane, and the other ideological zealots. Until about 1990 knowledge and analysis of Israel and the United States in the Arab world were both superficial and incomplete: even the tiny number of specialized institutes and individuals had very small audiences and, in the absence of free discussion and debate, a general current was maintained in which Israel was an enemy and its existence—despite Camp David—publicly decried, or ignored. So the various meetings, seminars, debates that took place as Gamil Mattar has described them were in effect closeted away from the scrutiny of most people, they did not seem to be coordinated, nor in the end were they useful to the Arabs, except, interestingly enough, as a way of surreptitiously getting closer to the Israeli power center. What policy-makers had in mind was not made clear and, in my own case as a member of several discussion groups between Israelis, influential (and we thought at the time) well-meaning American Jews, and a small handful of Palestinian intellectuals, I never felt that what we were doing was understood or properly assessed by the PLO. I was partly wrong of course, since behind our backs a whole program of cooperation, based on Palestinian concessions, was being set up: this led directly to Oslo.

Two important points need to be made about the present dilemma. One concerns the situation inside Israel, how it is read and interpreted. The other concerns the role of the Arab intellectual, which I would like to deal with first. There are two clear options here, so far as the intellectual's role is concerned (actually they are not so clear in real life, but for the purposes of analysis they can be construed as clear). One is to maintain a position of total independence and say you are going to talk about and act in a situation that directly confronts both Arab and Israeli political power, refusing to accept either of these as defining your role. Yet Mohammad Sid Ahmed said in a recent *Ahram* article about the debate over the current crisis that politics for politicians and their associated intellectuals is pragmatic and the art of the possible; in that case, you act as an intellectual whose purpose is to advance various interests, to influence and be involved in policy. I myself think that is a disastrous course: it has brought us to a situation where no values or principles are maintained, since being effective, influential, mainstream, and acceptable are the main criteria for action, with the further consequence that the intellectual is guided not by his/her sense of the truth of the situation, but by considerations of "the possible." Too often this has meant internalizing the norms of power, not those of genuine reflection and analysis, which answer, in my opinion, to more permanent, long-term considerations not immediately tied to implementation or to advancing policies and interests in the realm of the possible. Being far less powerful than either Israel or the United States—not only militarily, but also culturally and institutionally—we inevitably end up playing according to their agendas, as the last few years so shabbily attest.

The independent intellectual, I think, would therefore regard the impasse of today as an aspect of the larger problem, which is that Israeli society has maintained a rigorous denial of its own past toward the Palestinians in particular, and the Arabs generally. We have not made our voices heard inside Israeli society, that is, from a position that gets us attention as voices of conscience and challenge, rather than as petitioners or supplicants. Total refusal of what is now called "normalization" strikes me as unsubtle and inattentive to important currents within Israeli culture, currents that need to be supported, addressed, engaged. Why should critical voices like those of Israel Shahak be ignored just because they are not attached to power, or because we have a policy of not talking to Israelis under any circumstances? I do not think it is reasonable to expect Israelis to apologize in advance of a discussion for what Israel has done to Arabs and Palestinians, although it is, I think, possible to choose one's interlocutors and audience inside Israel on the basis of principle rather than proximity to power—hence, people like Shahak or Stanley Cohen, or the Alternative Information Center, as opposed to a Yossi Sarid or a Shimon Peres.

The main intellectual task is to confront the Israeli conscience with the serious human and political claims of the Palestinians: these require moral, intellectual, cultural attention of the most profound kind, and cannot be easily deflected by the common tactic of putting Israeli insecurity on the same plane. On the other hand I do think it is a mistake simply to rule out the whole history of anti-Semitism (the Holocaust included) as irrelevant. As Palestinians and Arabs we have not even tried to study this enormous subject, nor in any serious way have we tried to see how it impinges on the Jewish, and indeed Western, conscience as something all too real. Thus we need a discourse that is intellectually honest and complex enough to deal both with the Palestinian as well as the Jewish experience, recognizing where the claims of one stop and where the other begin. From that point on, we can then begin to discuss the mode of future coexistence between the two peoples, a coexistence that must rule out the possibility of any recurrence of the two great historical traumas that link us together. That seems to me a worthy goal, and a precondition for discussion.

Such considerations would then dictate one's interpretation of Israeli society, which is the first issue I raised above. If you look at it from the point of view of the Labor Party and its interests, which has been the tendency since the 1991 Madrid conference, then inevitably you will subscribe to an extremely limited ideological perspective.

Granted that every Labor Party member is not identical with every other one, and granted also that not every Laborite is limited by Party doctrine. Nevertheless it would be a mistake to accept the Labor Party as a reference point or as the main instrument of change in Israel, so far as Palestinians are concerned: the record is not an encouraging one, its relationship to power is necessarily inflected with militarism, colonialist attitudes, and a general heedlessness with regard to the Palestinians as a people. I see no reason to reward or endow it with miraculous capacities for change that end up as Peres did, by deceiving us. Israeli society is complicated and full of considerable fluidity, but in my view it cannot be studied to advantage without attention to its potential for real, as opposed to cosmetic, accommodation with Palestinian national rights in all their historical and moral richness. Here the constituency made up, for example, of the universities, independent artists and journalists, the Oriental Jewish community, is a genuinely more progressive agent of change than looking backward nostalgically to Peres and his party.

What I have been proposing here therefore is a very different approach from what is now available within Arab discussions of the crisis we are in. Genuine independence of opinion and approach are required for it, yet these seem unprovided for inside the political establishments that ponder and are trying to come to terms with our present situation. In short the situation seems to be especially ripe for debate, open discussion, and genuine process enacted by independent intellectuals. Are we up to the task?

Al-Hayat, November 5, 1996
Al-Khaleej, November 5, 1996
Al-Ahram Weekly, November 7, 1996
The Gulf Today, November 7, 1996

Chapter Seventeen

Whom to Talk to

As THE DEBATE over the role of intellectuals continues, I think it is extremely useful to provide a little more context and background on the type of ideological problem we face with regard to Israel. There has been far too general a rush to think of the Israeli Labor Party as a partner for peace, or as a possible group for Arab intellectuals to begin to lobby on the general question of peace, something on which of course Netanyahu's Likud, the far right, and the extreme religious parties that are the Likud's constituency have taken an extremely hard line. A more useful approach is to begin by asking what sort of peace it is that as Palestinians and Arabs we want, and whether or not there are deeply ingrained attitudes in the Labor Party's constitution and history that limit, if they do not altogether exclude, the possibility for Labor of ever accepting the kind of peace we would find acceptable and minimally just. It is very necessary to keep in mind that the current peace process was not negotiated abstractly or in a vacuum, but was the product of Labor's very specific political tradition and long-standing ideological as well as philosophical formation. The point to be made here is that unless those are understood as constitutively limiting what it is that Labor can accept and live with on the Palestinian side we will be repeating the same mistakes and drawbacks of the current peace process which, I have been saying in these pages, rests on a fundamental misinterpretation of what Labor is and what it can (and cannot) become.

What I propose to discuss are the foundations of the political phi-losophy of Labor as a liberal party in Israel; these suggest that it plays a particular role, it shares many things in common with other liberal constitutional parties, and it looks at the future within certain limits. What it is able to undertake for peace with the Palestinians is therefore a very specific thing; unless we accept that as a profound constraint on the kind of peace it will act on behalf of, then we will, I am sorry to say, continue to flounder in disappointment and deception. I have no doubt that the only acceptable form of peace between Israel and Pales-tine must really be a mutual one, in which Israel cannot enjoy benefits like sovereignty, security, territorial continuity, real political indepen-dence, and national self-determination, and Palestine not. Peace must be between equals, which is exactly what is wrong with the Oslo peace process. All one has to do is to look at the texts themselves, beginning with the exchange of letters of supposedly mutual "recog-nition" to note that whereas the PLO recognized Israel's right to exist—a formula hitherto unknown in international or customary law—renounced violence, and more or less said that it would behave itself, Israel contented itself with recognizing the PLO only as the rep-resentative of the Palestinian people, a rather limited proposition on the face of it. Moreover, in none of the hundreds of pages of texts that followed is there any indication that Palestinians would have the right to sovereignty, or that Israel would completely remove its army and settlements of occupation. Indeed, as I have been saying for too many months, the Oslo accords are designed to guarantee Palestinian subor-dination and dependence for the foreseeable future; like Peres, Netan-yahu has pledged himself to this formula, albeit in a harsher but in my opinion less hypocritical form.

Given all this, it would seem pertinent to ask whether there is any way in which the Labor Party, its intellectuals, functionaries, and gen-eral membership can be seen as prepared in some measure to accept the recognition of Palestinians as a people fundamentally entitled to the same rights as Israeli Jews. I am prepared to believe that such recognition might occur over a reasonable amount of time, and that a new process that envisions a really mutual recognition of Palestinians by Israelis, as well as vice versa, would have to take place step by step over a certain period of time. Is Labor therefore really a potential partner or lobby for peace in the real sense of the word?

My argument is that mostly it is not, and that we have to work outside the Labor Party for the kind of change that as Palestinians and Arabs we need to provoke. What are my reasons? As no one needs to be told, Israel is a very special kind of state with a very unusual form of democracy created by complex laws. It is the product of at least two historical currents, both of them feeding directly into the Labor Party, which has been the dominant party throughout the history of modern Zionism. The first of these currents is of course political Zionism, a form of Jewish nationalism whose goal since the nineteenth century has been the establishment of a state in Palestine (although for a time, other parts of the world were considered acceptable) exclusively for Jews. Anyone who has read the main documents or records of the principal debates within Zionism will be forced to conclude that hardly any time was spent discussing the role of non-Jews (Muslims, Christians, Palestinians, and other Arabs) in what was to become Israel: the Zionists were understandably focused on the problems faced by and concerned with Jews, and therefore spent no time at all looking around them, surely one of the most striking instances of political and moral blindness in the history of political thought. In addition to the all-consuming debates within political Zionism, there was also the tremendous importance of Jewish religious thought which, as Israel Shahak points out in his book on Jewish religion and history, has always been inimical, if not openly hostile, to non-Jews. So that when the state was established in 1948 a complex structure of laws was established more or less in accordance with Zionism and Jewish history. In the main it was a liberal nationalist edifice which allowed a large number of privileges for Jews while reducing the status of Palestinians juridically to that of "non-Jews." This lopsided situation still obtains today, even though there has been a continuous series of debates in the Knesset—some of which were reflected in judicial practice like the recent conviction of Israeli soldiers for killing an innocent Palestinian, then sentencing them to one hour in prison plus a fine of one agora—in which the religious and generally right-wing Revisionist Party has attempted to modify the state's juridical liberalism. The presence inside Israel of eight hundred thousand non-Jews (Palestinians who make up about 18 or 19 percent of the whole) has not appreciably changed their status for the better.

Except for its dreadful policy toward the Palestinians, Israel is considered today to be a Western liberal democracy. In my opinion, this is not an incorrect judgment so far as Jewish citizens are concerned. What Israel today shares in common with countries like the United States, Britain, and France is that the structure of laws protects citizens perceived as equals, and as real (that is, desirable) members of the state. Those people who do not fit the category, like Palestinians in Israel, or native Americans in the United States, may try to achieve equal rights through a process of pressure, bargaining, constant argument, and sometimes even direct action. Within each state there are three possible legal and authoritative positions taken by the courts and the parliament with regard to native rights, or the rights of groups not covered by the original constitution. One is a strict, traditionally nationalist position: only members of the majority, those perceived as authentically French, British, Israeli, and so on, can be recognized as members of the nation. The second position is the liberal one, which views the demand for recognition by minorities or non-integrated groups in the society as a danger to the association formed by the nation through common history, law, and outlook; the choice that liberals offer to native peoples is to tell them to try to integrate into the nation if possible, but if not (as is usually the case) the group must face the possibility of either leaving or seceding. Historically Israel has offered the Palestinians only the opportunity of leaving, since the state of the Jewish people cannot ever be the state of all its citizens, Arab as well as Jew. Hence, as the Palestinian academic and historian Dr. Nur Masalha has shown, the concept of transfer has been central to Zionist, and then Israeli thinking. Third is the position taken by members of the left-liberal school, who say that a certain amount of recognition of native rights is possible, but that the best solution is to let deprived natives develop their own community structures, within but apart from the main establishment. In my opinion, the so-called peace camp within the Israeli Labor Party led by people like Shimon Peres and Yossi Beilin, plus of course Meretz Party members such as

Yossi Sarid, have advocated this view, and in fact embodied it in the Oslo accords. There would be no real Israeli recognition of Palestinian independence and self-determination, but there would be a certain autonomy for Palestinians, who could then perhaps pretend to themselves that they had achieved something, whereas in fact their subordination to the majority community would remain absolute.

In no other liberal country, as Professor James Tully of McGill University in Canada has argued in his remarkable new book, *Strange Multiplicity*, has there been anything different so far as the national rights of indigenous people have been concerned. In Britain, as a case in point, it took six hundred years for the Irish to gain a measure of independence, although the Irish Protestant community in Northern Ireland remains in effect within Britain, plus of course a strong British military presence on the ground. In the United States the indigenous peoples have all but disappeared through genocide, diseases brought by the white man, slavery, and programs of deliberate dispersion. In places like New Zealand, Australia, and the American state of Hawaii important native movements have mounted a strong challenge to the constitutional authority of the nation, but those have yet to yield any fundamental change in the juridical authority that has essentially consigned native peoples and cultures to second-class status.

It is therefore a fundamental misreading both of Israel and of the various traditions and practices that have formed Israeli politics to expect that recognition of Palestinian rights would occur on anything like the level that is necessary for true peace. The outlook and history of the Labor Party is too entrenched, too tied to the liberal as well as nationalist positions that I have described, to make the move from denial to full recognition of full Palestinian rights. It is for that reason that a careful analysis of Israeli society would have to conclude that, in the absence of a credible military option, a more effective strategy would be to look to groups within the society that a) are themselves engaged in similar struggles for recognition or b) are not organically tied to the Labor Party. In the first group an obvious constituency is formed by the Jews from Arab countries who remain oppressed within the largely Ashkenazi-dominated Israeli system. In the second group are independent intellectuals, artists, university students and professors, whose social position and intellectual vocations permit a much greater degree of receptivity and tolerance for the idea of Palestinian national rights and independence.

Simply to repeat the cliché that the Labor Party is our only likely partner for dialogue and pressure is, I am sorry to say, a somewhat lazy reaction to the difficulties of the real task ahead of us. Moreover it must be strongly emphasized that Netanyahu's policies are an intransigent, ugly extension of what is always implicit, and sometimes very explicit, in Labor Party policies toward the Palestinians. I am certainly not saying that no change is possible within the Labor Party, nor am I saying that every Labor Party member or sympathizer is automatically against the real recognition of Palestinian national rights. But I am saying that it is a great deal more politically plausible to expect political change from elsewhere within Israeli society than it is to waste a great deal of energy on the historically solidified central ranks of the Labor Party, which by virtue of its far greater strength is in a better position to extract even more concessions from Palestinians and Arabs than the other way around. Why not then choose the more practical and morally acceptable tactic?

One further point needs to be made. As the great Italian political philosopher and working-class organizer Antonio Gramsci recognized, modern societies such as Israel's are not susceptible to putsches or revolutions such as occurred in countries with relatively underdeveloped civil societies such as ours or the Soviet Union. In the liberal Western tradition, democratic societies gain their strength and are able to resist change by way of institutions, voluntary associations, and traditional groups such as those provided by religion, the educational and independent judicial systems, the family, etc. There is hegemony in those societies rather than rule by force; hegemony in this case is the set of opinions, ideas, and institutions provided by civil society which, in the case of Israel, has so far been impervious to the recognition of Palestinian rights. To gain influence in this hegemony one must do a great deal of intellectual and cultural work of the kind that Gramsci talked about in his *Prison Notebooks*. This, as Arabs and Palestinian intellectuals we have not done, although I think it is true to say that the kind of intellectual and cultural work done during the intifada was an extremely promising start in persuading many

Israelis that Palestinians really existed as a people and required serious attention.

I shall have more to say about the nature of intellectual and cultural work that can result in social change in future articles. What I want to end with here, however, is to emphasize the limits of what the official Palestinian and Arab establishments can do and have indeed done. Since our societies are basically undemocratic and are ruled not by the hegemony that derives from argument, persuasion, and consent, but rather by direct force, censorship, intelligence services, and the absence of freedom of expression, I think it would be a serious error to expect Yasir Arafat's Authority, as an excellent case in point, to do anything very much about Israeli military occupation and settlement policies except complain and try to get more money from donor countries to pay for its corruption. If we are going to be accurate about Israeli society in the future we must of course be equally accurate and honest about our own. Until that time, we will continue to view the Labor Party simplistically as a lobby for peace within Israel.

The Gulf Today, December 4, 1996
Al-Khaleej, December 4, 1996
Al-Hayat, December 4, 1996

Chapter Eighteen

The Real Meaning of
the Hebron Agreement

T HE HEBRON AGREEMENT SIGNED with such fanfare and excitement a few days ago was of course really signed in September 1995, as part of the Oslo Two accord celebrated with all the usual flourishes and patched-together ceremonials on the White House lawn. When I visited Hebron last July I paid a call on an old friend, Mayor Mustafa Natshe, to find out from him what he saw as the future of his town. Among other things he told me that he had pleaded with Yasir Arafat and his men during the summer 1995 Taba negotiations that led up to Oslo Two not to sign an agreement that would give a Palestinian seal of approval to the 450 illegal settlers—most of them fanatics of the sort that had nurtured Baruch Goldstein and were soon to produce the lamentable Noam Friedman—squatting with such offensive, even murderous, insistence in the center of what in fact is an Arab town.

"It isn't just the principle of the thing that is so galling," he said, "but the fact that giving them this foothold in our midst by partitioning the town makes it possible for them to use Hebron as a precedent for staying in all their other settlements, extending their reach further all over the West Bank." Natshe's pleas went unheard, as Arafat and his team pressed ahead with their Israeli peace "partners" (the word has now entered official Palestinian discourse) who of course consolidated their gains with, I suspect, a sense of disbelief. How else could even the most hardened Israeli explain the fact that the Palestinians had accepted a formula for "coexistence" in Hebron which gave about 450 people (no one knows the exact number) who sat there with the Israeli army guarding them the choicest 20 percent of the town's commercial center, whereas the 120,000 resident Palestinians were expected to be happy that they got an 80 percent that was so bogged down with conditions, reservations, and stipulations as to make it virtually a peripheral part of the Israeli enclave. What sort of "strategic" calculation on the part of the Palestinian leadership produced acquiescence in that bizarre mathematics whereby an Israeli settler population of less than .03 percent got 20 percent of an Arab city, were allowed to carry their arms, were abetted by Israeli patrols who were given virtually the run of the hills surrounding the town, while the Palestinian police were limited to a few poorly armed men, theoretically subject to Israeli restraints in everything they did?

Nevertheless, there seemed to be genuine euphoria among Hebronites, for whom the presence of Israeli settlers and soldiers has been so unpleasant an ordeal; just seeing some of them leave in the hope of not having them come back on quite the same basis as before supplied a good day's worth of celebration. But there, alas, much of the jubilation will be as short-lived as it was when Ramallah and Nablus went through the same happy catharsis eighteen months ago. Despite super-magnified Palestinian cheers and exultant announcements, Hebron was not liberated. Eighty percent of it was given the right to administer municipal affairs (sanitation, health, postal delivery, education, local security, and traffic) under the Palestinian Authority's jurisdiction, with Israel still in charge of security, entrances and exits, water, and overall sovereignty. The ambiguities of the situation are evident in reports from Hebron carried recently in the press. On the first day, there were reports citing Netanyahu and Sharansky as to how Hebron is still Israeli, backed up by facts and figures showing continued Israeli control over the city. The next day, one could read editorials and news stories predicting a Palestinian state emerging soon from the messy Palestinian "archipelago" (the word is perfectly apt) that has left both the West Bank and Gaza divided into lots of little parts without territorial continuity or sovereignty. This schizophrenic scenario must also be afflicting Palestinians who want to believe that they are moving forward at the same time that all the evidence points in an opposite direction.

On U.S. television the de rigeur scene of Arafat and Netanyahu shaking hands with American mediator Dennis Ross between them showed a grim-faced Arafat anxious to speed away into the night. What he had held out for was supposedly a series of U.S.-Israeli guarantees that there would be a timetable of Israeli army withdrawals, or rather deployments from Area B (rural areas and Palestinian villages that constitute about 23 percent of the West Bank, an area which is now jointly patrolled by Israeli and Palestinian detachments although Israel controls security there) and even, according to some wishful thinking, from Area C, or the 73 percent of the West Bank (minus Jerusalem) totally controlled by Israel because C contains all the settlements, roads, military areas, etc. What he got instead was a series of "remarks," as they were instantly dubbed, that had absolutely no binding power on Israel. True, he did get a timetable of dates for redeployment from Area B, but they were stretched out over an extra year and, worse, no specific areas were mentioned. As the *New York Times* coyly put it in its jubilant report of how well things went, the actual amounts of land to be ceded to the Palestinians were left entirely to "Israel's discretion." Now this is precisely how things were left in the Oslo Two documents, since just before the Washington signing the Israelis calmly removed the specific areas of re-deployment already agreed upon between them and the Palestinians and simply left out the timetable. Apparently Arafat strenuously demurred at this, but under American pressure was made to sign anyway. His latest heroics during the Hebron negotiations were clearly meant to make up for what had happened earlier, but he failed again. No wonder he didn't particularly want to answer any questions.

It has been no secret that the United States, which has subcontracted out its Middle Eastern policy to Dennis Ross and his little coterie of experts, placed Arafat under impossible pressure. Israel's political concerns, its exaggerated obsessions with security and terror, the notion that one armed settler deserved more consideration than thousands of Palestinians: all these were adopted by the U.S. middle men who were acting as anything but honest brokers. There was also an important confluence of strategic aims that united Netanyahu and Ross, namely that there should never be anything resembling real Palestinian self-determination. And indeed to this day, three and a half years after Oslo began, "autonomy" for Palestinians is all that has been achieved, and achieved in tiny enclaves throughout the West Bank whose roads, access, and exits are controlled by Israel. In addition, an important town like Ramallah is now surrounded by settlements on three sides. Sovereignty in the true sense of the word remains in Israel's hands, and will remain so for the foreseeable future.

One might well ask then why so many Israelis seem upset by this agreement which after all keeps them firmly in charge throughout the still-occupied territories. The reason is an ideological fanaticism so deep and all-encompassing that most Western and even Arab readers do not have an adequate sense of what its imperatives are. Despite the presence in Palestine of millions of Palestinians, they have always been considered aliens, to be tolerated at most, to be driven out or treated either as nonexistent or as juridical inferiors in most cases. In addition, the land of Palestine is considered to be the land of the Jewish people entrusted to Israel; no non-Jews are doctrinally allowed to use or have this land. This is why Netanyahu, more honest than Peres, has always refused to accept the formula "land for peace," and why at no point in the negotiations, now or in the future, is sovereignty accorded to non-Jews as an admissible concept. I believe these positions are also shared by the "acceptable" Israelis (including the ubiquitous Amos Oz) whose views are routinely aired in the Western media as representative of the peace camp, and do a brilliant job of concealing their real views of Palestinians (not so different from Likud's) beneath a carpet of conscience-rending, anguished prose. They never bring up sovereignty for Palestinians either. Yes, many of them (including the egregious Henry Kissinger) speak of having a Palestinian state, which they say they would accept, but never has any of them specified sovereignty and real self-determination for Palestinians. Yes, they say, you can have your little insignificant state, but it must be demilitarized, we will keep our settlements, we will be in charge of security, we will control exits and entrances, the economy, and a few other things like water; otherwise you can call it anything you like, even a state. We retain sovereignty in all cases.

Trying to put myself in the shoes of the PLO men who continue to produce such, to put it mildly, disadvantageous agreements that do nothing to change the course of Israeli policy, I keep asking what our leaders must be thinking (they certainly do not do very much talking about what they are up to, and share very little with their people beyond the usual triumphalist nonsense). All I can come up with is a series of unflattering rationales for going on as before, with equally bad results and equally tragic consequences for the whole people. One rationale is that so long as the peace process guarantees the centrality of the PLO and its leader, then more or less anything goes. A second is that being so outmaneuvered, outgunned, outsmarted by Israel, you feel you have no choice but to go on trying to brazen it out vis-à-vis your own people, with a lot of hopeful but ultimately misleading speeches and promises; meanwhile you surround yourself with supporters who tell you what you want to hear and are anxious to help you set up more feel-good things like a bagpipe band, a few luxurious cars and houses, postage stamps with your face on them, and so on. The best thing of all is to go on as many state visits (few of them necessary) as possible: one day Stockholm, another Paris, another Beijing, another Cairo. Third is the tactic of making more concessions, accepting all the humiliating Israeli conditions in the wishful fantasy that some day you'll either stop having to make concessions or the Israelis will give you a few things back. Fourth is the rationale that this is politics, a dirty business, and so we proceed with the Israelis like partners in crime; never mind that they get all the advantages, a lot of commercial deals have come our way.

There may be one or two more possibilities, but none of them explains the Palestinian streets' acceptance of this appalling situation, which seems to be getting worse daily. Many of Arafat's advisers are intelligent men and women, quite a few of them with long histories in progressive politics. Why are they so silent? And why do the most gifted so willingly accept a few material advantages (a car, an office, a position, a VIP designation) in return for continuing to work with a man whose tactics they loathe and whose mistakes over the past few years they know, and have said openly, have brought us as Palestinians and as Arabs to one of the lowest points in our history? Why silence, and why cooperation? Do they feel no obligation toward the truth and to alleviating the misery of a people whose continuing dispossession could have been arrested a thousand times more effectively than the PLO has done?

In the meantime Netanyahu, Madeline Albright, and Dennis Ross will manage the peace process with the same results. Most people in the United States and in Europe genuinely believe that peace has improved things for the "area," and that for the first time in thirty years the Palestinians are getting their freedom. This is the cruelty of the Palestinian dilemma. On the one hand we want to show that we desire peace, whereas on the other, because of that "peace," the daily lives of all but a tiny handful of wealthy businessmen, security chiefs, PA employees have become a good deal worse. For at least six months now the mainstream media in the United States and Europe (this is equally true of print outlets, radio, and television) have been filled with stories about the diplomatic front, the negotiations, the impasses, and the final breakthroughs, and completely void of anything that portrays Palestinians' lives on the ground and in reality. There has been no coverage whatever of the thousands of students in Gaza who cannot go back to their schools and universities on the West Bank (forbidden by Israel), nothing about the large number of Palestinian prisoners still festering (and in some cases being tortured to death) in Israeli prisons, nothing about the horrors that a large family in Gaza with an unemployed father and eight children must go through just to survive, nothing about the systematic, almost daily reprisals against Palestinians who try to prevent their own dispossession by Israeli settlers and army, nothing about what it means for a Palestinian to try to get in and out of Gaza, or the case of all West Bankers who have been forbidden entry into Jerusalem for a year, nothing about the checkpoints that make the little West Bank enclaves seem like stifling ghettos, nothing about life under Arafat's dreadful regime, with books, newspapers, and magazines censored or banned, threats from the security services to average people, corruption on an operatic scale killing the possibility of regular daily business, nothing above all about the total absence of law or the rule of law in the Palestinian autonomy areas. The *New York Times* never reports on any of this with the kind of frequency that would make it the true background to the diplomatic stories it much prefers to repeat every day. How often do Western news consumers get a chance to see before their eyes the map that Israel has imposed on Palestinians, the crazy patchwork of Areas A, B, and C, demonstrating Israel's intent to destroy even the possibility of a Palestinian national existence.

Given all this, plus of course the sense of frustration and hopelessness felt by every Palestinian at the cruel farce our leaders are forced to enact, it becomes an absolute duty to describe the actualities of quotidian life under the peace process, unadorned and in the greatest detail possible. The world must be told by us what our people under occupation are still going through under the totally misleading reports—Israeli, American, and official Palestinian—of the peace process, whose most recent episode in Hebron is surely one of the most ironically cruel. This is not a matter of money, but of discipline and will. If every one of us first took it upon him/herself to be informed about what people in Ramallah or Hebron or Bethlehem or Jerusalem are going through, and then attempted somehow to break through the official and media silence—a letter to the editor, a call to a radio or TV station, the setting up of groups to do this kind of work systematically and collectively—then we will be begining our attempt at liberation, a minuscule and even laughably modest attempt, it is true, but surely a great deal better than passivity and collective silence. The present situation cannot last. There are too many inequities and injustices right at the heart of Palestinian life, and the Israeli scene, with its mad settlers and religious fanatics, simmeringly angry army brass, inept government, and frustrated well-intentioned civilians who are tired of tension and frustration, is too volatile for another Hebron-style negotiation not to produce more violence, more suffering, more incoherence. Who is preparing for the next phase?

Al-Ahram Weekly, January 23, 1997

The Gulf Today, January 27, 1997

The Guardian, February 15, 1997

Journal of Palestine Studies, Spring 1997

Al-Khaleej, January 27, 1997

Al-Hayat, January 27, 1997

Chapter Nineteen

The Uses of Culture

I GATHER THAT Samuel Huntington's recent book, *The Clash of Civilizations*, has been causing a good deal of discussion (and fun, I hope) here and there in the Arab world. His article on the same subject, which appeared three and a half years ago, seems to have stimulated more discussion than his ponderous, overwrought book has done in the United States, partly because the essay was short, had a catchy title, and was designed to shock his readership into some response at least; by contrast, the book has the plodding graduate student manner of someone wandering all over the place on uncertain territory, trying to be careful with things like definitions, "facts," and statistics, at the same time that he feels his professor's ire about to descend. There are so many things wrong with the premises of Huntington's argument (for example, that civilizations exist the way he says they do as vast and permanent blocks, rather like icebergs), so many embarrassing mistakes about the way cultures operate, so many infelicitous descriptions of what distinguishes the West from Islam, or Confucianism, or anything else, and at the same time so unexamined and uncritical a set of assumptions about the unique glory of Western civilization, most of which such nonsense went out with Montaigne and Hume, that it is genuinely hard to read him with serious attention.

Strangely enough, his shortcomings are most striking in his discussion of his own civilization, the West, although it is plain enough

that what he says about Islam, for example, is full of material bor-
rowed from unreconstructed Orientalists like Bernard Lewis. Huntington's fundamental mistake is to perceive the West as possessing an
unchanging essence, a kind of absolute core which remains as it is
from century to century. He says that civilization is comprised of the
major books, heroes, values that are central to it; this then forces him
to take the position that everything about the West confirms these
essences and values, as well as vice versa, a determinism that scarcely
allows for diversity or change in the real sense of both those words.

My own reading of the West would place emphasis not on the per-
manences and essences that give Huntington such evident pleasure,
but on the discontinuities and disruptions in it as in all cultures and
civilizations, in addition to all the various mixtures and hybrids that
in fact compose cultures and civilizations. The authoritarian and dogmatic interpreter will, like Huntington, see Socrates as an important
historical figure whose method, metaphysical inquiries into the true
and the good, constitute one of the permanent glories of Western civilization. To a genuinely brilliant and imaginative reader like Friedrich
Nietzsche, what made Socrates interesting was that by his methods
and "his great rolling critical eye" he was a disruptor of values, an
overturner of accepted ideas, someone who threatened all authority.
This is clearly why Socrates was put on trial, condemned, and left with
no recourse but to take his own life. And indeed, it is possible to argue
that one of the key elements in modern Western culture was the emergence and dominance of philosophies such as those of Nietzsche,
whose great thrust was in fact the overturning of even the ideas of
good and evil and the attempt to eliminate any faith in the concept of
a stable identity. For Huntington, civilizations have a fixed and constantly, perpetually recognizable identity, whereas the proper critical
question to be asked at the end of the twentieth century is "Which
West, or Islam, or Confucianism do you mean? There are dozens, all
of them in conflict, irreconcilably opposed, endlessly in flux. Is it
really possible to speak of *the* West, or of one Confucianism, since the
evidence of extraordinary diversity within each culture wreaks immediate havoc on any attempt to reduce the culture or civilization to a
simple, unitary phenomenon?"

A second mistake running throughout Huntington's book is that he does not at all take seriously the extent to which all cultures, as well as civilizations, are mixed, hybrid, full of elements taken from other cultures. So much so, in my opinion, that it really is intellectually irresponsible to argue as if there were a pure, unmodified culture that is totally at one, self-identified with itself. Nothing could be more fruitless than seeing the West as somehow standing apart and above from the civilizations of Africa, Islam, India, and Latin America. True, there are specific ideological attempts in all cultures to pretend that some pre-existing essence defines the culture once and for all, but that is ideology, not history or the serious interpretation of culture. I happened the other day to be reading about a new book on the emergence of calculus whose argument was that that indispensable mathematical tool sprang up full-blown in the seventeenth century and emerged simultaneously in Leibniz and Newton; according to the author, this amazing occurrence was a direct consequence of Greek science suddenly reappearing in the seventeenth century. I would call this an ideological, rather than a true historical, interpretation of what happened. To eliminate from this description of "Western" scientific genius any mention of the crucial role played by Arab mathematicians, without whose work neither Leibniz nor Newton could have formulated their mathematics, is to try to maintain the fiction of a pure, self-enclosed West, whose dominance and power are entirely its own, and whose history in the final analysis has no real connection with any other culture or civilization.

Huntington's equivalents exist in all cultures today as a consequence, in my view, of nationalism, or at least that aspect of nationalism that is defensive, xenophobic, politically amenable to the kind of manipulation that has produced ethnic and religious conflict as well as partitions of multicultural societies into separate little entities who can snarl at each other across their barbed-wire borders. Huntington himself writes from the point of view of someone who wants to manage such conflicts: he is an intellectual serving the interests of the last superpower (he is actually quite frank about this), whose preeminence as a world power he is set on serving and maintaining. The real subject of his work therefore is not how to reduce the conflict of cultures, but how to turn them to American advantage, as a way of conceding to the United States the right to lead the whole world. Yet none of his grandiose rhetoric can conceal the fact that this style of thought derives from the same polluted source to be found in all cultures, the notion that *my* way of life, *my* traditions, *my* way of thinking, *my* religion or civilization can neither be shared with anyone nor understood by anyone who does not have the same religion, color of skin, etc. India, Pakistan, Bosnia, Ireland, South Africa, Cyprus, Lebanon, and of course Israel-Palestine bear the ravages of such a logic, which in the end leads to more, not less narrowness, misunderstanding, violence. The point of course is that there is nothing inevitable about these ideas, despite what Huntington and others like him have been preaching. Although he shares very similar ideas with right-wing Zionists who believe that they have a superior right to the land of historical Palestine and are prepared to battle Palestinians until doomsday, he is taken more seriously because the United States has greater power than any other country today, a fact which scarcely validates the soundness of his argument.

No culture today is pure. Huntington writes about the West as if France were still made up of exclusively of Duponds and Bergeracs, England of Smiths and Joneses. This is fundamentalism, not analysis of culture, which, it bears repeating, is made by humankind, not decreed once and for all by an act of divine genesis. Every identity therefore is a construction, a composite of different histories, migrations, conquests, liberations, and so on. We can deal with these either as worlds at war, or as experiences to be reconciled. It is one of the prerogatives of power historically to classify lesser peoples by placing them in eternal categories—the patient Chinese, the servile Black, the devious or violent Muslim are well-known examples—that condemn them to solitude and apartness, the better and more easily to be ruled or held at bay. This is precisely what the "separation" of Arabs from Israelis is all about, in the past and during the peace process. Is that the only way for civilizations to coexist?

I think not. Another way of using difference in culture is to welcome the "other" as equal but not precisely the same. Most of the great humanistic scholars of our time, from Erich Auerbach to Joseph Needham, Louis Massignon to Taha Hussein, saw in the past and in different cultures an opportunity to overcome the alienation of time and distance. Reading Dante, Auerbach caught that poet's relationship to the fourteenth century, as well as to our own. The idea therefore is to study culture not nationalistically, but in order to understand how it is made, and how it can be remade for others. In this it is the critical humanist or intellectual, not the Huntingtonian crisis manager, who has something to offer, as well as a more authentic vision of the possibilities for human community.

I have spent thirty-five years of my life teaching young people the arts of interpretation, that is, how one reads, understands, and connects the products of human culture with other human activities. This has enabled me, I think, to understand politics better, since interpretation teaches one that all human activity takes place in history, is *of* history. The goal of interpretation, in my opinion, is to learn how to connect things with each other—different cultures, different peoples, different historical periods. That is an act of choice, the very opposite of the choice made by Huntington and others in the West and in the Islamic world, to see cultures in terms of opposition and clash. The clash of civilizations thesis is presented as if it is inevitable, whereas of course it is imposed upon a world filled with uncertainty and potential as well as actual discord. But we always have a choice to work for conflict, or against it. We must not be fooled by Huntington's martial accents into believing that we are condemned to ceaseless strife, because in fact we are not.

Al-Ahram Weekly, February 13, 1997
The Gulf Today, February 14, 1997
Al-Khaleej, February 13, 1997
Al-Hayat, February 13, 1997

Chapter Twenty

Loss of Precision

FOR THE PAST seven or eight weeks I have been plagued by a series of infections that inflicted more or less persistent pain on me, in addition to the necessity of remaining at home all the time, unable to teach my classes (which had to be cancelled for the semester), and enduring the kind of despondency and discouragement that a patient feels when he believes that he has suffered too long and too much. Despite that, I was able to experience something of the effect of what it must be like for an American to watch television for long periods of time. In too much discomfort to read anything for very long, unable to listen to or play music, I found myself all too frequently resorting to the handy television remote which so easily and seductively seems to bring the world to life on a small screen with the mere pressing of a button. People who live in New York must subscribe to a cable service (there is only one, a monopoly owned by Time-Warner), since without the cable the presence of so many high buildings makes even minimum reception totally impossible. So as you lie on your bed of pain you have flitting before you no fewer than about seventy-five channels, with films, news, sports, documentaries, talk shows, and many more varieties than I can enumerate here, available twenty-four hours a day. At first, I derived pleasure from looking at old movies—a few weeks ago one channel offered twenty-four hours of 1940s Universal films about the Middle East, most of them starring Jon Hall, Maria Montez, Sabu, Yvonne de Carlo, and Turhan Bey, movies like *Sudan, The Arabian Nights, Scheherezade,* in which Hollywood's conception of what the Orient was supposed to be like is given amusing, if grotesque, realization (to simulate the Middle East in these now long-forgotten films one always had to have lots of sand, galloping horses, cruel sultans, and dancing girls)—but after watching three or four of them I couldn't bear to watch another for even a second.

In what turned out to be a relatively short time I had exhausted my patience with television. One had to wait hours, perhaps days, for a decent, usually imported, film or documentary to appear; the chat shows were tiresome, unbelievably stupid, gossip; the news as delivered by CNN, the national networks, or the local channels was almost entirely about the United States, and usually copied from one network by another; CNN I found unwatchable since there are too many commercial breaks, too many shows about cooking and fashion to be worth the time spent waiting for an item of real news; endless sports programs proliferate, usually basketball and football, but punctuated with all kinds of bizarre new attractions like women's boxing and barefoot water-skiing.

Most of the airwaves, however, are polluted with three types of program. One is a general category that purports to be entertainment: this runs the gamut from cartoons to soap operas to weekly hourlong dramas and films. Intended to appeal to audiences of twenty million and more, these are usually sensationalist, extremely simple to follow, sentimental, vacuous. Most Americans tend to watch these shows round the clock, even as they work, and certainly after coming home from work one imagines these silent gatherings around the TV set replicated all over the country, with lots of popcorn-eating, beer-drinking, and the like, as entire families sit around the main TV set (every house, except for the very poor, has more than one set) transfixed by what is being watched. Second is the vast category of talk show, in which an interview takes place between a "host" and various invited guests, usually celebrities, but often people with peculiar problems (women who go out with their sons' girlfriends, men who always fall in love with extremely fat women, etc.), or "news-makers," that is politicians, or important visiting dignitaries like Princess Diana, but also Benjamin Netanyahu. So self-referential has television become and so powerful are its personalities that very frequently the top journalists interview each other, with the result that "the news" is what these characters say it is. Lastly there are the religious programs, which probably outnumber the other two categories. The enormous proliferation of these religious programs is one small index of how the United States is by far the most religion-obsessed country in the world. According to a recent poll, 88 percent of the American public believes that it is loved by God. Television religion includes all the standard denominations enacting their services, but that is minuscule compared to the weird cults and sects that proclaim their secret pathway to God on the air the rest of the time, from Christians who believe that a true understanding of God is available through a decoding of the structure of the Great Pyramid at Giza (I have actually seen these people on television, so you must believe me) to the various faith healers who purport to make the blind see and the lame walk in full view of millions of witnesses.

Even this quick summary is enough to suggest that American television, now exported all over the world, is from the point of view of a moderately well educated individual a deeply unsatisfying source of information or, in the real sense of the word, of entertainment. For one, because of its extraordinary prodigality of programming and availability, it imposes on the mind a sense of dependency and passivity. Most people feel that they can avoid, or perhaps even solve, their problems by simply flipping on the television and getting lost in the daydreams and fantasies that very soon acquire both a familiarity and reality that is more attractive than their own world. As for growing children, there is nothing easier for parents than to plant their three- or four-year olds in front of the TV set as a way of pacifying them for hours. In all sorts of obvious ways, then, television can become a kind of drug to be used with greater dependency once the habit gets started. Above all, from the perspective of someone who is interested in why so few people in this society—or for that matter, in the Arab world—refuse to accept the various abuses and lies of their governments, and why we seem now to be led by mediocre leaders who are simply not doing their jobs correctly, television provides an answer. It disarms critical or moral thought by its totality, by its all-enveloping, easy accessibility, and by its underlying ideological message, which is that this is America, the greatest society on earth, where all problems are as easy to deal with as opening a bottle of Coca-Cola.

I do not at all want to suggest that television does not present anything except silly farces: on the contrary, local news channels, for instance, are mainly full of murders, rapes, fires, and natural disasters. The medium has an amazing way of distorting reality so that where news programs are concerned you get the feeling that because it is on TV, a story is therefore real; conversely if it is not, then it does not exist. I would say that the percentage of news reported contains at most 3 or 4 percent about international issues, most of them, however, usually reported because of a crisis which as soon as it passes erases the issue from memory. Rwanda and former Yugoslavia make extremely rare appearances these days; in most minds, they are now only associated with the idea of "trouble" and little else. But by comparison, the amount of time devoted by television (and in effect by all the media) to the various O.J. Simpson trials has distended and bloated the story into something beyond all reason or even emotion. It has become virtually impossible to see the world as *not* principally about Simpson, his lawyers, victims, and legal predicaments. And the problem is that the story itself is fed not only by TV itself, but by a public that cannot get enough of what in reality is a sordid case of wife-beating and murder. In other words, the mind has lost its power to resist an onslaught of irrelevance and gross distortion of reality.

I am convinced therefore that television dependency has played not only a great role in inducing an absence of critical thought but an even more crucial role in reducing the capacity of the mind for precise and exact uses of language, language being what it is we think with and in when we think about our world. Television images are a form of magic that work by quick shifts from one place, image, time, and subject to others; they depict the world as subject to sudden magnifications and equally unlikely arrests that give us a reassuring sense that what we have before us, whether as soap operas, news broadcasts, sports spectacles, or journalists chatting authoritatively to each other, *is the world,* and its life is being lived, explained, and transmuted for us, without any effort on our part. Individual consumers of TV have no choice in what is before them, although of course they can switch

from one program or channel to another. Gradually, then, the reper-
toire of images and verbal discourse derived from television becomes a
substitute for the processes of one's own mind, whose laboriously
built-up capacities through education begin to atrophy and then finally give up. Instead of thinking concretely and self-consciously then,
you rely instead on what you heard or saw on television, which simply
floods in as you are looking for a word or thought. It articulates your
thoughts, provides much of the vocabulary, constructs sequences, and
reduces complexity to simple images.

In this way, over the years the image of the Arab or Muslim has
been essentialized down to the one simple meaning, *terrorist*. For the
time being, I am sorry to say that we are stuck with that identity in the
American consciousness, regardless of how moderate and concessive
our leaders appear, and irrespective of how many times they appear
for photo opportunities at the White House. It should also be kept in
mind that there is virtually nothing—and I mean this literally—in
what one sees on television that can provide a viewer with even the
possibility of doubting that the United States is God's country, has
never done anything wrong, and is basically a force for good in the
world. The phrase "our country" or the pronoun "we" has acquired
an unassailable positive force, so that even the word "America" in
common discourse is an ideological term, not just a simple national
designation, and is used as such on television. Most individual vo-
cabularies today therefore tend to be assaulted constantly by pre-
packaged terms like "we are going forward," "the great opportunities
that God has given us," and so forth, most of them safeguarding unrestrained capitalism even though the majority's interests are being harmed. A perfect instance of this is the chorus of attacks on
"government," which now means "big government," i.e., socialism.
During the abortive debate three years ago about health care—one
must remember that over forty-five million Americans have no health
coverage, since the government doesn't provide any; one must either
be wealthy or be enrolled in a corporate health plan—the one alternative never seriously discussed was national health insurance. Here
even the thought was never analyzed, because that kind of national
medical care had been polluted and transformed into the idea of

socialism, a concept which still has a very potent negative resonance for the average American.

What I have been saying about America is also true about the Arab world, where rote learning in school, radio, and television, plus an almost completely corrupt or at least counterfeit public discourse on matters having to do with the state of society, makes it very difficult to express oneself clearly and concretely. The noted West Bank educational activist Munir Fashie some years ago did an analysis of the prose produced by high school students. Two things stood out in every case: one, the student's inability to write concretely about any subject, two, a total incapacity to write about oneself directly. Thus, when requested, for instance, to write about specifically what the student saw and felt walking to school, the young people were only able to say extremely general things about the weather, about the street, about the need to go to school, all of them very conventional, and very imprecise so far as that individual was concerned. Very often the framework was provided by a few political slogans—we are winning our independence, the importance of a Palestinian state, etc. Some of this, of course, had to do with the difficult circumstances of life for these students, but the loss of precision and concreteness, the tendency to give up clear conceptual thinking and process, are to be found in the prose of my students here, in a major American university. The phenomenon, therefore, is a universal one, and of central importance during the coming years when of course the power and influence of electronic communication in all its forms will grow and acquire more authority over the individual mind and will.

Thus the worldwide market system—call it the IMF or World Bank model—seems to have produced alongside itself a communications apparatus whose effect is to lessen resistance, whether to political or to commercial ideas, on the part of the individual. For me the test of the individual consciousness is how quickly, or easily, it can be made to accept what is presented on television or in public discourse, even though the reality is not only more complex but totally different. The great precedent in the United States was the 1991 Gulf War, which, quite aside from Saddam Hussein's illegal occupation of Kuwait, was fought as a global projection of U.S. power. That war was in effect a war without a popular constituency in the United States. Between September and December of 1990 a consensus was built up laboriously over television, persuading citizens that Saddam was an evil demon who threatened "our" freedom, and that his aggression must be stopped by "us." No one asked about *our* aggressions, or who exactly had appointed *us* as the guardians of world order. Most minds were prepared by years of ideological insistence that "we" always did the right thing, and that sordid economic, political, or strategic motives could not be attributed to "our" actions. More to the point, the war was planned and fought as a clean "surgical" electronic war on television; viewers were persuaded that, yes, there were American forces in the desert, but since they were being watched at home the war itself was without "real" damage or cost to anyone, except those evil Iraqis. The frightening thing was that for the few who actively opposed and spoke against the war, it was impossible to break through into the mainstream media, which in cooperation with the government, had created an electronic wall around what was being done.

In short, an imprecise, not very concrete hold on language and reality produces a more easily governable, accepting citizen, who has become not a participant in the society but an always hungry consumer. Literate, critical education has an extraordinarily important role to play in providing the instruments of resistance to this and, it must be said plainly, in providing a means of self-defense. Otherwise the picture of billions of people whose volition has been pacified and whose consciousness and will have been usurped is a truly frightening one.

The Gulf Today, February 24, 1997
Al-Ahram Weekly, February 27, 1997
Al-Khaleej, February 24, 1997
Al-Hayat, February 24, 1997

Chapter Twenty-one

The Context of
Arafat's American Visit

I HAVE JUST SPENT the last two days reading the manuscript of
Raja Shehadeh's devastatingly sad and powerful new book, *From
Occupation to Interim Accords,* which thanks to a Dutch publisher is
soon to appear in print. As I said earlier, Shehadeh himself is a
remarkable man, unusual for the care and deliberation of what he says
and writes, courageous and modest in manner, serious and apparently
without illusion. He is the son of the late Aziz Shehadeh, a distinguished Ramallah lawyer (originally from Jaffa) who was one of the
first to say publicly after 1967 that Palestinian self-determination
should be sought on a West Bank and Gaza state. I recall that he was
greatly attacked for his views at the time. Raja was educated in literature at the American University of Beirut, a fact that has always given
a literary dimension to what he writes, especially in his diary of life
(sumud) under a brutal military occupation. He did his law studies in
England, then returned to the West Bank in the 1970s both to join the
family law firm and to become one of the founders of al Haq, to this
day the most credible and well-considered of the Palestinian human
rights organizations. Written in a clear, analytic style without exaggeration or bombast, al Haq's studies, including Raj's own analysis of
the system of laws imposed by the military and civil authorities entitled *Occupier's Law,* stand as ineradicable records of Israel's systematic strategy for controlling the Palestinian territories for a very long
time. I recall several discussions with him about this during the 1980s

when he lamented the fact that the PLO didn't seem to understand that the Israelis were not just passing laws here and there but were operating with a plan and a vision for bringing these territories—which they clearly never planned to give up—under the rule of law for their purposes. He was the first, I think, to understand the legalistic character of Israeli thinking, and he remains a member of that small minority of Palestinians who always try to grasp the overall structure of domination that gives Israeli thinking about Palestinians and their land its coherence and power.

I recall being delighted that after the 1991 Madrid Conference Raja Shehadeh was appointed as legal adviser to the Palestinian delegation that came to Washington that autumn to negotiate with the Israelis. But I also recall seeing Raja in London a few months later when he told me with great despondency that he had decided to resign: it was clear to him that the Tunis PLO under Arafat was undermining the work of the delegates from the West Bank and Gaza, and he therefore felt that there was no use in continuing. That was the first inkling I had that Arafat and his men were probably trying to make a separate and secret deal with the Israelis to guarantee that the outside PLO, and not the West Bank and Gaza delegates, would be the ones to become Israel's interlocutor. Raja was always disciplined enough to draw conclusions and then act definitively on them. From that time (it was late 1992 I think) he has withdrawn from politics and now concentrates on his law practice.

His new book is therefore, he says, a kind of unhappy postmortem of what happened from the Washington talks until the present, in which he documents in great detail the concessions and the massive inattentiveness and incompetence of what the Palestinians were doing; this, he makes clear at every juncture, is in absolute contrast with the Israelis, who used the negotiations according to carefully prepared plans to consolidate their hold on the territories and by no means to concede sovereignty or self-determination to the Palestinians. "Peace" in this context was a very misleading word. What the Palestinians seem never to have grasped was the nature of the Israeli context, the schemes, legal maneuvers, and meticulously prepared negotiating tactics that drove them forward first in Washington and then much more seriously in Oslo. In order to have understood this context the Palestinian leadership would have had to study Israel carefully, understand the dynamics of its politics and ideological commitments, and taken a much more active and demanding position vis-à-vis the Israeli negotiators. Instead, as Shehadeh shows in painstaking detail, they were always anxious to show the Israelis (especially after the defeat of Arafat's policy of alignment with Saddam Hussein during the Gulf crisis) that they were willing to concede major Palestinian positions on, for instance, settlements and Jerusalem, just to prove to the Israelis that they would make willing partners. On one occasion in 1993 in order to test Palestinian intentions Rabin submitted fifty questions to the Palestinians, all of which were answered positively by Arafat and Abu Mazen (who emerges from this whole story as a catastrophically uninformed and ignorant man willing to give everything up just to stay in power). Even Rabin was surprised at their answers, and more surprised still when it was clear that the Palestinians never asked questions of the Israelis, never challenged them, never effectively probed their intentions.

I have gone on at such length about Shehadeh's book because precisely the same situation obtains today between the Palestinian Authority, i.e., Arafat and his group, and the Americans. Arafat came on a so-called state visit to this country during which he saw President Clinton, Madeline Albright, and a few members of Congress in Washington; after that he came to the UN for a reception, a meeting with Jewish leaders, in addition to a speech at the Council of Foreign Relations, and then visits to George Bush in Texas and Jimmy Carter in Atlanta. Of course he seemed generally delighted to be welcomed to the United States on his own, to be treated by the government and media with elaborate courtesy, and to be the center of attention. Beyond that both he and his entourage seemed oblivious to the political and intellectual context in which they were being manipulated by the Americans. Clinton made one statement, just one, indicating his displeasure with the Israeli announcement that a new settlement was going to be constructed in Jabal Abu Ghneim; the State Department spokesman made one statement criticizing Israel's intention to close down four Jerusalem offices that were allegedly "political." And that was it. At exactly the same time as Arafat's delegate in the United Nations, his nephew Nasser al-Qidwa, was putting forth a Security

Council resolution that had the unanimous consent of the members in which Israel was condemned for Jabal Abu Ghneim, the Americans made it absolutely clear to the PLO that if the resolution came to a vote they would veto it, which of course they did.

Moreover Arafat seemed uncomprehending, or at least unaware, of how gently he was being treated by the media which a very short time ago had compared him as a mass murderer of innocent Jews with Hitler and Stalin. He appeared on an evening talk show with Larry King, a devoted Zionist, who asked him questions about his *kuffiyeh* and whether there was democracy of the press and other freedoms in the Palestinian territories. Yes, answered Arafat shamelessly, we have a full democracy, which King clearly knew was a lie but which he passed over so as to spare Arafat the disgrace of exposure. Never once in all his media appearances did Arafat say a word about the sufferings of his people, or about 1948, or about the closures, or the thousands of prisoners still held by Israel. He was a creature of a context he neither understood nor tried to change: for in fact Arafat was in America not to advance the cause of his people but rather to play a small role in American politics as a reformed terrorist who was here to testify to the power and goodness of America, and to further the cause of American interests in his part of the world. He seemed to have no consciousness at all of the fact that his posturings as a military commander or as a major political actor were tolerated because in the American political context—which did not give him much in the way of promised money—he had already conceded his people's aspirations to be free and to have real self-determination. This was the price he had paid to be treated with respect by Clinton and Albright. In the American context he was only a local enforcer of the peace that Israel and the United States had imposed on him, a peace which, as Raja Shehadeh's work very clearly shows, is a consolidation of Israel's territorial gains in Gaza and the West Bank. His submission was apparent in the colorless language he and his various assistants used (it was sad to see the gifted and brilliant Hanan Ashrawi reduced to the status of his translator and linguistic helper).

The worst thing of all during his American visit was that Arafat seemed to have no idea who his real supporters were, the African-Americans, the students and professors, the various Arab-American organizations and other civil rights groups who have defended Palestinian self-determination for years in this country against extremely difficult odds. He paid no attention to any of these, contenting himself at a large and expensively pointless UN reception with shaking a lot of anonymous hands. In the American context he was no longer a fighter for his people's rights, but a curiosity who made a series of appearances and then left. This, I believe, is an extremely reckless way to behave for someone who represents himself as the head of a nascent Palestinian state. He ought to come here as someone who knows and makes others aware of how much damage the United States has done to his people, to challenge Americans, to ask difficult questions, to enter into the life of this country not as a mindless petitioner, but as the representative of a cause and a people which the United States and Israel have done everything to destroy. But, as Raja Shehadeh concludes, it may be too late for us. So long as the present Palestinian leadership remains we shall lose more and more, and alas, our leaders will appear more pacified, tame, and uncomprehending than ever, even as (ironically) they seem to be getting a Palestinian state stripped of most of the attributes of sovereignty.

And yet there are signs here and there among the Palestinian people that the leadership's attitude is not theirs. The popular attempts to prevent further building of Israeli settlements is one such sign, and there will soon be others as Arafat's tyranny against his long-suffering people increases.

Al-Hayat, March 17, 1997
Al-Khaleej, March 17, 1997
The Gulf Today, March 20, 1997
Al-Ahram Weekly, March 20, 1997

Chapter Twenty-two

Deir Yassin Recalled

M Y PARENTS, SISTERS, and I left Palestine for the last time
during the latter part of December 1947; in addition to the
family business in Palestine of which he was a partner, my father
was in charge of the Egyptian branch, so in effect when we left Jerusalem for Cairo we were returning to somewhere familiar, to a home,
schools, friends, etc. The rest of my extended family was not so lucky.
By mid-spring of 1948 every one of them on both sides, paternal and
maternal—uncles, aunts, cousins—had become refugees scattered
throughout the Arab world. Most went to Jordan, a few to Lebanon,
my paternal aunt and most of her grown children to Egypt, where
they joined my father in the business of which they too were partners.
I recall quite vividly that though I was twelve at the time, I neither was
told much about nor was able fully to grasp the nature of the catastrophe that had overtaken us as a people; I am not even sure that I
thought of us as members of a specific people. Our household was
totally depoliticized, although we came to feel the difficulties of Palestinian refugees in Egypt as somehow involving us. This was natural
enough, since I remember it was quite common to see relatives in very
reduced circumstances, worrying about how they were going to pay
the rent, find jobs, and so on. During the course of 1948, however, it
dawned on me imperfectly and incompletely, I am sure, what a true
misfortune had befallen Arab Palestine.

No small role was played in this growing awareness of the question of Palestine by the fragmentary reports I heard around our dinner table in Cairo during the spring and summer of 1948 about the Deir Yassin massacre, which took place on April 9, 1948. My aunt and her daughter in particular had been in Jerusalem (about four kilometers away from Deir Yassin) at the time, but had heard only the desperate and horrified accounts of the ordeal of those 250 men, women, and children—innocents all of them—ruthlessly murdered in cold blood by "the Jews," as everyone called them. More than any single occurrence in my memory of that difficult period it was Deir Yassin that stood out in all its awful and intentional fearsomeness—the stories of rape, of children with their throats slit, mothers disemboweled, and the like. They gripped the imagination, as they were designed to do, and they impressed a young boy many miles away with the mystery of such bloodthirsty and seemingly gratuitous violence against Palestinians whose only crime seemed to be that they were there. Yet it was not until almost a decade later that I was able to understand the context and real meaning of what happened at Deir Yassin.

It used to be thought that the massacre was a deliberate but somehow random terrorist incident planned and executed by Menachem Begin's Irgun. What we now know is that according to Benny Morris the "operation" at Deir Yassin was not only abetted and participated in by the Haganah, but was part of an overall Zionist plan (Dalet, first written about by Walid Khalidi) to systematically empty Palestine of its Arab population. Deir Yassin, because of the sheer horror of its murderousness had, says Morris in his book *The Birth of the Palestinian Refugee Problem, 1947–1949,* "the most lasting effect of any single event of the war in precipitating the flight of Arab villagers from Palestine" (p. 113). The fact of course is that it was not just "Arab villagers" who left for that and similar reasons, but two-thirds of the entire Palestinian population, about eight hundred thousand people. Recent, extremely important work by the Palestinian-Israeli scholar Nur Masalha on the concept of "transfer" in Zionist thought shows how persistently the Zionists imagined, planned for, and implemented programs to rid their "promised land" of the native people. His first book, which treats Zionist ideology from 1882 to 1948, is *Expulsion of the Palestinians;* his second, and only just published, is a terrifyingly graphic account of the period between 1949 and 1996: *A Land*

Without a People: Israel, Transfer and the Palestinians, 1949–96. The
material he presents in his second volume is even more compelling,
since not only is it based mainly on Zionist sources, but it shows how
deeply, how thoroughly, and how determinedly Israeli politicians,
military men, and intellectuals continued well after 1948 to prosecute
the same policy of trying to get rid of the Palestinians, either by actual
transfer, by massacre (as in Kafr Qasim), or by forcing submission on
them as a whole. The entire idea has always therefore been to reduce
the Palestinian actuality to nil, to efface Palestinians as a people with
legitimate rights, to render them alien in their own land. And indeed
Israel has so far succeeded in its own mind. The Oslo peace process,
the settlements, the arrogant defiance of Netanyahu: these all derive in
a straight line from events like Deir Yassin and the idea that made Deir
Yassin into the massacre it was.

   Yet the question remains: Why has Deir Yassin mostly been forgotten, and why has 1948 been removed from the peace agenda by Palestinian leaders and intellectuals? After all, we are dealing with Israeli
Jews who constantly, and justly, remind the world of the evils of anti-
Semitism and the Holocaust, and of the reparations thereby made
necessary. In his book *Silencing the Past: Power and the Production of
History,* the Haitian historian Michel-Rolph Trouillot discusses how
in Western accounts of the Haitian revolution of 1798 the Westerners
always seem finally destined to win, the Haitians to lose; in addition,
most accounts of that period simply ignore what happened in Haiti.
He refers to "the silencing of the Haitian revolution," which he says
happens because the narrative of Western global domination makes
the defeat of native people seem inevitable, unless there is an attempt
by native peoples to retell the history of Western domination and thus
provoke "a fundamental rewriting of world history." As Arabs and
Palestinians we are very far from that stage. Our history is written by
outsiders, and we have conceded the battle in advance. Our leaders
negotiate as if from a tabula rasa. The agenda is America's and Israel's.
And we continue to concede, and concede more, and concede again,
not only in the present, but also in the past and in the future. Collective memory is a people's heritage and also its energy: it does not
merely sit there inertly, but it must be activated as part of a people's
identity and sense of its own prerogative. To recall Deir Yassin is not

just to dwell on past disasters, but to understand who we are and where we are going. Without it we are simply lost, as indeed it seems we really are.

Al-Ahram Weekly, April 17, 1997
The Gulf Today, April 25, 1997
Al-Khaleej, April 25, 1997
Al-Hayat, April 25, 1997

Chapter Twenty-three

Thirty Years After

ONE OF THE most daring books of historical research and argument to emerge in the United States is by Arno Mayer, a Princeton professor, who in 1981 published *The Persistence of the Old Regime: Europe to the Great War*. Mayer's argument is that after 1789, and despite a century of revolutions against the monarchy, aristocracy, and church, Europe's established, quasi-feudal structure persisted well into the early twentieth century with the old elites, the traditional high cultures, and the rituals of authority guarding their preeminence against the inroads of industrialization, the ascendant bourgeoisie, and an irresistible trend toward mass democracy. If there was ever another case of an old order persisting well past its time it is to be found in the post–1967 Arab world. To every Arab and Israeli at the time, the June War was one of the great turning points in contemporary Middle Eastern history. In a matter of hours the Egyptian and Syrian air forces were destroyed on the ground by a preemptive Israeli military strike; vast tracts of land—Sinai, the West Bank and Gaza Strip, the Golan Heights—were occupied by the Israeli army; many thousands of Arab soldiers lost their lives, some of them (we have learned in the last two years) massacred as defenseless prisoners of war by Israeli troops; a whole structure of militarist ideology was discredited in the Arab world, though vindicated in Israel; the Jewish state became the dominant regional power thanks in part to its alliance with the United States, whereas the Soviet Union, whose weapons and political support had backed the Syrian and Egyptian regimes, was very much the loser until during the 1973 war its regional allies somewhat recouped their reputations.

The great irony is that every Arab regime of consequence is still essentially unchanged today, thirty years after the greatest collective defeat in Arab history. True, nearly every government has switched its allegiance to the United States, and formerly belligerent Egypt, Jordan, and the Palestine Liberation Organization have signed peace agreements with Israel. But the structure of power in the Arab world has remained in place, with the same oligarchies, military cadres, and traditional elites holding precisely the same privileges and making the same general kind of decisions that they did in 1967. A few days ago King Hussein commemorated the 1967 war's anniversary with a radio broadcast to his people; the war, he said, had been a regrettable mistake, the result of poor planning, poor coordination, ill-considered strategies, and strident propaganda. The observation he did (or perhaps could) not make was that the Arab situation today was not really any better than it was in 1967. If the airwaves in late May 1967 were filled with the propaganda of Arab victory in war, they have been replaced today with the vociferous, but no less fraudulent, chorus of praise for the "peace process," which has yet to receive any widespread popular support or any advantages except for Israel. Almost every one of the large and important Arab countries has had elections and has parliaments, but democracy in the true sense of the word is still manifestly absent: the ruler is still in charge of foreign policy, defense, budgetary matters, and overall security. Freedom of expression remains a luxury, as controlled newspapers, television, and radio continue as the norm for the overwhelming majority of citizens. And when it comes to personal freedoms, the record is no less dismal, no less undeveloped than it was in 1967. Torture, summary arrest, and deplorable prison conditions exist everywhere, as do secret police teams who operate on the basis of an antiterrorism routinely associated with Islamism, the common scourge of Arab rulers and their Western and Israeli counterparts.

The sheer longevity of the old order is even more astonishing when we go over the turbulence of the past thirty years. For not only did Israel in effect maintain its occupation of the West Bank and Gaza

(90 percent of the former and 40 percent of the latter) despite the peace process, but a major war was fought in 1973, followed by an oil embargo that raised the price of oil to undreamed of heights, the fruits of which have not significantly increased prosperity in the Arab world; the PLO emerged as a political and, for a time in Jordan, a military force to be reckoned with, until the 1970 Black September civil war in Jordan put an end to its presence there and gave it renewed life in Lebanon; the Lebanese civil war began in 1975, consumed the country and an estimated 150,000 lives before the Ta'if agreement settled matters in 1990; Israel invaded Lebanon in 1982 (there had been a previous full-scale intervention in 1978), expelled the PLO, destroyed and then occupied a part of South Lebanon at a cost of about 20,000 civilian casualties, which included the many hundreds of defenseless Palestinian refugees slaughtered in the Sabra and Shatila camps; Iran's Islamic Revolution brought a new factor into post–1967 politics, first as a supporter of Palestinian resistance, then as a sponsor of local guerrilla groups such as South Lebanon's Hizballah, which alone among Arab military movements has fought Israel's occupying forces to a stalemate; the Palestinian intifada began in 1987 and for the first time since the conflict between the Palestinian people and Zionism compelled Israel's leaders to a new acknowledgement of this people's political inevitability.

As much as the turbulence and volatility seemed to portend the most radical change, the striking feature of the political landscape has been the power of the Arab old order, the United States, and Israel to contain and head off any serious challenge. Each successor to a major predecessor has been a diminished version of what came before. Abdel Nasser was followed by Anwar Sadat, Sadat by Hosni Mubarak, one military figure after another, with less flair and charisma as the line progressed. Arab nationalism was succeeded by local patriotisms that tailored geography to more tightly patrolled, less generous borders. Nowhere was this tendency more desperately and criminally opposed than by Baathist Iraq for whom its neighbor was the stuff that debased Bismarckian dreams were made of. The Iraqi occupation of Kuwait in 1990 and the Gulf War of 1991 constituted the greatest of the post–1967 crises, the one that exposed the terrible rifts between Arabs, that dramatized the moral vacancy in so-called Arab "radical" thought, and that finally introduced the United States as an actual military presence in the heart of the Arab world. Out of American ascendancy, as well as the tragically misguided policies of the PLO's Arafat, who preposterously aligned himself with Saddam Hussein and was thereafter forced by his own cowardice and shortsightedness both to end the intifada and accept his people's subjugation, came the famous Oslo peace talks and the new agreement between Zionism and the head of the Palestinian national movement.

The inequities and shortcomings of what began in September 1993 in a blaze of exaggerated publicity on the White House lawn have brought the famous peace to a complete standstill, but not before Israel has secured every one of its historic strategic gains and reduced Palestinians to their lowest ebb. Personal income on the West Bank and Gaza has dropped by 50 percent, while 40 percent unemployment, widespread poverty and frustration, food shortages, and continued incursions by Israeli military forces against civilians have ground Palestinians further down. Meanwhile, about four hundred fifty thousand refugees in Lebanon remain stateless, given no permission to work or move, and face mass deportation; almost the same number or more refugees in Syria are quarantined in camps without adequate attention to their needs, and over a million in Jordan, and several thousand more in various other Arab countries linger in a limbo without respite. In the Palestinian autonomy areas (it should be remembered that the Oslo accords specify autonomy but leave sovereignty, exits and entrances, resources like water and land, as well as overall security entirely in Israeli hands) a corrupt, cruel, and incompetent regime of autocracy under Arafat rules Palestinians for the benefit of a small handful of cronies. There are monopolies on fuel, building materials including wood and cement, tobacco, and nearly every commodity and consumer item, all of them shamelessly enriching Arafat, his lieutenants, and their children. This corruption has become an international scandal. A popularly elected Legislative Council has been unable for three years to pass any laws or make any constitutional inroads on a despot who controls the budget, in addition to his twenty security services who torture, kill, imprison critics and ban their books at the whim of Palestine's overweening tyrant. Nor is this all. The Palestinian population of about seven million people is at the mercy of an incompetent man who serves as the implementer of Israeli occupation and dispossession, and who can do nothing more for his people except oppress and deceive them. It is rarely noted that Arafat now in fact is able to represent a minority of his people (the inhabitants of Gaza and the West Bank), whereas 60 percent of all Palestinians reside outside and must seek redress for the injustices done them in other ways and with new leaders, new thought, new purpose.

It is an insufficiently remarked irony that Arafat's corrupt peace with Israel forgave the Zionist movement everything that it did to Palestinians, beginning with the destruction of their society and the forced expulsion of 70 percent of their numbers from Palestine in 1948. To compound the irony, the PLO essentially ignored the devastation of thirty years of Israeli military occupation, accepted the annexation of Jerusalem and the presence of 140 settlements on expropriated Palestinian land, and more or less said let bygones be bygones. And this while confronting a people which never let the world forget injustices done to them, received huge reparations from Germany for the Holocaust, and today seeks out former Nazis and countries like Switzerland who have been accused of collaborating with fascism. There is a fundamental blindness in the Israeli conscience which the PLO encouraged, instead of forcing responsibility on Zionism for its crimes against an entire people. There can never be peace between Palestinian Arabs and Israeli Jews (and their many diaspora supporters) until public acknowledgment of Israel's dispossession, and continuing oppression of the Palestinian people is recognized as a matter of state policy.

Thanks to the efforts of courageous Israeli and Palestinian revisionist historians, the stark record of what transpired is now easily available. We know that every major Zionist figure since 1897 has dreamt of ridding Palestine of its indigenous Arab inhabitants in order to keep alive the myth of a land without people for a people without land. We also know that the war of 1948 was fought by Zionist forces with an end to driving out as many civilian Palestinians as possible; the late Yitzhak Rabin was personally responsible as the Haganah commander who emptied the Palestinian towns of Lydda and Ramleh of sixty thousand men, women, and children. After 1948 one Israeli leader after another took part in the effort to suppress and defeat every attempt at Palestinian self-determination, usually by attempts at forced exodus (over three hundred thousand refugees were created in 1967 alone) or, more recently, by closures, curfews, roads built on Palestinian land for settlers, etc. By the admission of many of its leaders, including the super-hawkish Begin, Israel had no real need to fight the 1967 war, except for the desire to add more land to its territory while keeping the Palestinians subdued. An apartheid system today exists on the West Bank, where there is no continuity between the Palestinian areas, which are divided from each other by barricades, settlements, bypassing roads, many of them built as part of the peace process. For every one of his exits and entrances to and from Gaza, Yasir Arafat must get Israeli permission, a condition which is more harshly administered for the average Palestinian. East Jerusalem is closed to inhabitants of the West Bank and Gaza; as for those Palestinians with official residence permits there, Israel is trying methodically to cancel them, in order to proceed with its Judaization of the city.

Given all this, it is little short of amazing that the Palestinian leadership persists in its illusion that negotiations with Israel on the basis of the Olso accords can deliver land for peace. They cannot, and they were never intended to. The Labor Party made no secret of this, and certainly Benjamin Netanyahu's extremist government has made its intentions very clear to colonize and steal more Palestinian land in the name of a fraudulent right to settle anywhere in "the land of Israel." There seems to be little intention on the part of the Clinton administration to do anything more than support Israel "unconditionally," as Vice President Al Gore put it recently.

It is therefore evident that on both sides the inclination toward a real peace with justice and equality is lacking. Israelis feel that after thirty years of military supremacy they can do what they want in either peace or war; Palestinians refuse to reconcile themselves to a state of permanent subjugation despite their leaders' weakness. So long as the fundamental reality is denied or avoided—that Israel exists as a Jewish state by virtue of its having supplanted the rights of all Palestinians with a "superior" Jewish right—there can neither be reconciliation nor true coexistence. If the past thirty years have taught one lesson, it is that a yearning for peace and self-fulfillment amongst Palestinians cannot be abrogated or totally suppressed, no matter how militarily and politically powerful Israel is. What is now needed is a change of consciousness: Israelis must realize that their future depends on how they face up to and deal courageously with their collective history of responsibility for the Palestinian tragedy. And Palestinians, as well as other Arabs, must discover that the struggle for Palestinian rights is indivisible from the need to create a real civil and democratic society, to invest massively in innovative education, and to explore modes of secular community now unavailable in the "returns" either to Judaism, Christianity, or Islam which are characteristic of contemporary religious fundamentalism.

Al-Hayat, June 19, 1997
The Gulf Today, June 20, 1997
Al-Ahram Weekly, June 26, 1997
World Times Focus, July/August 1997
El Pais, September 16, 1997

Chapter Twenty-four

The Debate Continues

URING THE EARLY part of 1997, a meeting between various Arab and Israeli intellectuals was held in Copenhagen with the help of the Danish government. Let us accept the notion that these really were intellectuals, even though one of the Israeli participants was an intelligence operative who had many years of well-documented service throughout the Arab world (especially Lebanon), and the Jordanian contingent was reportedly made up of military officers designated for this task by the government (which was unable to find independent civilians to participate in the Copenhagen meeting). Immediately after the meeting a declaration was issued which was supposed to chart a course toward peace between Arabs and Jews; the claim was that all participants in the meetings were representative of a wider, more popular movement than the few who had gathered in Copenhagen. No evidence was given for this. Nevertheless the document and news of the meeting were widely circulated and debated in the Arab world, with only one or two references to it in the U.S. media, which treated the whole matter as a nonevent. A few issues raised there seem interesting and worth looking at, especially if one can avoid the frequent name-calling and invective used to discredit adversaries, a most disagreeable aspect of the whole business.

Although I was referred to and briefly discussed in an interview with the celebrated Egyptian journalist Lotfi al-Kholi—a protagonist at Copenhagen—I myself have had nothing to say about the meeting

before now. The interviewer, Nuri al-Jarrah, asked Kholi whether my
views on the peace process might have had a bearing on the meetings.
Mr. Kholi responded by saying that even though he respected me as a
literary scholar, I was not after all a political person, which seemed to
imply that because I was literary I had little qualification for anything
else. Far be it from me to suggest that I am a political expert or intellectual like Mr. Kholi, or that I have any of his considerable accomplishments. But it does not seem to be enough of a reason to dismiss
someone's views just because he is not accredited by an expert. The
whole point of engaging in political debate, I have always thought,
was that it was actually the duty of every citizen, not just the prerogative of certified professionals like Mr. Kholi.

One of the main issues in the debate over Copenhagen has been
the question of change in Israeli political thinking: is there a constituency for real peace? Have the conditions in Israel changed sufficiently to warrant hope and a serious Arab political investment in the
process of transformation? All the evidence available from history,
from Israeli political behavior and the like, points most discourag-
ingly away from positive answers to these questions. In the various
apologias on behalf of the peace process as well as the propects for
peace with Israel, there seems to be little Arab awareness that in
speaking about, dealing with, or analyzing Israel we are confronting a
unique political phenomenon. Israel is not an ordinary state, nor was
it ever meant to be. It is "the state of the Jewish people," not of its citizens, who include about nine hundred thousand non-Jews, which is
the official Israeli designation for the Palestinian minority in the state.
As Professor Israel Shahak said in the *Ahram Weekly* a few days ago:
"The history of modern Zionism has shown a singleness of purpose
which is unmatched by any other contemporary movement. So powerful have been the motivations of its leaders and adherents, so deep is
their certainty in the rightness of their course and cause, that violations of morality, law, and human decency have repeatedly been
accepted as unfortunate but unavoidable consequences of the fulfillment of their destiny—reclaiming the Biblical Jewish homeland and
establishing the Jewish state of Israel."

Were this description simply a matter of ideological conviction in
an abstract sense it would be bad enough, but it is also an accurate

characterization of Israeli action since the founding of the state in 1948. I have had occasion in these pages to mention the work of Nur Masalha, the Palestinian-Israeli scholar who has written two books on the centrality of the concept of "transfer" in Zionist thought and practice. His second book, *A Land Without a People,* published in England (but not in the United States) this year, ought to occupy enthusiasts of the peace process and Copenhagen somewhat more than ill-considered general encomia to the need for new thought and a new Arab mind. Masalha traces the actions of the Israeli government against the Palestinians from 1948 until the present, showing how the exodus of 1948, the attempts during the 1950s by Ben-Gurion and his associates (Dayan, Rabin, Peres, Allon, Yadin, Hertzog, and the others) to redraw the map of the Middle East so as to eliminate or dissolve Syria, Lebanon, Jordan, Iraq, the military occupation after 1967, the policies toward Palestinian Israelis, the settlements, and even the Oslo accords, were all aspects of much the same obsession: to rid Palestine of its original Arab Palestinian inhabitants by expulsion, repression, colonization, and a kind of willful blindness toward them as human beings. For example, the Israeli Attorney General wrote in 1971 about deportations by Israel of Palestinians from their homes to Jordan: "Deportation of a person to Jordan is . . . neither deportation to the territory of the occupying power nor to the territory of another country. It is more a kind of return or exchange of a prisoner to the power which sent him and gave him its blessing and orders to act" (p. 131). According to Masalha there has been a long-standing effort to force Palestinians to emigrate, and even to provide funds for them to go to Argentina, Venezuela, and elsewhere in Latin America.

During the 1980s a powerful right-wing extremist movement gradually gained power and influence over politics in Israel, encouraged of course first by Begin, then by Shamir, and now by Netanyahu. Groups like Gush Emunim, the Kach, Tehya, and Moledet parties, and the Whole Land of Israel Movement have openly advocated not only annexation of Palestinian land, but also an unyieldingly hostile view of Palestinians as "aliens" in the land of Israel. True, Masalha concedes, there have been liberal Israeli critics of these tendencies and parties, but not enough of them to stop such groups or to make them modify their extreme views. Besides, it should be obvious that the influence of the right wing has been greater than that of the liberals, who at times seem to have diminished in size and influence since Oslo. Moreover, the Oslo accords do not obviate the desire on the part of Labor as well as Likud to stunt Palestinian development, to annex most of the West Bank, and, above all, neither to give back settlements nor to concede any Palestinian rights in Jerusalem. In that city, the deputy mayor, Shmuel Meir, is on record as planning to "devour Arab east Jerusalem and reduce its Arab community to an insignificant minority." The plan includes demolishing more Palestinian houses, more settlements, more stripping Palestinians from Jerusalem of their identity and residence permits.

A great deal has been made by Copenhagen and peace process enthusiasts of people like Yossi Beilin, who is routinely considered to be a dove and something of an ally of the Palestinians. Having myself heard Mr. Beilin last year in Washington defend the Cana massacre, I am somewhat less convinced, but it is true that he has had cordial dealings with Palestinian leaders like Abu Mazen. The two of them produced a "secret" document on the final settlement supposedly acceptable to both sides. Not only was the document leaked everywhere, but Beilin made a similar agreement with a Likud Knesset member in which it was decreed that there would be no uprooting of settlements (which will be annexed by Israel), no return to the 1967 borders, no Palestinian state (but only a demilitarized "entity"), and the Jordan valley will remain an Israeli security zone. He put it quite plainly in *Ha'aretz* on March 28, 1997: We will have a "demilitarized Palestinian entity, with limited sovereignty, in return for a whole and undivided Jerusalem." He said even more on a television roundtable on March 17, 1997: "I am in favor of building everywhere in Jerusalem, including the building of Har Homa, since this is our right; the question is one of timing and clever tactics. We [the Rabin government] increased settlements by 50 percent, we built in Judea and Samaria, but we did it quietly and with wisdom. You [the Netanyahu government] proclaim your intentions every morning, frighten the Palestinians and transform the topic of Jerusalem as the unified capital of Israel—a matter which all Israelis agreed upon—into a subject of worldwide debate. The main thing is to get the Palestinians to agree that Jerusalem is the capital of Israel. Without their agreeing to this, there will be no agreement."*

With so reliable and honest an ally, Arabs have very little to worry about: the Israeli peace camp is lined up and ready to march with us! What bothers one about Arab commentators and intellectuals who support Copenhagen and the peace process is why they never confront people like Beilin and Kimche with *public* questions about their real attitudes. After one hundred years of unbroken Israeli-Zionist hostility to the native Palestinians, and fifty years of mostly successful attempts to destroy their corporate social and political existence, dispossess them of their land, reduce their actuality to that of blacks under apartheid or native American Indians on reservations—with the active collaboration of an incompetent, discredited, and totally corrupt Palestinian leadership—one would have expected a little more skepticism from Messrs. Kholi and company than the stream of insult and abuse directed against honest Arab critics of Israel and the peace process. Why do Mr. Kholi and his friends not direct their energies toward trying to change Zionist practices, especially since at present they show very little knowledge of how either Israel or the Zionist movement has treated Palestinians? Why this unseemly enthusiasm for peace with an ideological state that has shown scarce inclination, if at all, to concede either on matters of doctrine or on the ground?

The other major issue in the post-Copenhagen debate has concerned an entity obscurely referred to as "the Arab mind," as if one could speak responsibly of so vast, not to say stupefyingly general an object with any degree of sense. So let us begin by saying that by attacking the Arab mind in so racist a way, accusing it of derangement and simple "madness," the pro-peace pro-U.S. Arab commentators, mostly expatriate former leftists, contribute only to the general demoralization that has overtaken Arab political and social discourse. For them, being modern is being opportunistic. Very little is said about the policy either of Israel or the United States, while a great deal that is defamatory is said about individuals whose views are taken to

---

*Quoted in Tikva Honig-Parnass, *News from Within*, April 1997.

be retrograde, unmodern, basically stupid. In a typical piece of transparently illogical rhetoric one of them accused Arab intellectuals of not having a new enough style of the kind of thought that is required to think about peace; even Palestinians, he says, think too much about the wrongs done them and not enough about the future. As if one could separate the past from the future, particularly when one is dealing with an opponent whose main raison d'être is a realization of the Old Testament, which is nothing if not a style of thought rooted, indeed frozen, in the past. So completely has this individual intellectual separated himself from the past that in 1991, in a prominent American journal of opinion, he advocated an American invasion of Baghdad and the military occupation of Iraq by the U.S. military. If this is an example of new futuristic thinking, one would be right in dismissing it as a fraud, and seeing in it only the old complexes of people for whom the White Man's power is to be worshipped, fawned upon, emulated at all costs.

Clearly we need more, not less, debate in the Arab world. But we cannot accept as debate and free expression of opinion anything that is coercive and has the authority of official thinking to enforce its claims. The real burden has to be put back aggressively on Israel, to require of its citizens and intellectuals a qualitative change from a political ideology that has never deviated from extreme chauvinism, and downright aggression against Arabs, both Palestinian and non-Palestinian. Unfortunately, however, the real tragedy is that in the Arab world we have neither the social and political institutions to carry on an open debate with equals, nor the unity and sense of purpose to confront a ruthless and ruthlessly single-minded opponent. Until we do, the distorted claims and counterclaims that have emanated from the aftermath of the Copenhagen meeting and declaration will probably continue with no effect at all on the Israeli advance toward the total appropriation of Palestine.

The Gulf Today, March 6, 1997
Al-Ahram Weekly, May 8, 1997
Al-Hayat, May 7, 1997
Al-Khaleej, May 7, 1997

Chapter Twenty-five

The Next Generation?

I T IS HARD for any Arab aged between fifty and seventy not to feel that his or her generation has *not* made an *all* around mess of things. Ours was the generation that supported and lived through the first decade of post–World War II independence which brought to power the very regimes—surprisingly durable—that run things today: the armies, the undemocratic societies, the intelligence services, the hopelessly backward and unreformed educational systems, the growing gap between a small elite and a vast number of disadvantaged citizens, the dependence on the United States, the almost total absence of a thriving civil society, the sinking rate of nearly all forms of productivity. Ours is also the generation that announced all sorts of wonderful slogans about liberation, creating a new society, and freedom from the shackles of a colonial past. The dream was to be Arab unity, a phrase that has become almost a term of abuse, replaced instead by all kinds of fancy formulations about a new Middle East that was supposed to get us out of the traps of that illusory hope of unity. Worse yet, the ideal of cooperation and planning has been withered down into a string of jealous nationalisms that have now reached the end of their promise. And to top it all, we all live under Israeli hegemony. The longest military occupation in the twentieth century continues its unabated rule, now in its thirty-first year; a set of flawed, deeply unpopular peace agreements with an Israel that has neither bothered to define its borders nor to modify its racist anti-Arab laws, were the lamentable result of a failure of Arab military, political, and social policy. Israel got its way in most things, with the result that today "peace" is only a word shunned by most Arabs as a trap, celebrated by a small minority of their number as a hope, and essentially rejected by the most reactionary and brutal government in Israel's history.

This is not a record to be proud of, obviously enough, nor is it something in its present form that we can confidently hand down to our children. And it certainly is not a matter of becoming more, or less (as various Islamic movements have argued) Western. Most of the advisers to Arab leaders today are Western trained and educated. A fair number of Arab university and college professors were trained in American and European universities. Many of them were contemporaries of mine, many gifted and full of promise, and many went back to their countries of origin full of hope about serving their people. Yet today's Arab world is dominated not by them but by a class of profiteers, bureaucrats, and time-servers; Harvard- and Oxford-educated advisers end up by going along with policies that produced various Arab civil wars (including the Gulf War) and one losing proposition after another. Within my own limited experience I have been struck that so many talented humanists, social and natural scientists whom I either know or taught in the United States returned to comfortable positions as faculty members in Arab universities only to become unproductive and lazy, perhaps because of the vast demoralization overtaking so many parts of secular Arab society.

Our generation is now reaching the end of its tenure without, alas, having very much to hand on to our children. But there are grounds for hope, hope in unexpected places. Three weeks ago I gave a lecture on the relationship between imagination and imperialism at a distinguished university near Boston. It was the first lecture I had given after four months of illness and confinement at home, so I was quite apprehensive about how it would be received, and about how I would be able to deliver it. The lecture went reasonably well, there was a spirited question and discussion period after it, and then we were all invited to a reception next door. The discussion continued for quite a time afterward, most if not all of it sustained by a sizable group of young Arab men and women, students at places like Harvard, MIT, Tufts, and Boston University. All of them seemed to be between the ages of twenty and thirty, with a preponderance of younger people in that range. Part of the joy of meeting them was, first of all, to encounter the children of old friends, parents of my generation, whose sons and daughters I vaguely remembered as noisy little figures running around the living room. They had now become lively young university students, hungry for ideas, brimming with theories and questions, critical and yet very engaged with the Arab world.

Not all of them were Arab-Americans, although most of them were in fact the product of good secondary schools in the eastern United States. There were a fair number of young scholars from countries throughout the Arab world, including the Gulf. I spoke to sociologists, economists, literary scholars, poets, political scientists, and one or two people in the natural sciences. The one thing that impressed me about every one of them was the almost total absence in what they said of the clichés and vague formulas that were the stock in trade of my generation. None of them seemed to have any system of answers to our problems: rather they were full of questions about why we were that way, and full also of a kind of healthy skepticism about easy answers or solutions. None of them seemed disengaged from the Arab world, even those who were born or brought up in the West. But their connection, although very real, was unsentimental. All of them were essentially bilingual, fluent and at home both in English and Arabic, which the Americans among them had learned the way my son learned the language, on their own, the hard way; and there was a mastery of both Arab and Western discourse that suggested an ease unavailable to my generation, which I have always thought got the worst of both worlds, mostly resentful and hostile about a West that had seemed to reject them, sentimental about an Arab world that an unhappy expatriation had painted in falsely rosy colors.

It is important to mention that the whole group of about forty young people, graduate and undergraduate, seemed to be in the care of Professor Elaine Hagopian, a marvelously kind and generous teacher of sociology at Simmons College in Boston. She is certainly the most dedicated and modest person I know; she never boasts or talks about herself, and most commendable of all, she has made it her personal responsibility to care for these young Arabs in Boston, all of whom regard her not only as a senior professor but as an older sister.

She is completely egalitarian, and so, as one of them told me, she never makes them feel inferior or somehow less important a person than she. What she does she does without money and without official support. No wonder, then, that all the young people I met, all intelligent, all articulate and eager for some work to do to help our Arab world, seemed so indebted to her. In my generation it was and still is the case that the older and more significant you feel yourself to be, the more you bully the young, prevent their rise, are jealous of their success, repress enthusiasm and initiative whenever possible. Professor Hagopian is the exact opposite, a genuine mentor.

For the first time in years I felt my gloom about our condition lifting. Here was a new generation that had suddenly emerged (there must be many like them in the Arab world and elsewhere) despite the miserable failures of the past and present. In my opinion one of the great things about this generation is its ability to exist comfortably in more than one world; gone is the paranoid defensiveness of the past, when a blanket of hatred of the West coexisted both with fear and ignorance of it, along with a secret subservience to its every dictate. I felt it was my duty to announce to our disheartened people that a new generation of fine young people was present and needed careful support and nurturing. Can we follow Elaine Hagopian's example, or are we going to follow the example of our generation? Yes, it is a new generation, but we bear responsibility for its ascendancy. I hope we can do the right thing.

Al-Hayat, May 21, 1997
Al-Khaleej, May 21, 1997
The Gulf Today, May 22, 1997

Chapter Twenty-six

Are There No Limits to Corruption?

W HILE I WAS IN LONDON a few days ago I attended the annual fund-raising dinner for Medical Aid for Palestine (MAP), an important British charity that supplies medicine, training, and hospital equipment to Palestinians in Lebanon, the West Bank, and Gaza. Most of the audience (and indeed many of its supporters) was Arab generally, Palestinian in particular, but there was also a considerable British presence as well. The two main speakers were Lord David Steel, MAP's current president, a former Member of Parliament and leader of the Liberal Party, and Clare Short, Minister for International Development in the New Labor cabinet of Tony Blair. Both are well-known supporters of Palestinian rights and, though they spoke approvingly of the now defunct Oslo accords, were emphatic in lamenting the current state of affairs in which Palestinians continue to suffer the denial of their rights. The striking thing about both speeches, however, was the reference made by each speaker to the misuse of public funds by the Palestinian Authority. Steel and Short stressed the need for accountability and transparency, in effect saying that what is now a universally known aspect of the PA's rule should stop, given that Palestinians are an oppressed people still in need of financial aid and support.

These remarks came at a very difficult time for all Palestinians. Not only has the peace process worsened economic and political conditions in the occupied territories, but the extreme right-wing government of Benjamin Netanyahu has intensified the provocations and outright robbery which is the core of its settlement campaign. In addition the United States Congress—acting in accordance with *its* policy of being more unconditionally loyal to Israel than to any other country—has passed a resolution giving Israel total sovereignty over Jerusalem. There has been very little help to Palestinians from the Arab states, and internationally the cause of Palestine has lost a great deal of its luster; there are, after all, many other problems in the world.

Thus it is entirely correct to say that Palestinians feel embattled and isolated: they are either forgotten refugees, or prisoners of Israel's occupation. But it would be entirely wrong to conclude that *all* their problems derive from their enemies. Some responsibility for the disastrous state of affairs must be laid at the door of the Palestinian Authority and its head, Yasir Arafat. When a report issued by his own internal auditors states flatly that 40 percent of the Authority's budget has either been wasted or misused, it would be absurd to blame Israel, or to say that all Middle Eastern governments are corrupt and inefficient and so why should we be different. Nor is it the case that Palestinian official malfeasance is an invention of the pro-Zionist Western media. A few weeks ago the *Guardian*'s senior correspondent, David Hirst, a lifelong sympathizer with the Palestinian tragedy and a first-rate reporter who has devoted his life to living in and writing about the Arab world, wrote a devastating report entitled "Shameless in Gaza" in the *Guardian* on "the open corruption of the Palestinian Authority." He described the enormously ostentatious and expensive villas being built on the coast by Abu Mazen and Um Jihad, the company called "al-Bahr" which, true to its name (the sea), swallows up property and businesses for Mr. Arafat's interests, the nightclubs, the luxurious limousines, the commercial abuses of various high officials, all of them going on at a time of huge unemployment in Gaza, the protracted misery of the thousands of camp dwellers, the total paralysis of the Palestinian economy, and the complete breakdown in any sort of advance in Palestinian rights.

When asked about all this in a more than usually disgraceful interview with *Newsweek,* Mr. Arafat said it was not true, and that there was no money in the Authority, which he said is under the thumb of the donor countries for its budgetary activity. Every time he was requested to explain an embarrassing aspect of his regime (e.g., Daoud Kuttab's summary arrest and ten-day detention), either he would say that he had appointed a committee to look into it, or he would object to the questions by saying "Do you realize that you are speaking to Yasir Arafat?" For not only does Mr. Arafat have no notion of proper governmental responsibility and accountability, but he believes he can fool everyone with his prevarication and bluster. No one needs to be reminded that Mr. Arafat's word in the Territories is law; he is the Authority and very little can get done without him; he is the sole source of patronage, and only he knows the full scope of the budget.

We have now become an international scandal. In April, *Ha'aretz* published a fifteen-page supplement on the Authority's characteristic double-dealing. This year 1.5 billion shekels ($500 million) will be transferred from Israel into the PA's secret accounts in Israeli banks; this is referred to as *al-sandooq al-thani,* and comprises remittances on VAT taxes, import duties, and pension fund deductions paid by Palestinians which Israel returns to Arafat, but since only he and assistants of his, like Mohammed Rashid (Khalid Slam), know the exact amounts and accounts, he is at liberty to dispose of this money basically to buy people's loyalty and complicity. In the face of virtually no productivity and no public works, Arafat simply inflates the size of his bureaucracy and security forces now totalling about 90,000 people, many of them without real jobs except for a title (750 directors-general of ministries to cite just one example) and a salary. To survive, Palestinians must become servants of a despotic tyrant who has nothing real to offer his unfortunate people except himself, more failure, more corruption, and mediocrity.

The really serious theft is the system of monopolies operated by Arafat and his cronies, including his ministers, their children, wives, uncles, and aunts. There are now monopolies on wheat, cement, petroleum, wood, gravel, cigarettes, cars, gasoline, cattle feed, and a few other commodities; all these compel the ordinary citizen to pay inflated prices several times greater than the price under direct Israeli occupation. Thus a ton of cattle feed used to be 120 dinars; it is now 300 dinars. No one knows exactly how much money is made in this way, nor who gets it, or how it is spent. There are no laws for companies or investments, and consequently no requirement to register companies, nor to hold bidding competitions and offer tenders. There is no way of regulating mortgages, no orderly routine for collecting debts, no laws for recording joint companies, and so on. In such a deliberately chaotic situation Arafat and his associates can do what they please, with neither a legal system nor an aroused independent media to inhibit their appetites. Many of the security chiefs and their services are used for enforcement or extortion, and above all for threatening anyone who dares to object.

The results of all this are uniformly negative. No real development can take place, no institutions can develop, no prosperity can occur. When ministers and their assistants charge their home expenses to the Authority, own four cars, insist on traveling first class, all this sits badly for a society that is still under occupation and for whose majority life is extremely difficult. Besides, these are all abuses of public funds and the public trust that demoralize and cheat people for whom the "peace process" from the beginning was a fraud and who are still entitled to yearn for justice and freedom.

During hard times, leaders are expected to set a high standard of personal conduct and commitment. In the Palestinian case, the tragedy of a dispossessed and militarily occupied people is compounded by a leadership that made a "peace" deal with its more powerful enemy, a deal that serves Israel's strategic purposes by keeping Palestinians, whose land has been practically lost to Zionist conquest, in a state of depression and servitude. The leadership of Yasir Arafat *perpetuates* rather than alleviates this horror: he delivers security to Israel by punishing his own people, lying to them that he is bringing us nearer to self-determination, deceiving them into believing that he acts in their name and interests. With his corruption he has stripped his own people of their resources, squandered their wealth, abused their lives further. What right does he claim to do all this while robbing his people, forcing them to accept monopolies, allowing himself to be accountable to no one as he bribes, bullies, corrupts everyone in his way.

The fact is that by his behavior Mr. Arafat no longer represents the majority of Palestinians, and now survives without dignity by virtue of U.S., Israeli, and Arab support. He has no use for his people and, if they were free to say so, neither have they for him. The cause of Palestine can only be served if he resigns. I said this right after the Oslo accords were signed, and I am sorry to say that time has proved me right. Yasir Arafat neither has the vision nor courage to lead anyone anywhere except into more poverty and despondency.

The Gulf Today, July 2, 1997
Al-Hayat, July 2, 1997

Chapter Twenty-seven

Reparations: Power and Conscience?

THE DRAMA OF Swiss banks being forced to reveal the contents, amounts, and numbers of their secret accounts continues day by day. For years these extremely powerful and prestigious institutions took the position that their absolute secrecy as to the identity of holders of bank accounts would never be broken: the country's credibility was at stake, as was its continued prosperity as the recipient of funds deposited there as a refuge from foreign scrutiny, persecution, or generally unwelcome attention. But for quite some time now the phrase "a Swiss bank account" has been synonymous with cheating or wrongdoing; the idea that there was one very safe place on earth where illicit money could be kept in absolute secrecy has appealed to every dictator and criminal throughout the world, with results for Switzerland itself that assured it both of affluence and a reputation for a dubious "neutrality." It is also worth recalling that for at least two decades there has been a determined Swiss opposition to the bank secrecy laws. The courageously outspoken Swiss intellectual and parliamentarian Jean Ziegler attacked his own country's policy as immoral since, he said, whatever benefits accrued to Switzerland came at the expense of the poor and oppressed in the Third World. Others joined Ziegler's campaign to do away with bank secrecy, but to no avail—until through a combination of American political pressure in alliance with the World Jewish Congress earlier this year Switzerland was persuaded to open up its banking records.

As I write these lines, today's *New York Times* (July 23, 1997) contains two full pages of names and accounts totaling two thousand unclaimed amounts. This could not have happened without the pressure exerted on Switzerland by influential members of the U.S. Senate plus distinguished Jewish Americans. Last winter there were several days of congressional hearings in Washington in which witness after witness declared his/her knowledge of accounts held by Switzerland whose owners were Holocaust victims, but whose descendants or relatives were alive and competent to take over the funds. In time a commission was appointed by the Congress, headed by Paul Volker, a well-known economist and former head of the Federal Reserve. Its mandate was to secure as much knowledge and information as possible about these World War II accounts, to make them public, and obviously to get hold of the money for both Jewish and non-Jewish beneficiaries. A great deal was made of this in the international and especially the U.S. media, and as pressure on the Swiss government mounted, various officials felt it necessary to resign in the face of growing public outrage at what was seen as Swiss greed and obduracy. The case for disclosure was greatly helped by the defection of a Swiss bank security guard who smuggled out lists of names and accounts to the United States; he later had to leave Switzerland but was immediately welcomed to America, given a hero's reception, and then a lucrative job. Feeling itself shamed before the entire world, the Swiss government has given up on its secrecy so far as World War II accounts are concerned. (It is an interesting anomaly of the situation that General Mobutu of Zaire, who made off with several billions of his country's treasure, has so far not been required to declare what his Swiss accounts are; a cursory search by independent experts has revealed only about $14 million hidden in Switzerland, but since the United States has not taken a position on his larceny, there has been no pressure to divulge the actual amount.) In a few weeks a referendum of Switzerland's entire population will be held in order to determine whether the country ought to establish an additional endowment fund for "charitable purposes" that will include restitution to Jewish as well as non-Jewish Holocaust victims.

Although it is quite clear that various individuals have been involved in this campaign against Swiss banking secrecy for entirely selfish, even cynical reasons, the whole thrust of what has taken place strikes me as entirely justified. Not all the pressure has come because of Jewish influence. Clearly the United States is trying to end the Swiss practice of accepting drug money in secret accounts, and clearly also the European Community has little patience or use for Switzerland as an independent economic and banking center inside, but not of, Europe. Be that as it may, one must also admire the persistence of the World Jewish Congress in pressing the case for reparations to Jewish Holocaust victims. Why should the victims of persecution and geno-cide also be deprived of their worldly goods, and why should their persecutors be given an additional victory? This is not a matter of revenge, but of an injustice rectified. As to whether the Swiss bankers and people themselves feel that justice has been done, that is another question, since there is no doubt that only the enormous power of the United States could have extracted the concessions that have finally emerged. The main thing to be lamented is that this same power has not regularly been deployed on behalf of other victims of injustice.

Analysis cannot end here, however. Israel is in a sense the state of Holocaust survivors and the victims of Western (especially Christian) anti-Semitism. Theodor Herzl's arguments on behalf of Zionism always included the wish to end the persecution of Jews by creating a place for them where they would be the majority, not an oppressed and often despised minority. Many Western supporters of Israel believed that in taking Israel's side in its dispute with what were always referred to very generally as "the Arabs," they were compen-sating for what their societies had historically done to the Jews. The facts of the matter are not so accommodating, since after all Palestine was an already inhabited country, whose natives were subsequently displaced and dispossessed, their society destroyed, and their remnant either hounded into exile or the rest of their territory militarily occu-pied since 1967. A debate has been developing inside Israel on what the Haifa University psychologist and historian Benjamin Beit Hal-lahmi has called Israel's original sin—its treatment of the Palestinians from the Zionist movement's very inception through 1948 and 1967. There is now considerable evidence from research done in Israeli archives, in addition to the testimony and research produced by Pales-tinians, to ascertain that the tragic fate of the Palestinian people for the past fifty years has derived in large measure from Israel's behavior—Israel, that is, acting as the state of the Jewish people. An article in the July 19–25 issue of *The Economist* entitled "the Unchosen People"—a reference to the Palestinians as victims of Israel—describes the Israeli historians' debate about what role and what blame should be assigned to Israel's wars and to its army. This is an important development in that for the first time since 1948 the wall of official denial has been penetrated, and the silence about what took place in 1948 has been broken despite the fact that some intellectuals still refuse to acknowledge the factual evidence. *The Economist* concludes as follows: "The war of Israel's historians is fated to continue. That is probably, on balance, a good thing. Nobody can deny that, whatever the original intentions of Zionism's leaders, their project turned out to have calamitous consequences for the Arabs of Palestine. It may be that by accepting their portion of the blame Israelis will find it easier to reach a reconciliation with the Palestinians. But not, it is to be hoped, by rewriting their country's history."

Against the background of Swiss compliance with the World Jewish Congress's legitimate wish to have secret bank accounts of Holocaust victims uncovered, it is plain that the Palestinian claim for losses to Israel ought at least to be addressed. It is hypocritical for Israel to require justice in one instance and refuse it in another, especially since nearly everyone of the seven million surviving Palestinians today incurred major losses because of deprivation, dispossession, military occupation, bombing campaigns, and terrorism. To say that the only reason that the Swiss were forced to open their bank records was that the power of the United States and the World Jewish Congress made it possible is to tell only part of the truth. Undoubtedly, power played a significant role, something the Palestinians have no hope of emulating. But it is also true that were it not for Swiss acknowledgment of injustice, there could have been no redress of World War II evils. The conclusion arrived at seemed inevitable, whether for reasons of power or of conscience or both. Israel has never been required to face its own past. Its claim to have survived for fifty years as a state embodying the innocence of the victim is of course utter nonsense. Palestinian losses for which Israel is directly responsible are estimated at many billions of dollars, considering that in 1948 the Zionists had only succeeded in buying 6 percent of Palestine's land area; the rest came by conquest and by driving out as many Palestinians as possible. Thus the Jewish victims of anti-Semitism and the Holocaust produced their own victims, the Palestinians; even though it is difficult to formulate the claims of the victims' victims the fact is that such a claim must be formulated by Palestinians above all, but also by other Arab peoples and other supporters of human rights.

For the past half century, Palestinian struggle has focused principally upon armed conflict for understandable but, in my opinion, insufficiently analyzed reasons. The myth of the heroic freedom fighter was allowed to stand on its own; hence it was easy for Israeli propaganda to turn Palestinians into terrorists, thus voiding our claims for justice and reparations. From militancy and armed struggle our leadership jumped directly into the concessions that have produced the disasters of Oslo, for which the large majority of Palestinians are today paying the exorbitant price. More important than peace for us is acknowledgment of our past losses and sacrifices, and this, I am sorry to say, both the Arabs generally and Palestinian leadership in particular have simply forgotten about. But today's world is neither like that of 1948 nor that of 1967. There is an aroused moral conscience everywhere apparent in today's world, which is why the intifada of 1987–91 achieved significant moral and political successes, and why the South African victory, the crumbling of the Berlin Wall, and the coming of democracy to various Latin American countries have had such resonance. The point here is not just to blame the Palestinian leadership for another of its failings but to suggest that we should start to rethink our strategy for peace beyond the cul-de-sac of Oslo. Haidar Abdel Shafi's call to put the Palestinian house in order is a central part of the strategy, since one cannot wage a struggle for national rights without belonging or appearing to belong to a just cause. Corruption, torture, abuses of power, and a bankrupt rhetoric have no place now and should no longer be tolerated, any more than collaboration with an authority that practices such things can be tolerated. But the next step is in fact for us to turn ourselves into a community of conscience and to stand before Israel and its supporters not as supplicants or as petitioners for pity, but as a people demanding that their presence and past be acknowledged for what they are. We must remain true to the principles of our history and of our losses, which cannot be sidetracked by such things as the ridiculous "Allon Plus" plan offered by Netanyahu and his right-wing supporters. Peace can only come with reconciliation and restitution.

In short, we need an entirely new strategy of peace, a new peace movement on the basis of equality, reconciliation, and justice, and a rhetoric that puts our history on the world's agenda for the restitution of past wrongs. This cannot occur simply by going out begging. It has to be organized using the plentiful resources of the Palestinian diaspora community, which include money, talent, and a mobilized will. In the end, though, there is no substitute for finding a new national language that does not bear within it the tired slogans of the past, nor the inadequate concepts of the American-Israeli peace process. Sooner or later this generation of leaders is going to pass. We should start to think about the future constructively from now on, but we cannot do so until we anchor ourselves in our real history and agenda. We have had one century of loss and failure. Surely, since even the Swiss banking system has had to change, we too can change.

Al-Hayat, August 10, 1997
Al-Khaleej, August 11, 1997
Al-Ahram Weekly, August 7, 1997
The Gulf Today, August 11, 1997

Chapter Twenty-eight

Bombs and Bulldozers

I T HAS TAKEN almost exactly four years for the Oslo peace process inexorably to peel off its cosmetic wrappings in order to reveal the stark truth hidden at its core: there was no real peace agreement, only an agreement to keep Israeli hegemony over the Palestinian territories safeguarded by hypocritical rhetoric and military power. In this, as I have been saying for a long time, there was a lamentable Palestinian failure to judge Israeli motives—especially under Labor—and to preserve a degree of skepticism. Instead we entered an appalling spiral of loss and humiliation, gulled by the United States and the media into thinking that we had at last achieved some measure of respectability and acceptance, all of which has impoverished our people whose per capita income has been slashed by half; we have lost our ability to move around freely, confined to the dreadful little Bantustans (about 3 percent of the West Bank) that we insist on calling liberated zones, obliged to watch more settlements being built and more land taken, more houses destroyed, more people evicted, and sadistic collective punishments meted out without proportion or reason. Western liberals must remember that Oslo was not a fresh start: it was built on twenty-six years of Israeli military occupation and, before that, nineteen years of Palestinian dispossession, exile, oppression. If Israel has all along insisted that it is not responsible for what has been visited on the Palestinian people since 1948, then it should explain to us why we, alone of all people, should forget the past, remain uncompensated, our travails unacknowledged, even as all other victims of injustice have the right to reparations, apologies, and the like. There is no logic to that, only the cold, hard, narcissistic indifference of amoral power.

I have not heard one Palestinian applaud or even mildly approve the marketplace bombs of last week. They were stupid, criminal acts that have brought disaster on our people. Yet the media and the Israeli and U.S. governments, united with Micronesia in the UN (a marvelous alliance), have insisted that Palestinian terror and violence be stopped. The predictable Amos Oz has demanded that we decide between peace and violence, as if Israel had already grounded its planes, dismantled Dimona, stopped bombing and occupying South Lebanon (two seventy-year-old Lebanese men were killed by Israeli planes at the time of the marketplace bombings: why is that not violence and terror?), and withdrawn all its troops out of the 97 percent of the West Bank it still controls, along with the military checkpoints that it has planted between every major Palestinian center. Israel and its American supporters have rarely troubled themselves with any of these facts, which Israel is entitled to fabricate or annul on the ground and in the media as it suits its purposes. Neither of the two suicide bombers has been identified; neither, it is practically certain, came from the Palestinian territories; no recognizable party or group has claimed credible responsibility for the crime. On the contrary, Israel, in its mania for security, has retained control of every exit and entrance into the territories, and it alone is responsible for West Jerusalem, where the attack took place. How dare the egregious Netanyahu and his chorus of American minions demand that Islamic militants be summarily arrested, and Israeli security be guaranteed? Who does he think he is addressing as his bonded servant, and by what standards of human decency does he dare assume that the hundreds of Palestinians murdered during the intifada, the victims of the Sabra and Shatila massacres—all of them directly the responsibility of Israel—are nothing compared to Israel's "security" needs? Only a few weeks ago the Israeli justice system ruled unilaterally that victims of Israel's military during the intifada were not entitled to pursue their claims against the state since it was a "war" situation. Who do those people think they are, that they can make light of or ignore what they have done to us and still wrap themselves in the mantle of "the survivors"? Is there no

term limit, is there no sense of respect for the victims' victims, is there
no boundary to what Israel can do while continuing to demand the
privileges of the innocent?

As Anthony Lewis put it on August 11 in the *New York Times,*
Israel holds most of the cards; to blame the Palestinians for every misfortune or incident inside Israel is to jumble up blame with illusion.
He is absolutely right, and right also to admit that there isn't much
hope for peace in such circumstances. I have been unsparing in my
criticism of Arafat and his associates for what they have done during
the past five years: now, I must say, I concur fully with their policy of
refusing to negotiate on "security" as Israel defines it (i.e., rounding
up "Islamic" suspects to Israel's satisfaction) until Israel fulfills the
terms of Oslo that it has so far either blatantly violated or simply
brushed off. When Bill Clinton and Madeleine Albright repeat the formula now used as frontline propaganda by the Israeli lobby, "there is
no equivalent between bombs and bulldozers," they need to explain to
a recently evicted Palestinian family or Palestinians under curfew or
Palestinians whose houses have been destroyed or whose young men
and women languish in Israeli jails or who are strip-searched by Israeli
soldiers or driven out of Jerusalem so that Russian Jews can be settled
in their homes or killed in massacres or deprived of any right to
resist Israeli occupation policies, what *is* the equivalent of an Israeli-
American bulldozer in such a context? There is a simple racist premise
underpinning the "peace process" and subsequent rhetorical am-
bushes set in its name that Palestinian and Arab lives aren't worth as
much as Israeli Jewish lives. Last year, when 100 Lebanese civilians
hiding in a UN shelter were deliberately targeted and killed by Israeli
jets and helicopter gunships, there was no Israeli apology, no demand
from the United States that Israel should curb its bombers, no willingness even to accept the UN Secretary-General's report. Is there any
real merit to the notion that the United States and its army of former
Israeli lobbyists who now are in charge of the "peace process" can still
continue to claim that they are somehow for "peace" and are even-
handed negotiators?

The only peace worth its name is an exchange of land for peace on
the basis of rough parity between the two sides. There can be no peace
without some genuine attempt on the part of Israel and its powerful

supporters to take a step toward the people they have wronged, a step they must take in humility and reconciliation, not in clever talk and cruel behavior. Very few of us want back everything we lost in 1948, but we do want some acknowledgment of what we lost, and of Israel's role in that mass dispossession, which so many of Israel's new historians have themselves excavated with courage and assiduity. Many Palestinians do not want to return to their land, but they ask, why is it that any Jew anywhere has the theoretical right of return, whereas we have none at all? And Israel's citizens and its friends need to ask themselves openly whether they think that Israel can go on abusing and humiliating Palestinians, showing contempt for Arabs, flaunting its brazen actions before the world and at the same time enjoy real recognition and acceptance. The sad fact is that both the United States and Israel are so out of touch with Arab actualities, so enamored of clichés about Islamic terror and Arab radicalism and anti-Semitism, that they seem to have missed the fact that Arabs want peace, that Palestinians want also to lead a decent life of independence and democracy as much as the common Israeli or American. Why then lay up stores of resentment and hatred that will surely delay peace for Israelis and Arabs for years more?

Terror bombing is terrible, and cannot be condoned. But the bulldozers of forgetfulness and righteous arrogance are terrible also. Israel's constant demands for security conceal, I think, a deep insecurity about Israel's "original sin," the fact that there was always another people in Palestine, and that every village, kibbutz, settlement, city, and town had an Arab history also. Dayan used to admit it publicly. This generation of leaders hasn't his honesty. The worst are Israel's lobby and the scads of pro-Israeli organizations in the United States who repeat the dreadful clichés and celebrate Israel without a trace of awareness that there is tragedy beneath every road, every act of military prowess, every settlement. What sort of hypocrisy is it to rail against Islamic fundamentalism and to say nothing of Jewish fundamentalism that dehumanizes every non-Jew and relies on biblical promises that go back two millennia?

To mouth phrases about getting the negotiations going in such a context is to play King Canute, as if only State Department planners and Israeli policy-makers are capable of defining history and reality.

The air needs to be cleared, language shorn of its worn-out phrases, honesty and simple fairness given a chance. Yes, Palestinians want peace, but not at any price and not the way Netanyahu and company define it, with endless conditions concealing an iron rejection of the desire for Palestinian equality. People respond to a call for justice and the end of fear and oppression, not to the lumbering heaviness of something called a "peace process," in which Israel has all the advantages (plus a nuclear arsenal) and demands that Palestinians are there only to give it "security." I fear that at present the atmosphere is too inflamed by lies, too corrupted by illusions and self-fulfilling incapacities to allow us all to move forward. But a start needs to be made somewhere and somehow, blame apportioned accurately, and responsibility assigned proportionately. One cannot always expect a people without statehood, without rights, without hope, to act like well-dressed diplomats sitting in seminar rooms talking about scenarios and confidence-building measures as so many abstractions. What we need now—and certainly the United States can take the step—is a restatement of the basic premise that there is peace only when land is given back, and that, for the short time that it may be still possible, the goal is independence and statehood for two peoples in Palestine. Start from that, and it might be possible to move toward the goal in as many steps as are necessary. But one cannot expect peace and security while Palestinians continue to suffer and not one word is said about the causes of that suffering.

Al-Ahram Weekly, August 14, 1997
The Nation, September 8, 1997
The Gulf Today, August 19, 1997
International Herald Tribune, September 11, 1997
Al-Hayat, August 19, 1997
Al-Khaleej, August 19, 1997
Le Monde, September 5, 1997

Chapter Twenty-nine

Strategies of Hope

CERTAINLY THE LIST of negatives against Oslo is a long one, and as we reflect on it during this fourth anniversary of the signing ceremony in Washington, the horrendous balance sheet makes it almost impossible to understand why so many Arab and Western leaders keep referring to it with such enthusiasm. But in the wake of Benjamin Netanyahu's reign, his scorched earth policy has in fact delivered up a landscape of singular bleakness even when compared with Oslo's intended devastations. Yet enough has been said about economic, social, and political deprivations for Palestinians during the past four years (all of them attributable to the Oslo peace process) without sufficient attention paid to the human factor, surely the most important. For in the age of globalized capital and the triumph if not of the actual then of the theoretical market model, most analysts tend to reproduce one of the ideological correlatives of this triumph, which, I believe, is the conviction that there is no alternative to it. If you now think that only the IMF, the World Bank, market economics, which favor the wealthiest transnationals and countries, count in the world today, and that more equitable distribution and social justice are sentimentalized aspects of socialism's defeat, then you will also be condemned to think that there is no alternative but to compete in the market. Individual will and agency recede in importance, while the sheer power of market economics seems to dominate every individual everywhere. So it has been with Oslo, which has been a triumph for the powerful, in which Israel and the United States have convinced Palestinians and others that what has taken place since 1993 is not only the best, but the single remaining solution to our extremely grave problems. So the attitude today is "Let us get Oslo back on track, since anything else is unthinkable."

At such a juncture it becomes evident that Oslo's greatest expense for Palestinians has been the loss of faith in what I called above the human factor. We need to remind ourselves that political struggles are always contests of will, in which one side attempts to persuade the other side to give up, to lose the will to resist and fight on. This is not a military but a political and moral matter. I therefore think that the task for Palestinian intellectuals today is the reactivation of will and, just as important, the revival of belief in the possibility that what human beings do can make a difference. The tragedy of suicide missions is that they stem from hopelessness; they cannot be part of a program for national revival since what they promote is negation for its own sake. The problem with the present impasse is not that Madeline Albright and the United States are unwilling to pressure Israel enough, but that the leadership is caught up mainly in the effort to survive rather than in the effort to mobilize as many Palestinians as possible to resist what Israel, in its arrogant heedlessness, is trying to do to us as a people. This attempt at survival is understandable but insufficient as the core Palestinian strategy, since the good of the many, the good of the nation, is of far more significance than the well-being of a few. What then are the imperatives?

Some of them are obvious and scarcely need insistence here. *Sumud*, standing fast, is crucial, as is the building of civil institutions by and for Palestinians, quite independently of what the Palestinian Authority may or may not have in mind. For we have a tendency to think only in literal terms, not sufficiently in symbolic and moral ones. The greatest victory of Zionism has been a sustained one for a whole century: to persuade Jews and others that "a return" to an empty land is the proper, indeed the only solution for the afflictions of genocide and anti-Semitism. After spending many years living, studying, and being active in the struggle for Palestinian rights, I am more convinced than ever that we have totally neglected the effort—the human effort—required to demonstrate to the world the immorality of what was done to us: this, I think, is the essential task facing us as a people now. Unless we mobilize ourselves and our friends and, above all, our voices so that the Zionist project can systematically be shown for what it is and was, we can never expect any change in our status as an inferior and dominated people. Even as Arafat and his men try unsuccessfully to deal with Israel's actions, they seem to have forgotten that no voice (or voices) speaks for the suffering of the Palestinians, no effort is made to record systematically the wrong we suffer, no energy is expended on trying to organize our various expatriate communities so that they can undertake the task of dramatizing and finally defeating the legitimacy of the plan to take the whole of Palestine, every significant inch of our land, every aspect of our past as a people, every possibility of self-determination in the future. For at bottom our struggle with Zionism must be won first on the moral level, and then can be fought in negotiations from a position of moral strength, given that militarily and economically we will always be weaker than Israel and its supporters.

The importance of this was first borne out for me when I visited South Africa in May of 1991. Mandela had already been released, exiled leaders of the ANC had been repatriated, and the stage was set for the huge political transformation that was to ensue with democratic elections four years later and the victory of the "one person one vote" program of the ANC. When I was there I visited the ANC's headquarters in downtown Johannesberg; a scant few weeks earlier the organization had been considered as terrorist, and no legitimacy at all attached to it. I was stunned by the complete reversal. Speaking to Walter Sisulu, who had been exiled for almost thirty years and was second only to Mandela in authority and prestige, I asked him how the transformation had been possible. What exactly did the ANC do to turn defeat into victory? "You must remember," he said, "that during the eighties we were beaten in South Africa; the organization was wrecked by the police, our bases in neighboring countries were routinely attacked by the South African army, our leaders were in jail or in exile or killed. We then realized that our only hope was to concentrate on the international arena, and there to delegitimize apartheid. We organized in every major Western city; we initiated committees, we prodded the media, we held meetings and demonstrations, not once or twice, but thousands of times. We organized university campuses, and churches, and labor unions, and businesspeople, and professional groups." He paused for a moment and then said something that I shall never forget as long as I live: "Every victory that we registered in London, or Glasgow, or Iowa City, or Toulouse, or Berlin, or Stockholm gave the people at home a sense of hope, and renewed their determination not to give up the struggle. In time we morally isolated the South African regime and its policy of apartheid so that even though militarily we could not do much to hurt them, in the end they came to us, asking for negotiations. We never changed or retreated from our basic program, our central demand: one person, one vote."

Let me add one footnote. On the basis of my South African experience I organized a seminar in London for every leading Palestinian activist-intellectual that I knew, including a few who have since become ministers in Arafat's government. I invited the ANC ambassador in England, whom I had met in Mandela's office and who was on the same plane with me out of Johannesberg, to address one of our sessions, and he gladly accepted. The idea was to impress on everyone, a mere matter of weeks before Madrid, that we should all tirelessly focus on the same facts about what had happened to us as a people, and should not get deflected into discussions about policy and grand negotiating tactics with the Israelis and the United States and so lose sight of the political-moral goal of isolating the Israeli occupation and delegitimizing through a carefully organized movement in Europe, North America, the Arab world, and elsewhere. There was some resistance to listening to the ANC representative talk about his experiences. "We are not blacks," said a distinguished young Palestinian political scientist who thought we should be addressing Oxford or Harvard experts behind closed doors, not wasting our time on trying to create a grassroots movement of support for Palestinian human rights. I remember saying that we should always make it a point to be as concrete as possible—to talk about daily life under Israeli occupation, to talk about the humiliations of checkpoints, of how our houses were blown up, and how our trees were uprooted—and not to talk to audiences as if we were negotiating theoretical issues. But all in all I and my co-organizers of the seminar felt that we had made some progress. But the moment Madrid gave us an opportunity to appear in public, we all started to speak like James Baker, forgetting that our status had more weight as representatives of a moral cause than as members of a diplomatic delegation. And of course the goal changed, so much so that in the Oslo negotiations and in the period after them we forgot not just our values but our own history.

I am convinced that we have no recourse now but to return to the discourse of the oppressed and use what Netanyahu is now doing to us as an initiative to put his policies in direct connection with the history of Zionist policies toward the Palestinians. After all, he speaks in a straight line of descent from what every major Zionist theoretician has declared: that Jews have a superior right to Palestine despite the presence and existence of Palestinians. We must not only contest what is now being done to us, but also take our moral presence directly into the Israeli and Western, and even the Arab, consciousness. But this confrontation cannot be undertaken by individuals acting alone: it must be a job of organizing and then implementing such a plan by the worldwide community of Palestinians. Yasir Arafat and his coterie have never understood this. They have always supposed that if they could get the attention of the President or Secretary of State, or even of various prominent Jewish leaders in the United States, these influential people could be persuaded to do "something" for the Palestinians. I have always refused the premise that what we demand as a people ought to be conceded to us charitably, or in bits and pieces as a reward for our good behavior. This is to diminish ourselves and what we stand for, since our position as a dispossessed people is morally unassailable.

I am not at all saying that we should advocate the destruction of Israel, nor the dispossession of Israelis. Our movement gains its moral stature by its humane dimensions, its sincere willingness for coexistence, its firm belief in respecting the rights of others. What I am talking about is a new peace initiative designed over a long period of time to bring parity between us and the Israelis, who so far overpower us now as to make the moral dimension our only field of struggle. We must show Israel and its supporters that only a full acknowledgment by them of what was done to us can bring peace and reconciliation. To do this, therefore, we must have a policy of concrete detail, not one of broad, abstract statements that are not fully engaged in the struggle

for opinion. It would be good, for example, to remind readers of journalistic articles that various sites in Israel were once Arab sites from
which their original inhabitants were expelled. Thus, in a recent
profile of Anatol Scharansky, in *The New Yorker* magazine, David
Remnick mentions casually that the Soviet activist now resides in
Qatamon, "an old quarter in West Jerusalem," without adding that it
was an Arab quarter emptied of its inhabitants by force in the early
months of 1948. Similarly, when Madeline Albright cites her appreciation of "Palestinian suffering" we should be challenging her to do the
arithmetic in public: how many Palestinians need to suffer, and for
how long and in what way, for Israel's security anxieties to be allayed?
Or yet again, in a recent issue of the *New York Times Sunday Magazine* which contained a profile of Jibril Rajub by Jonathan Goldberg,
who admits to having served in the Israeli army, we should be publicly
challenging the appropriateness of an ex-Israeli soldier to write fairly
of a Palestinian activist. The examples can be multiplied infinitely, but
all of them rest on the assumption that there is a full-scale moral argument that as a people we carry what has never been fully heard or
taken into account. What we ask for is acknowledgment, not destruction; equality, not subordination. I think also that we must always be
very clear in our understanding of Jewish suffering and in making it
apparent that what binds us together is a common history of persecution, which must be shown not to be the exclusive possession of the
Jewish people.

Only by raising our voices in concert and registering moral victories can we then further encourage and empower our compatriots in
Palestine or in the various refugee camps in the Arab world. We should
be voices of courage and honesty, both of them credibly connected to
an ongoing effort to gain real self-determination for the Palestinian
people. I know that skeptics will say that words are not as effective as
deeds, and that only the experience of facing Israeli settlers on the
land is what counts. But that, I think, is sadly to miss the moral dimension that must be expounded on wherever there are people to listen
and unjust power to engage with directly. The greatest victories of
Zionism were not simply that they had better armies than we did, but
that they had organized opinion to accept and even support the idea
that settling Palestine with incoming Jews was a morally positive idea.

We must now undertake the same laborious task, first of delegitimizing Israel's military and colonial policy in Gaza and the West Bank, then of giving our quest for self-determination the authority it still lacks. We should be prepared to ask academics and professionals to boycott visits to Israel unless they make an effort to visit and support Palestinian universities and institutes; we should also be mounting a campaign to ensure that tourists to Israel who think of it only as an "interesting place" should begin to see it as a land whose two peoples must live together peacefully and equally. In other words, what we now have before us is a commitment that far exceeds anything that Oslo either foresaw or promised, and if we do not take up the challenge I fear that we will be the very compromised and much impoverished permanent losers.

Al-Khaleej, September 25, 1997
Al-Hayat, September 25, 1997
The Gulf Today, October 1, 1997

Chapter Thirty

Israel at a Loss

A NYONE ACQUAINTED WITH Israel's history since 1948 will be
aware that its leaders have always arrogated to themselves the
right to intervene unilaterally in the affairs of other countries. This
has been true not only for Israel's neighbors, but also for countries like
the United States and Italy, friends and even allies of the Jewish state.
The Pollard case of recent memory apparently did immeasurable
harm to American security, so much so that even the repeated appeals
to the United States by Israeli prime ministers (Rabin, Peres, and
Netanyahu most recently) have been turned down. Mordechai Vanunu
was kidnapped off the streets of Rome and brought to Israel, where
he has been serving a life sentence in prison ever since. The list of
invasions—in addition to assassinations, bomb outrages, kidnap-
pings, and the like—against Arab countries is far longer; these rankle
in the minds of most Arabs, for whom Israel's actions testify not only
to that country's supreme bellicosity and arrogance, but also to Arab
impotence and defenselessness. Against that background, then, suicide attacks on Israeli civilians stand forth as the desperate acts of the
weak, morally inexcusable but understandable humanly. Yet Israel's
most recent attempt against an Arab citizen in the capital city of the
most friendly and pacific of Arab countries, Jordan, is mystifyingly
obtuse and downright stupid. For not only was the assassination plan
extremely bizarre, but its method of implementation peculiar in the
extreme. Why try to kill someone by pouring poison into his ears (a

method last employed by Claudius against Hamlet's father), and why antagonize the government of Canada by supplying the terrorists with forged and stolen Canadian passports?

The overriding impression is one of clumsiness and contempt, as if Israel's leaders had decided to throw caution to the winds and indulge their most primitive fantasies, with no other end in mind except to assert their power and humiliate the Arabs. Netanyahu's excuse for the caper—that it was part of Israel's unrelenting war against terrorism— simply made matters worse, not only because it demonstrated every intention to go on in this fashion, but also because it suggested that the *goyim* had it coming to them: after centuries of anti-Semitism, it was now "our" turn to push people around. That was it, since there was no possible advantage to attempting so coarse a gambit on the streets of Amman: "we shall do what we please, and hang the consequences."

To speak about Netanyahu's bungles as a sign that Israel has lost its way is of course to suggest that it had a way once. Under the country's historic leaders—Ben-Gurion, Golda Meir, Menachem Begin, Yitzhak Rabin, and Shimon Peres—there was always evident a will to dominate, and Israel did this not only by overwhelming military power, accumulated and nourished over years and years, but also by a qualitative attention to its own Jewish citizens and society. This meant that education received high priority and that many of the institutions of civil society, such as the media, the courts, the universities, the labor movement, developed generally along Western European lines. There were always hidden and unacknowledged rifts within the society, between Ashkenazi and Sephardic Jews, for instance, and between Jewish and non-Jewish (i.e., Palestinian) citizens, but Israel could claim to the world that its people in the main fared better there than they had in the pre-1948 diaspora (except for American Jews, who prospered in the United States as nowhere else). Israel's eternally postponed problem, however, was always its actual place and status in a part of the Middle East that was predominantly Arab and Islamic. Ben Gurion, we now know, felt in the beginning that it was better for Israel to reject Arab peace overtures after 1948 and well into the early sixties; he thought that the state of siege was materially beneficial to the country while at the same time allowing Israel to insulate itself against Levantinization, Arabization, and the like. So state policy could follow from the idea that Israel was a sort of cultural and political fortress developing its own interests and strengths *against* its Islamic and Arab surroundings. As a result Israeli identity had specific content as something assertive and collective at the same time, something that could be shaped and formed over time as a separate Jewish identity freed from its burdensome past and its immediate context in the eastern Mediterranean.

I have never agreed with Israel's politics, but at least until the late 1970s I could at least understand the logic that drove them. It is not difficult to put oneself in the place of a people whose centuries of persecution and weakness required restitution, they felt, by means of a new political identity that was the opposite of what Jews had been in the past. Yet so great was the power that Israel was able to accumulate since the 1967 war, and so remarkable were its successes for diaspora Jews, that it soon outstripped the Arabs economically, culturally, and socially. What had been a beleagured and uncertain national state became a nuclear power and, more significantly, an occupying power, ruling over several million Arabs which it persisted in treating as inferior and alien. The stunning thing is that as one reflects on the past two decades Israel's policies emerge as fundamentally unwise, foolish in fact, as if all considerations of prudence and normal human caution had been dismissed by the country's leaders and its electorate as so much unnecessary nonsense. There is no question that Israelis want acceptance and the normalization between themselves and their neighbors that all human beings depend on for their security. But as the colonization of the West Bank and Gaza increased, as the grandiose international adventures multiplied (for example, during the invasion of Lebanon, and the continuing occupation of the South), as political gains were squandered, it was as if the country lost its bearings and drifted without sense of proportion or of self-preservation. I used to imagine myself addressing Rabin or Begin with the question. "Where do you expect all this violence against Arabs, all this willful humiliation, all this reckless expenditure of your power, to lead? Do you think that in the end we will say, yes, you are wonderful and we accept you? Do you expect all of us to forget the past?"

The import of such a question is totally missing in Israeli politics today, with the exception of a small group of individuals whose consciences and sense of reality are activated by the havoc all round them. It was extremely significant that for the first time ever as a result of a Palestinian terror-suicide raid, an Israeli voice was raised in accusation not of the perpetrators but of the Israeli government. General Matti Peled's daughter, whose own daughter was killed in the market bomb attack, wasted no effort on railing against Palestinians, but vented her wrath on the willful policies of her government which, she said, actually create terrorism. I knew her late father very well, and recall that in 1983 in Geneva, at a UN conference on the question of Palestine I asked him what caused him to accept the difficult fate of a lone Israeli voice speaking out against his former military colleagues and his own government for their inhumanity to the Palestinians. "Remorse," he said simply and definitively. That his legacy should be passed on so demonstrably to his daughter in her hour of terrible grief testifies to the power of a sentiment which, while largely absent in the society at large, is still there and can be fanned and encouraged. Except for the Peleds, Israel Shahak, Leah Tsemel, and a few others like them, Israel seems now to be flailing around destructively without much policy or intelligence. The country has lost its sense of purpose, and can only react instinctively against a "terrorism" it categorically refuses to investigate as having anything to do with its behavior toward Palestinians particularly and Arabs in general. There is a failure of reason and an incapacity to understand that acceptance and normalization cannot be imposed by obdurate military force.

There is a deeper problem. There seems to be a battle inside Israel and the diaspora today between Orthodox authorities and the more liberal Reform and Conservative segments of the Jewish people. Many secular and liberal Jews bewail the emergence of Orthodoxy as the consequence only of local Israeli politics, but they miss, I think, the inescapable outcome of establishing a state whose main purpose is to establish and enshrine Jewishness alone as its raison d'être. The crisis in Israel today is a crisis of what Jewish identity is, if it is not the extremist, inordinately backward and primitive brand of Orthodoxy that has come to the fore. These people say that they embody Judaism, or at least the Judaism that Israel was designed to perpetuate. Their opponents have very little to offer by way of serious response, since they cannot claim that as a Jewish state Israel in the end can do more than make sure that non-Jews are simply kept down or kept away. Liberal Zionism as represented by the Labor Party of Rabin and Peres failed the test when it came to Oslo; in the end, they too wanted Jewishness to prevail at all costs, never mind the changes required for a real peace with the Palestinians. Oslo failed not only because it was unjust to the Palestinians but also because Israeli leaders were unable to take a real step forward out of their historical policies of humiliating the Arabs into submission. Rabin and Peres (as well as their American patrons) were simply blind to the real meaning and the real possibilities of peace. They should have seen that what was being offered was the possibility of a new way, one that put Israelis and Arabs on an equal footing in charting the future; instead of conceiving of a common destiny, Rabin and Peres took the easy way of consolidating their territorial and military gains by other means (i.e., so-called autonomy) and basically proceeded as they always had in the past, by force and with the contempt for the Arabs that characterized much of their previous history.

Palestinians and Israelis together stand today at the edge of a precipice. Neither people is blessed with a leadership of vision or moral courage. But the Israelis face a more severe and difficult challenge. They must define Jewish identity in such a way as to permit them to live intelligently and productively in the future by coexisting as equals in an Arab and Muslim Middle East. But unfortunately there is little in the official Israeli past to draw on for such a task. And, alas, the Palestinian and Arab leadership is too powerless and morally bankrupt to offer anything significant for the Israelis to work with. It is left to a small number of intellectuals and visionaries to articulate a new theory of coexistence which, in the current impasse, might offer a way out of the quandary. I shall discuss this in my next article, but in the meantime, Netanyahu bungles on, rash, heedless, destructive, and essentially unregenerate.

Al-Hayat, October 21, 1997
Al-Khaleej, October 23, 1997
Al-Ahram Weekly, October 23, 1997
The Gulf Today, October 23, 1997
Dagens Nyheter, December 10, 1997

Chapter Thirty-one

Bases for Coexistence

ONE OF THE most important differences between Arabs in the Arab world and those who live in the West is that on a daily basis the latter are forced to confront the Jewish experience of anti-Semitism and genocide. Year after year new books, films, articles, and photographs pour out in ever-increasing volume. Last year was the year of *Schindler's List*, the Steven Spielberg film that put the horrors of the Holocaust before literally hundreds of millions of people. There have been numerous controversies about the reasons for the German catastrophe, how an eminently civilized nation that had produced Europe's greatest philosophers and musicians, and among its most brilliant scientists, poets, and scholars, could have descended into not just the madness of Nazism but one of the most awful programs of human extermination in history. Anyone who now lives in the United States, France, or elsewhere in Europe cannot ever escape the pictures of Auschwitz and Dachau, the constant reminders of Jewish suffering and torment, the ceaseless evidence of mass inhumanity directed against principally one people, the Jews, who despite their achievements and contributions to culture were reduced to the status of mere animals, to be gassed and cremated by the millions.

It is certainly true that a great deal of this history is not only circulated everywhere in universities, schools, museums, and public discourse in the West but is also the stuff of controversy, provided most recently by Daniel Goldhagen's book *Hitler's Willing Executioners.*

Goldhagen's thesis was that every German, not just the Nazi party nor
only the psychopaths among Hitler's entourage, was prepared to and
indeed did support the genocide against the Jews. Most historians
have disagreed with this extreme view, but the question of European
and more particularly Christian mass guilt continues to exercise
the Western world. Among Jewish Americans whose community was
spared the horror of what happened in Europe, the Holocaust is fer-
vently studied and memorialized; it is noteworthy, for instance, that
Washington is the site of an extremely lavish Holocaust Museum and
not the place where the extermination of native Americans or the slavery of millions of Africans is commemorated. To some extent, therefore, the Holocaust is used retrospectively to justify contemporary
political actualities. Routinely a connection is made by critics between
the history of Jewish suffering and the triumph of the American Jewish community, or between the Holocaust and Israel, one leading to
and vindicating the other. And certainly there has been enough history uncovered to show that the mainstream Zionist movement was at
times less interested in saving the whole Jewish people from elimina-
tion than in rescuing some for settlement in Palestine; by the same
token right-wing Zionists (e.g., Shamir) during the Nazi period did
contact the Germans for support and help.

All in all, though, the sheer enormity of what took place between
1933 and 1945 beggars our powers of description and understanding.
The more one studies this period and its excesses, the more one must
conclude that for any decent human being the slaughter of so many
millions of innocents must, and indeed should, weigh heavily on subsequent generations, Jewish and non-Jewish. However much we may
concur, say, with Tom Segev in his book *The Seventh Million,* that
Israel exploited the Holocaust for political purposes, there can be little doubt that the tragedy's collective memory and the burden of fear
it places on all Jews today is not to be minimized. Yes, there were other
collective massacres in human history (native Americans, Armenians,
Bosnians, Kurds, etc.) And yes, some were neither sufficiently acknowledged by the perpetrators nor adequately compensated. But there is
no reason at all, in my opinion, not to submit oneself in horror and
awe to the special tragedy besetting the Jewish people. As an Arab in
particular I find it important to comprehend this collective experience

in as much of its terrible concrete detail as one is capable: this act of comprehension guarantees one's humanity and resolve that such a catastrophe should never be forgotten and never recur.

Such a view of Jewish suffering was afforded Arab commentators during the trial of Adolf Eichmann in Israel early in the 1960s, when the trial was used by Israel to lay out the full horrors of Nazi genocide. Right-wing Lebanese Phalanges commentators claimed that the whole business was baseless propaganda, but elsewhere in the Arab press of the time (in Egypt and in the mainstream Lebanese press) the Eichmann affair was reported with due consideration given to the appalling events in wartime Germany. Yet according to a study of the period by Dr. Usama Makdisi, a young Lebanese historian at Rice University in Houston, Texas, Arab reports of the trial concluded that though what was done to the Jews in Germany was indeed a crime against humanity, Israel's crime of dispossessing and expelling an entire people constituted no less a crime of the same kind. Dr. Makdisi discovered that there was no attempt to equate the Holocaust with the Palestinian catastrophe; only that, judged by the same standards, Israel and Germany were both guilty of heinous crimes of enormous magnitude. My own feeling is that perhaps the Eichmann trial was useful to the Arab side during the psychological battles of the 1960s as a way of exposing Israeli callousness to the Arabs and not especially as an attempt to acquaint Arab readers with details of the Jewish experience.

Yet except for a few Jewish intellectuals here and there—for example, the American Jewish theologian Marc Ellis, or Professor Israel Shahak—reflections by Jewish thinkers today on the desolate history of anti-Semitism and the uniqueness of Jewish suffering have been inadequate. For there is a link to be made between what happened to Jews in World War II and the catastrophe of the Palestinian people, but it cannot be made only rhetorically, or as an argument to demolish or diminish the true content both of the Holocaust and of 1948. Neither is equal to the other; similarly, neither one nor the other excuses present violence; and finally, neither one nor the other must be minimized. There is suffering and injustice enough for everyone. But unless the connection is made by which the Jewish tragedy is seen to have led directly to the Palestinian catastrophe by, let us call it "necessity" (rather than pure will), we cannot coexist as two communities of detached and uncommunicatingly separate suffering. It has been the failing of Oslo that it planned in terms of separation, a clinical partition of peoples into separate, but unequal, entities, rather than grasping that the only way of rising beyond the endless back-and-forth violence and dehumanization is to admit the universality and integrity of the other's experience and to begin to plan a common life together.

I cannot see any way at all (a) of not imagining the Jews of Israel as in decisive measure *really* the permanent result of the Holocaust, and (b) of not also requiring from them acknowledgment of what they did to the Palestinians during and after 1948. This means that as Palestinians we demand consideration and reparations from them without in any way minimizing their own history of suffering and genocide. This is the only mutual recognition worth having, and the fact that present governments and leaders are incapable of such gestures testifies to the poverty of spirit and imagination that afflicts us all. This is where Jews and Palestinians outside of historical Palestine can play a constructive role that is impossible for those inside, who live under the daily pressure of occupation and dialectical confrontation. The dialogue has to be on the level I have been discussing here, and not on debased questions of political strategy and tactics. When one considers the broad lines of Jewish philosophy from Buber to Levinas and perceives in it an almost total absence of reflection on the ethical dimensions of the Palestinian issue, one realizes how far one has to go. What is desired therefore is a notion of coexistence that is true to the *differences* between Jew and Palestinian, but true also to the common history of different struggle and unequal survival that links them.

There can be no higher ethical and moral imperative than discussions and dialogues about that. We must accept the Jewish experience in all that it entails of horror and fear; but we must require that our experience be given no less attention, or on perhaps another plane of historical actuality. Who would want morally to equate mass extermination with mass dispossession? It would be foolish even to try. But they *are* connected—a different thing altogether—in the struggle over Palestine which has been so intransigent, its elements so irreconcilable. I know that at a time when Palestinian land is still being taken, when our houses are demolished, when our daily existence is still subject to the humiliations and captivity imposed on us by Israel and its many supporters in Europe and especially the United States, I know that to speak of prior Jewish agonies will seem like a kind of impertinence. I do not accept the notion that by taking our land Zionism redeemed the history of the Jews, and I cannot ever be made to acquiesce in the need to dispossess the whole Palestinian people. But I can admit the notion that the distortions of the Holocaust created distortions in its victims, which are replicated today in the victims of Zionism itself, that is, the Palestinians. Understanding what happened to the Jews in Europe under the Nazis means understanding what is universal about a human experience under calamitous conditions. It means compassion, human sympathy, and utter recoil from the notion of killing people for ethnic, religious, or nationalist reasons.

I attach no conditions to such comprehension and compassion: one feels them for their own sake, not for political advantage. Yet such an advance in consciousness by Arabs ought to be met by an equal willingness for compassion and comprehension on the part of Israelis and Israel's supporters, who have engaged in all sorts of denial and expressions of defensive non-responsibility when it comes to Israel's central role in our historical dispossession as a people. This is disgraceful. And it is unacceptable simply to say (as do many Zionist liberals) that we should forget the past and go on to two separate states. This is as insulting to Jewish memories of the Holocaust as it is to Palestinians who continue in their dispossession at Israel's hands. The simple fact is that Jewish and Palestinian experiences are historically, indeed organically, connected: to break them asunder is to falsify what is authentic about each. We must think our histories together, however difficult that may be, in order for there to be a common future. And that future must include Arabs and Jews together, free of any exclusionary, denial-based schemes for shutting out one side by the other, either theoretically or politically. That is the real challenge. The rest is much easier.

Al-Hayat, November 5, 1997
Al-Ahram Weekly, November 6, 1997
Jeune Afrique, December 16, 1997
Dagens Nyheter, December 11, 1997

Chapter Thirty-two

Iraq and the Middle East Crisis

THE PRESENT CRISIS concerning Iraq contains all the elements of the much larger situation—one of almost desperate complexity and fragmentation—now beginning to overtake the region, perhaps irrecoverably. It would be a mistake, I think, to reduce what is happening between Iraq and the United States simply to an assertion of Arab will and sovereignty versus American imperialism, which undoubtedly plays a central role in all this. However misguided, Saddam Hussein's cleverness is not that he is splitting America from its allies (which he has not really succeeded in doing, for any practical purpose) but that he is exploiting the astonishing clumsiness and failures of U.S. foreign policy. Very few people, least of all Saddam himself, can be fooled into believing him to be the innocent victim of American bullying; most of what is happening to his unfortunate people who are undergoing the most dreadful and unacknowledged suffering is due in considerable degree to his callous cynicism—first of all, his indefensible and ruinous invasion of Kuwait, his persecution of the Shias and Kurds, his cruel egoism and pompous self-regard in his persistent aggrandizement of himself and his regime at exorbitant and totally unwarranted cost. It is impossible for him to plead the case for national security and sovereignty now, given his abysmal disregard of it in the case of Kuwait and Iran. Be that as it may, U.S. vindictiveness, whose sources I shall look at in a moment, has exacerbated the situation by imposing a regime of sanctions which, as Sandy Berger, the

American National Security adviser has just said proudly, is unprecedented for its severity in the whole of world history.

Since the Gulf War, 567,000 Iraqi civilians have died mostly as a result of disease, malnutrition, and deplorably poor medical care. Agriculture and industry are at a total standstill. This is unconscionable, of course, and for this the brazen inhumanity of American policymakers is also very largely to blame. But we must not forget that Saddam is feeding that inhumanity quite deliberately in order to dramatize the opposition between the United States and the rest of the Arab world. Having provoked a crisis with the United States (or the UN dominated by the United States), he at first dramatized the unfairness of the sanctions, but with his continuing defiance the issue has changed and has become his non-compliance, and the terrible effects of the sanctions have been marginalized. Still the underlying causes of an Arab-U.S. crisis remain.

A careful analysis of that crisis is imperative. The United States has always opposed any sign of Arab nationalism or independence, partly for its own imperial reasons and partly because its unconditional support for Israel requires it to do so. Since the 1973 war, and despite the brief oil embargo, it had been Arab policy up to and including the peace process to try to circumvent or mitigate that hostility by appealing to the United States for help, by "good" behavior, by willingness to make peace with Israel. Yet mere compliance with the U.S.'s wishes can produce nothing except occasional words of American approbation for leaders who appear "moderate": Arab policy was never backed up with coordination, or collective pressure, or fully agreed upon goals. Instead each leader tried to make separate arrangements both with the United States and with Israel, none of which produced very much except escalating demands and a constant refusal by the United States to exert any meaningful pressure on Israel. The more extreme Israeli policy becomes, the more likely the United States has been to support it, and the less respect it has for the large mass of Arab peoples whose future and well-being are mortgaged to illusory hopes embodied, for instance, in the Oslo accords.

Moreover, a deep gulf separates Arab-Islamic culture and civilization from the United States; in the absence of any collective Arab information and cultural policy, the notion of an Arab people with traditions, cultures, and identities of their own is simply inadmissible in the United States. Arabs are dehumanized; they are seen as violent irrational terrorists always on the lookout for murder and bombing outrages. The only Arabs worth doing business with for the United States are compliant leaders, businessmen, military people whose arms purchases (the highest per capita in the world) are helping the American economy keep afloat. Beyond that there is little feeling at all, for instance, for the dreadful suffering of the Iraqi people, whose identity and existence have simply been lost sight of in the present situation. Consider also the general indifference to Bosnian Muslim deaths.

This morbid, obssessional fear and hatred of the Arabs and Islam has been a constant theme in U.S. foreign policy since World War II. In some way also, anything positive about the Arabs or Islam is seen in the United States as a threat to Israel. In this respect, pro-Israeli American Jews, traditional Orientalists, and military hawks have played a devastating role. Moral opprobium is heaped on Arab states as it is on no others. Turkey, for example, has been conducting a campaign against the Kurds for several years, yet *nothing* is heard about this in the United States, which effectively supports the Turkish military. Israel occupies territory illegally for thirty years, it violates the Geneva conventions at will, conducts invasions, terrorist attacks, and assassinations against Arabs, and still, the United States vetoes every sanction against it in the UN. Syria, Sudan, Libya, Iraq are classified as "rogue" states. Sanctions against them are far harsher than against any other countries in the history of U.S. foreign policy. And still the United States expects that its own foreign policy agenda ought to prevail (e.g., the woefully misguided Doha economic summit) despite its hostility to the collective Arab agenda.

In the case of Iraq, a number of further extenuations make the United States even more repressive. Burning in the collective American unconscious is a puritanical zeal decreeing the sternest possible attitude toward anyone deemed to be an unregenerate sinner. This clearly guided American policy toward the native American Indians, who were first demonized, then portrayed as wasteful savages, then exterminated, their tiny remnant confined to reservations and concentration camps. This almost religious anger fuels a judgmental attitude that has no place at all in international politics, but for the United States it is a central tenet of its worldwide behavior. Second, punishment is conceived in apocalyptic terms. During the Vietnam war a leading general advocated—and almost achieved—the goal of bombing the enemy into the stone age. The same view prevailed during the Gulf War in 1991. Sinners are meant to be condemned terminally, with the utmost cruelty, regardless of the agonies they suffer. The notion of "justified" punishment for Iraq is now uppermost in the minds of most American consumers of news, and with that goes an almost orgiastic delight in the gathering power being summoned to confront Iraq in the Gulf. Pictures of four (or is it now five?) immense aircraft carriers steaming virtuously away punctuate breathless news bulletins about Saddam's defiance and the impending crisis. The President announces that he is thinking not about the Gulf but about the twenty-first century: how can we tolerate Iraq's threat to use biological warfare (even though—and this is unmentioned—it is clear from the UNSCOM reports that he neither has the missile capacity, nor the chemical arms, nor the nuclear arsenal, nor in fact the anthrax bombs that he is alleged to be brandishing)? Forgotten in all this is that the United States has all the terror weapons known to humankind, is the only country to have used a nuclear bomb on civilians, and as recently as seven years ago dropped 80,000 tons of bombs on Iraq. As the only country involved in this crisis that has never had to fight a war against a foreign enemy on its own soil, it is easy for the United States and its mostly brainwashed citizens to speak in apocalyptic terms. A report out of Australia on Sunday, November 16, suggests that Israel and the United States are thinking about using a neutron bomb on Baghdad.

Unfortunately, the dictates of raw power are very severe and, for a weak state like Iraq, overwhelming. Certainly, U.S. misuse of the sanctions to strip Iraq of everything, including any possibility for security, is monstrously sadistic. The so-called UN 661 Committee created to oversee the sanctions is composed of fifteen member states (including the United States), each of which has a veto. Every time Iraq passes this committee via a request to sell oil for medicines, trucks, meat, etc., any member of the committee can block these requests by saying that a given item may have military purposes (tires, for example, or ambulances). In addition, the United States and its clients—e.g., the racist Richard Butler, who says openly that Arabs have a different notion of truth from the rest of the world—have made it clear that even if Iraq is completely reduced militarily to the point where it is no longer a threat to its neighbors (which is now the case), the real goal of the sanctions is to topple Saddam Hussein's government. In other words, according to the Americans, very little that Iraq can do short of Saddam's resignation or death will produce a lifting of sanctions. Finally, we should not for a moment forget that quite apart from its foreign policy interest, Iraq has now become a domestic American issue whose repercussions on issues unrelated to oil or the Gulf are very important. Bill Clinton's personal crises—the campaign-funding scandals, an impending trial for sexual harassment, his various legislative and domestic failures—require him to look strong, determined, and "presidential" somewhere else. And where but in the Gulf against Iraq has he so ready-made a foreign devil to set off his blue-eyed strength to full advantage? Moreover, the increase in military expenditure for new investments in electronic "smart" weaponry, more sophisticated aircraft, mobile forces for the worldwide projection of American power, are perfectly suited for display and use in the Gulf, where the likelihood of visible casualties (actually suffering Iraqi civilians) is extremely small, and where the new military technology can be put through its paces most attractively. For reasons that need restating here, the media are particularly happy to go along with the government in bringing home to domestic customers the wonderful excitement of American self-righteousness, the proud flag-waving, the "feel-good" sense that "we" are facing down a monstrous dictator. Far from analysis and calm reflection, the media exist mainly to derive their mission from the government, not to produce a corrective or any dissent. The media, in short, are an extension of the war against Iraq.

The saddest aspect of the whole thing is that Iraqi civilians seem condemned to additional suffering and protracted agony just as Bosnians and Chechnyans were. Neither the Iraqi government nor that of the United States is inclined to ease the daily pressure on them, and the probability that only they will pay for the crisis is extremely high. At least—and it isn't very much—there seems to be no enthusiasm among Arab governments for American military action; but beyond that there is no coordinated Arab position, not even on the extremely grave humanitarian question. It is unfortunate that, according to the news, there is rising popular support for Saddam in the Arab world, as if the old lessons of defiance without real power have still not been learned. Undoubtedly the United States has manipulated the UN to its own ends, a rather shameful exercise given that at the same time the Congress once again struck down a motion to pay a billion dollars in arrears to the world organization. The major priority for Arabs, Europeans, Muslims, and Americans is to push to the fore the issue of sanctions and the terrible suffering imposed on innocent Iraqi civilians. Taking the case to the International Court in the Hague strikes me as a perfectly viable possibility, but what is needed is a concerted will on behalf of Arabs who have suffered the United States's egregious blows for too long without an adequate response.

Al-Hayat, November 25, 1997
Al-Ahram Weekly, November 20, 1997
Al-Khaleej, November 25, 1997
Against the Current, May/June 1998
The Gulf Today, November 29, 1997
The Yemen Observer, March 16, 1998

Chapter Thirty-three

Isaiah Berlin: An Afterthought

NOVEMBER IS A mournful month in the history of Palestine. November 2 is the day of Arthur Balfour's 1917 Declaration, which opened the way to the establishment of Israel as a Jewish state. Framing November at the other end is the day in 1947 that the United Nations, under immense U.S. pressure, pushed through the partition resolution on Palestine, thereby conceding about 55 percent of the country to less than 30 percent of the population, which at that time had only gained ownership of about 7 percent of the land. The keynote of both these decisions was struck in a memorandum written by Balfour in August 1919 in which he said: "In Palestine we do not propose even to go through the form of consulting the wishes of the present inhabitants of the country. . . . The four great powers are committed to Zionism and Zionism, be it right or wrong, good or bad, is rooted in age-long tradition, in present needs, in future hopes, of far profounder import than the desire and prejudices of the 700,000 Arabs who now inhabit that ancient land. In my opinion that is right." British policy was therefore intent on transforming Palestine demographically during the Mandate, again despite the wishes of the indigenous inhabitants of Palestine. And for the period after 1947, Palestinians were intentionally swept aside by a movement and a rhetoric that neither had any use for them nor in effect saw them as more than a temporary threat to the colonization of Palestine.

In the fifty years since Israel came into existence as a Jewish state it not only consolidated its hold over the land (especially after 1967), but also painstakingly constructed a whole structure of opinion and discourse in the West that completed the obliteration of the Palestinians as a people that had any rights, or continuity of residence, or conceiveable national claims on the territory of historical Palestine. It is a striking fact that that task was undertaken by pro-Zionist Jews as well as non-Jews who stood at the very authoritative center of Western society, where their prestige as intellectuals, scientists, musicians, authors, artists, politicians, businessmen, and journalists gave weight and credibility to their support for the Zionist project. No comparable body of opinion or opinion-makers existed on the Arab side, with the result that for years the Palestinians were both invisible and silent insofar as their "desire and prejudices" (to use Balfour's disparaging phrase) were represented in the West. The only member of the British cabinet during Balfour's time who was opposed to Zionism was Lord Curzon, but he absented himself the day of the vote on Balfour's Declaration. But if one thinks of Churchill, Weizmann, Einstein, Freud, Reinhold Niebuhr, Eleanor Roosevelt, Truman, Chagall, the great conductors Otto Klemperer and Arturo Toscanini, plus dozens and dozens of others like them in Britain, the United States, France, and elsewhere in Europe, and then tries to produce a list of Palestinian supporters at the time who might have balanced this tremendous array of influence and prestige, one finds next to nothing.

Among the most famous of Israel's supporters in Britain in the period after 1948 was Sir Isaiah Berlin, a remarkable man who was born and grew up in Riga and St. Petersburg, but came to Britain in his late teens. He attended St. Paul's School in London, then went to Oxford and more or less remained there until his death at the age of eighty-eight on November 5, 1997. A philosopher by training, he was much more than that, a brilliant general intellectual renowned for his amazing powers of conversation (Churchill considered an evening with Berlin as the highest pleasure), his fabulous memory, his learning and gift for the most compelling of lectures, his charm, his connections with every famous and influential person in the Anglo-Saxon as well as Israeli-Jewish world, and above all his capacity for attracting to him talented students, professors, statesmen, journalists, intellectuals, philosophers, philanthropists, who revered and loved him. He was the only academic or intellectual who was always referred to by his first name: everyone knew who "Isaiah" was, and everyone considered him to be an ornament of Western culture.

Unlike great figures such as Toynbee, Bertrand Russell, Jean-Paul Sartre—like Berlin in that they had a universal reputation and were respected by specialists as well as by the general public—Berlin was not a prolific writer at all, and the author mainly of essays and three or four short books (including a rather thin and, in my opinion, inadequate study of Karl Marx). He was a consolidator of thought rather than an initiator of it. But he had a vast range, which with his excellent Russian, French, German, Italian he put to illuminating use in the history of modern thought, liberalism, opera, personal impressions, and especially his studies of the ninetenth-century Russian intelligentsia, two of whom, Turgenev and Herzen, were the subjects of his finest essays. His most famous book, which I recall reading when I was about twenty, is *The Hedgehog and the Fox,* a study of Tolstoy based on the distinction made by the Greek lyric poet Archilochus between the two animals. The hedgehog, the Greek poet said, had one big idea which he found everywhere; the fox was interested in many little ideas only. Berlin's thesis was that Tolstoy wanted to be a hedgehog, was possessed of a very large general vision of human history and destiny, but in effect, because he was a supremely endowed novelist, he was really a fox, ultimately committed to empirical detail, concrete experience, and observable behavior, the very contrary of what interested the hedgehog. In that book Berlin expressed his lifelong suspicion of and animosity toward systems of thought (like Marxism, for example) that promised a solution for everything. In his most famous essay, "Two Concepts of Liberalism," he elaborated a theory of realistic political freedom, negative (the right not to be persecuted) and positive (the right to positive liberties) which became the hallmark of the Western self-image during the Cold War years and the battle against Stalinism and the Soviet bloc. Berlin stood for balance, reasonableness, intellectual freedom, pragmatism, civilized behavior. He was the enemy of fanaticism, whether extremism took the form of unfettered rationalism or of dogmatic passion and system-building. For that reason, then, he found common ground with exiled Russian intellectuals whose skepticism made life impossible for them in their revolutionary homeland; it was also the reason for his interest in Vico, the eighteenth-century Italian philosopher, and Herder, the eighteenth-century German philosopher, whom he called enemies of the Enlightenment, which in both his and their opinion had overestimated the possibility of human perfectibility through science and reason.

Over the years I read his work with great interest, and never lost the opportunity to hear him lecture. He was a small man who stood in front of usually very large audiences with a sheaf of papers (which he never consulted) in one hand, and used the other to gesture as his prose poured out with lightning, often incomprehensible, speed: he was certainly one of the most remarkable speakers I have heard for his lucidity, the enormous amount of material he packed into his lectures, and the perfect shape of his English sentences, which were always pronounced with a slight trace of his native Russian. I met him a few times, and he was unfailingly cordial; the last time I saw him was a year ago in a London restaurant, where he called out to me and insisted on chatting briefly with me about Vico, a great comon interest of ours.

His death early in November brought forth a Niagara of obituaries, all of them affectionate, admiring, sorrowful, and yet celebratory since it was clear to all who knew him, including myself, that he found life itself a pleasure, a sentiment he was always able to communicate to his friends, audiences, interlocutors. The one discordant note for me about Berlin was that in public he was a fervent, unquestioning, and unskeptical Zionist, a true believer, whose close involvement with Israel as country and as cause contributed in a major way to the positive image and structure of feelings created in the West about the Jewish state. He was a close personal friend of Chaim Weizmann, whom he describes in an admiring portrait he wrote some years ago as one of the greatest men that he ever knew. Weizmann, Berlin said in that essay, "committed none of these enormities for which men of action, and later their biographers, claim justification on the ground of what is called raison d'état." There is a stunning blindness to this statement, which verges on the idolatrous: Weizmann presided over the colonization of Palestine, he knew about the eviction of the Palestinians, and of course he must have felt all along that had those things been done to Jews, he would have been the first to call them injustices.

In 1944 he told President Roosevelt that "we could not rest our case on the consent of the Arabs; as long as their consent was asked, they naturally refuse it." Berlin does not mention a word about this. In fact, having read practically everything he wrote, I found to my disappointment that to the best of my knowledge he never said a word about the Palestinians as a people. For him they seemed to have been the inevitable clutter that, once swept away in a higher cause, need never be mentioned or thought of again.

Berlin's last pronouncement, produced in London's *Guardian* on November 13 was surprisingly a declaration about Israel and the prospects for Middle East peace. Here too, there is no mention of the Palestinians at all; they are referred to as one of "two sides," as is partition which, Berlin timidly says, might produce a relationship of good neighbors. But he withdraws even from that because, he says, "there are bigoted terrorist chauvinists on both sides," as if it were the case that Palestinians held most of the territory but were prevented from compromise by Muslim terrorists. He says nothing about military occupation, nothing about settlements, nothing about invasions, killings, dispossessions. Instead, he concludes, we must have "reluctant toleration" as a way of preventing war. As for Jerusalem, Berlin concludes that "it must remain the capital of Israel with the Muslim holy places being extraterritorial to a Muslim authority," as if, for instance, Jordan or Saudi Arabia or maybe even Pakistan and Bangladesh could be members of that Muslim authority. Not a word about Palestinian national rights, or Christian rights, or anything of that sort. Palestinians, for the worldly Berlin, do not constitute a people, nor have they been victims of an injustice. They are either "the other side" or members of a group to be ruled over and represented by a "Muslim authority." As for the notion that there is something about Zionism that is exclusivist or discriminatory for the "non-Jews" who fall in its path, Berlin is silent.

It was not only that Berlin supported Israel and never raised a question about the morality of what it did in dispossessing and oppressing an entire people, it is also that he tried to prevent others from doing so, using his enormous prestige and influence to stifle dissent and silence opposition. Noam Chomsky told me two stories that are worth repeating here. In the late 1960s while giving a series of political lectures at Oxford, Chomsky devoted one to the Middle East situation and was extremely critical of Israel. The next morning Berlin visited him and said that even though he might have agreed with some of what Chomsky said, he had come to tell the celebrated intellectual dissident that Jews should not speak about Israel that way in public. Chomsky was of course unpersuaded, although the two men remained friends. The second incident took place in the mid-1980s, when Chomsky wrote a solicited article for *Index on Censorship* about the way Israel's actions either are not reported properly or are covered up in the Western media. From behind the scenes Berlin organized a campaign to try to stop the magazine from printing Chomsky's article; he got influential friends of his to write letters of protest, and in many ways attempted to harm the magazine (which did publish Chomsky after all) and even tried to get it closed.

The contradiction in all this is plain: that Berlin was a liberal, a man of fairness and compassion, of civilized moderation in everything except where Israel was concerned. There he acted with the kind of unblinking zeal that fanatics of either the Right or the Left might have felt, but which in all his work on other subjects Berlin deplored. In that sense Berlin was an organic intellectual for Israel, a man so closely allied with the interests of that state—especially when those interests overrode fairness and humanity—that his readers and admirers were led by his example to celebrate Israel and overlook the injustice of its actions. One cannot say that Berlin fabricated untruths on behalf of Israel. But he did lend himself to the same blindness that ordinary Zionists had for the Palestinians, whose only crime was that they happened to be in Palestine which, as Balfour said, was a piece of immensely significant geography that had too great an importance for the mere desire and prejudices of its native inhabitants.

There is an even greater misfortune for us as Palestinians in the fact that none of us—and I do not excuse myself at all—were able to engage with Berlin on the question of Palestine. I regret that I never brought the matter up in our conversations, and I regret that I can only do so in this manner, after his life and work have been accomplished. Berlin's legacy, however, lives on, and the best we can do now is to make sure that his disciples, friends, and colleagues in the Zionist movement will add a new and more realistic dimension to their thought about the future of Middle East peace.

Al-Hayat, December 9, 1997
Al-Khaleej, December 9, 1997
Al-Ahram Weekly, December 11, 1997

Chapter Thirty-four

Palestine and Israel:
A Fifty-Year Perspective

A s I W R I T E these lines from Calcutta, I am at the end of my first
visit to India, one of the countries for which I have always felt
a great affinity and have very much wanted to know. As a boy in
British colonial schools both in Palestine and Egypt, I studied India,
read Edmund Burke and Lord Macaulay on it, Kipling's novels and
stories, and understood its presence for the English as the jewel in the
crown, the cornerstone of the imperial edifice. The Arab world was, I
learned, important to the empire because in part it constituted the
route to India, crucial to be safeguarded and defended no matter
the cost. The British spent four hundred years here: they derived
enormous wealth and thousands of men for their armies from India,
they instituted a system of organizations and networks (educational,
bureaucratic, legal, military, religious) which they controlled through
hierarchies and often cruel measures stemming from their great power,
and in the end they left, having decided that Indian independence was
too strong a force to resist. At the height of its glory Great Britain
ruled 350 million Indians with less than a hundred thousand men.

Despite its overwhelming size, immense diversity of languages and
traditions, beauty and inspiring monuments, India is less strange a
country for me than, say, Sweden or Italy. Islam has played a very
important role in the subcontinent, never more impressive for the visitor than in the extraordinary dignity and grace of its remarkable
architecture. The Taj Mahal, for example, is both totally unusual and

at the same time familiar, its ethereal walls and soaring, clean symmetries echo the mosques in Andalusia, Egypt, and Syria. India, after all, is part of the same Orient conceived of by Flaubert, Burton, and Disraeli, and to some extent we Arabs are Orientals of the same kind, colonized and considered inferior, now struggling toward real autonomy and independence, loved and admired by some for our "classical" past, looked down on by others for our backwardness and technological insufficiencies, exploited alike by transnational corporations and greedy local elites. But in India the Arab can feel at home in a way that is impossible for us in Europe. There is of course the strong Islamic presence (between them India, Pakistan, and Bangladesh have a larger Muslim population than the entire Arab world), but there is also the warmth, sense of tradition, and generally unstressed sense of life that characterize so much of the non-Western world. We also share the same problems of poverty, ignorance, and disease, although India, unlike the Arab world, has an important middle class, a vibrant academic and intellectual community, a super-sophisticated electronic industrial sector, and a functioning democracy.

Perhaps the most striking parallel, though, is that both of us suffered the ravages of imperial partition. The year 1997 is the fiftieth year of Indian independence; it is also the fiftieth year of the country's partition into a Muslim Pakistan and a mainly Hindu India, whose 950 million people include 125 million Muslims, several million Sikhs, and numerous other smaller minorities (among them Christians in South India). It is also the year that produced a United Nations partition resolution for Palestine, with results in conflict between the Zionist movement and the entire Arab world that are too well-known for summary here. Ethnic and religious partition, however, has not produced the kind of stability or tranquility the Hindus and Muslims had hoped for, any more than it has delivered security and coherence between Arabs and Israelis, or even among the Arabs themselves. Independence has brought forth sectarianism, bloody civil war (as in Palestine, Lebanon, and Algeria), and the kind of instability that was supposed to have ended when the last colonial soldier left. In the Arab world the xenophobia and religious and ethnic intolerance represented by Israel has spilled out all over, some of it obviously deriving from Zionism itself, but a good deal also instilled by homegrown religious fanaticism, which alas has not been offset by the emergence of a true democratic society. And even in India, a virulent Hindu fundamentalism, as embodied in the BJP, a party dedicated to establishing India as a Hindu country—something that Gandhi and Nehru always resisted very strenuously—now appears to be the strongest single party after the recent dissolution of Parliament. Because of corruption and the usual bureaucratic abuses (much as the FLN's power in Algeria was dissipated), the old power of the Indian National Congress has dissolved so that today the country's oldest party, which won independence from Britain, is in what seems to be a permanent slump after many years of the Jawaharlal Nehru–Indira Gandhi dynasty. The government crisis lingers on as the elections draw near. A sense of foreboding has enveloped the country politically.

India thus provides a confirming perspective on, and a vast parallel for, the half century since Israel was established by conquest, the Palestinians were dispossessed, and the Arab world was militarized, bloodied by years of war, endlessly postponed democratic rights, religious extremism developing into a force to be reckoned with. There is no question in my mind that we are worse off than either India or Pakistan, which is more like the Arab countries in that the army, unlike India's, has played a major political role. As I said a few pages back, Israel's "solution" to the age-old Jewish problem has resulted in a sectarian debate within the country over the question of "who is a Jew?" as the country totters from crisis to crisis under Benjamin Netanyahu. The first generation of Arab, Indian, and, yes, Israeli leaders after independence were similar in that all of them—Abdel Nasser, Nehru, Ben-Gurion—however much we disagree with them today, were charismatic leaders, imbued with a comparatively secular, nationalist position which, less so in the Israeli case, was inclusive, moral, and informed by a powerful sense of justice. We now live within much narrower, even paranoid horizons, where local and sectarian, but essentially religious (or at least traditionalist) nationalisms rule the day, not by generosity of spirit or genuine leadership but by playing on the anxiety, insecurity, and defensiveness of peoples who feel that they have lost their way as they approach the new millennium. Take away from Israel the feeling that its citizens are an embattled minority facing a fearful "Islamic-Arab" enemy, and the question of what Israeli identity actually *is* revolves around a Talmudic debate presided over by backward-looking rabbis and dangerous zealots who consider Arabs as aliens in "their," that is, God's, country, the so-called land of Israel. And this kind of sentiment, whose root is an us-versus-them polarity, is replicated all too frequently throughout the Arab world, with democracy and civil society to all intents and purposes abrogated for the foreseeable future.

Since its new military pact with Turkey, Israel has been flexing its nuclear options in threats against Iran, and with mounting U.S. pressure against Iraq provides an outline of things to come in a new age of nuclear terror. There is now no immediate prospect of real Palestinian self-determination: thirty years of resistance against Israel have bled and finally coopted the Palestinian national movement, its leaders aged and ill, its people disorganized and despondent, its immediate future a combination of rule by security chiefs and second-rate figureheads. Militarily, the Arab states are still no real match for Israel and its allies. Syria may not be more than a second thought for Israeli hard-liners, and is certainly no deterrent, any more than any of the other regional powers are.

The Arab people have therefore lost the first half century of the struggle against Israeli expansion and domination without posting any significant gains on the other side of the ledger. We are more populous, but poorer; more threatened by illiteracy and widespread poverty; less free; less accomplished in science, culture, agriculture, and industry. Water, oil, and other natural resources are scarcer: we are soon likely to be bypassed by the Caspian Sea region in oil production; we have not sufficiently coordinated regionally on sharing water; and as for pollution, it is unregulated, running wild in big cities like Cairo, Beirut, Damascus, and elsewhere.

Israel was the result of many factors, of course, principally of the imperialist desire to divide and rule, allied with a Zionist program also determined to end anti-Semitic oppression. The various partitions that brought about the numerous independent states of the Middle East left behind, if they did not altogether destroy, the notion of Arab unity that was a guiding idea in the area for the first half of the twentieth century, and which is now a scarcely remembered, much maligned and insulted "dream" no one dares to defend in public. From the beginning of its existence—one recalls here the Lavon affair of 1954–5—Israel has been intent on helping to keep the Arabs divided not only from themselves but from the rest of the world. We are now so obsessed with Israel and the West that we have forgotten Africa, the Indian subcontinent, China, Japan, as well as the rest of Asia; these are rich cultures and histories well worth our being in close touch with (as the Arabs once were), but now ignored for reasons of racial prejudice, increasing appetite for Western consumerism, and uncritical dependence on the United States.

There is little real recourse for us as a people unless once again we re-establish our place in the world, as a culture, a civilization, and as a moral and political cause. The essence of that shift must be prompted by a vision not of inter-Arab competition and indifference, but of some sort of communal and regional cooperation, without which we shall sink further and further. If the past fifty years of Israel's life should teach us anything, it is that you cannot in the end resist an enemy if your society is crumbling from within. We have sacrificed years of our national life to buying arms we cannot properly use, millions of our people in wars they never thought seriously about winning, billions of dollars in projects that served commission agents and unscrupulous businessmen more than they did anyone else. *Needed: a concept of Arab citizenship,* an idea involving rights, obligations, responsibilities. Above all, it calls for service, and the entitlement of each citizen not to be tortured, imprisoned, killed unjustly, to speak and investigate freely, to elect representatives fairly, to live a life assured of basic necessity. Central to all this is, I think, a proper system of taxation. As the economist George Corm once said, the Arab world today is a tax-free zone for the wealthy, which in effect means that profit and plunder can go on without regard for the society in which one lives, while parliaments and assemblies exist to rubber-stamp the rulers' policies, most of them unpopular.

The real challenge of Israel, which has so far outstripped us in military, economic, and political power, is not just that it occupies our lands and in part decides our future unilaterally, but that it forces us back more and more upon our incompetence, absence of democracy, lack of will. I do not know how the turnaround will occur, or even if it can. But our present course is simply not the right one and, alas, none of us can escape responsibility. We need a collective goal and an unprecedented intellectual effort to face the next ten years: otherwise, as Ibrahim Abu-Lughod put in in 1991, the Arab states will end up as did nineteenth-century Africa, partitioned, incoherent, poverty-stricken.

Al-Hayat, January 6, 1998
Al-Khaleej, January 6, 1998
Panorama, January 9, 1998

Chapter Thirty-five

The Challenge of Israel: Fifty Years On

T HE SCARS ARE still unhealed, the wounds fester, the past will not be forgotten. And yet there is no overriding consensus in the Arab world as to what Israel represents, and how we should deal with it. Even using the collective pronoun "we" suggests a unity of views that is more presumed than actual. At some higher level of politics and ideology Israel is an objective ally of some Arab policies and politicians, not all of them right-wing Christian Lebanese. Jordan, for example, has signed a peace treaty with it, as have Egypt and the PLO: still, very few Arab writers, intellectuals, academicians, artists, and even policy-makers will say that they are ready for normalization with Israel, so long as it remains in occupation of Palestinian, Syrian, and Lebanese territory. An enormous grey area exists in our collective consciousness. Israel is there, but how are we to think about and above all act toward it? Everyone wants and speaks about peace, yet how, for Palestinians whose entire territory was captured and society destroyed, is one to declare a statute of limitations and say, what is past is past, let us reconcile ourselves to a future with Israel? When it comes to the present, how are we to say that we will coexist with a state that still has not declared its boundaries and still describes itself not as the state of its citizens but as the state of the whole Jewish people, entitled to the entire "land of Israel"? As for the future, where is the glimmer of a new Israel which is neither imperialist and exclusivist, but somehow at one with the Islamic Arab world in whose midst it has been planted as idea and as reality since 1897?

Israeli policy has always consisted of two parts. On the one hand, strenuously absolve yourself of any responsibility for the existence of a Palestinian "problem," and on the other, try to make compromises on the basis of that self-absolution with whatever Arab or Palestinian leadership exists at the moment, and continue to settle the land. The premise of both parts of this policy is the same, that given enough time and pressure Palestinians will forget, give up, or variously accommodate themselves to the permanent loss of what was once theirs. In the main, this policy has not really been successful, despite the existence of a peace process and two treaties with Arab states.

But the fantasy of somehow removing Israel and its people is equally unthinkable. Yes, they can be made to withdraw from the occupied territories, but it is a dream to expect that "they" will disappear or go back to Poland, Russia, America. There is now an Israeli nationalism and a society independent of what we think and independent also of the diaspora. Behind it, as I said in an earlier article, are memories of the Holocaust and centuries of Western anti-Semitism from which it would be folly for us to expect Israelis to disconnect themselves. But there is also a history of anti-Palestinian behavior which demands recognition as injustice and cruelty of the first order. Just as Jews require recognition from the world, we too must continue to make the same demands, not on the grounds of vengeance, but because justice requires it. Thus the misery of Oslo is that our leaders simply brushed off our history along with Messers. Rabin and Peres, whereas it behooves us to remember what Zionism did, and—no less important—what Britain, the United States, and other pro-Zionist Western governments who conspired in our dispossession have done.

The first challenge of Israel then is the need to exact acknowledgment from it for what it did to us and to other Arabs whose sons and daughters were killed in its wars, conquests, military occupations, settlements. This is a moral mission for each of us to pursue by not forgetting, by reminding each other and the world, by testifying to the continued injustice against us. I simply cannot imagine that history will ever excuse us for failing in this task. But then, I believe, we must also hold out the possibility of some form of coexistence in which a new and better life, free of ethnocentrism and religious intolerance, would be potentially available. It is the present poverty of Zionism and Palestinian nationalism that accounts for the void in vision and moral energy that we suffer from today. I am certain that if we present our claims about the past as enabling a form of mutuality and coexistence in the future (although the response will initially be negative and dismissive), a long-term positive response on the Israeli and Western side will develop.

It is also evident to me that we cannot detach our views of Israel from our attitudes and policies toward the United States. Since 1949 America has poured about $140 billion into Israel. Not only is this a major financial investment, but the American political establishment has a long-term investment in the country as well. To expect the United States to lessen support of Israel, or even to become critical of it—these are real possibilities in my view—is unthinkable without a massive campaign in the United States on behalf of Palestinian political and human rights. This is so obvious as not to require much insistence here. The only question to ask is why has this not been done before. Every one of us who knows the West knows full well that Israel's successes on the ground have been prepared for and supported by assiduous propaganda about Arab intransigence, the Arab wish to drive Jews into the sea, the Israeli desire for peace and tranquility, and, central to all this, that Israel as a Jewish state was created by the national liberation Jewish movement (Zionism), which found the place a desert and made it a garden. Zionism, along with all the other successful mass movements in the twentieth century (including fascism), learned the lesson of propaganda: that the battle for opinion is the most important one to win. This is something that we still have not completely grasped, and until we do we shall always be the losers.

In short, Israel is the measure of our failings and our incompetence. We have waited for a great leader for years, but none came; we have waited for a mighty military victory, but we were defeated roundly; we have waited for outside powers (the United States or, in its time, the Soviet Union), but none came to our aid. The one thing we have not tried in all seriousness has been to rely on ourselves: until we do that with a full commitment to success there is no chance that we can advance toward self-determination and freedom from aggression.

Take as a simple case in point the current Palestinian case, where the failures seem the most glaring and the remedies more easily at hand than anyone has suspected. We have been saddled with poor leadership ever since I can remember, and still we persist in supporting the same bankrupt group through all its mistakes and disasters. On the other hand, we pride ourselves on the many successes of our people—doctors, lawyers, engineers, entrepreneurs, businessmen, intellectuals, academics, artists. We claim that we want statehood and independence, yet none of the most basic institutions of statehood are in anyone's mind. There is no basic law where the Palestinian Authority rules today, the result of one man's whim not to approve such a law, in flagrant defiance of the Legislative Council. Our universities are in an appalling state, starved for money, desperately run and administered, filled with professors who struggle to make a living but have not done a stroke of research or independent work in years. We also have a large and impressive group of extremely wealthy businesspersons who have simply not grasped that the essential thing for any people is a massive investment in education, the construction of a national library, and the endowment of the entire university structure as a guarantee that as a people we will have a future. I have attended meetings for almost twenty years in which hundreds of little projects are funded, but without a central vision of what it is that as a society we need. The absence of a collective end to which all are committed has crippled Palestinian efforts not just in the official realm, but even among private associations, where personality conflicts, outright fights, and disgraceful backbiting hamper our every step.

Looked at from this perspective, the fundamental challenge that Israel poses is to ourselves—our inability to organize, our inability to dedicate ourselves to a basic set of principles from which we do not deviate, our inability to marshal our resources singlemindedly, our inability to devote all our efforts to education and competence, finally, our inability to choose a leadership that is capable of the task. It is no use blaming the failures of the current PLO on a few inadequate and corrupt individuals. The fact is that we now have the leadership we deserve, and until we realize that we are being driven further and further from our goal of self-determination and the recovery of our rights by that leadership which so many of us still serve and respect, we will continue to slide downward. Antonio Gramsci put it very succinctly: pessimism of the intelligence, optimism of the will. Yes, our situation vis-à-vis Israel is calamitous and under Netanyahu the situation will get worse. But we need to ask what it is that we can do, and then by an act of collective will we must do it. The rest is simply a waste of time. The choice of better leaders is an imperative, but we must also improve our own conditions so that our workers do not have to build Israeli settlements just to put food on their tables, and our students do not have to settle for incredibly backward curricula in an age when our opponents are sending people to the moon, and our people do not have to accept lamentable conditions of tyranny and oppression where dissent is punished and torture is used by our Authority to cow the citizenry, all in the name of national unity. Until we awake from the sleep of reason, we will continue to lose more land and power to Israel. But we cannot fight for our rights and our history as well as for the future until we are armed with weapons of criticism and dedicated consciousness. In this we need the support of the Arab intellectual and cultural community, which has devoted too much time to slogans about Zionism and imperialism and not enough to helping us fight the battle against our own failures and incompetence. The struggle of the twenty-first century is the struggle to achieve self-liberation and self-decolonization. And then Israel can be properly addressed.

Al-Hayat, January 12, 1998
Al-Khaleej, January 12, 1998
Panorama, January 16, 1998
Al-Ahram Weekly, January 15, 1998
The Progressive, March 1998

Chapter Thirty-six

The Problem Is Inhumanity

TWO CORNERS OF the Arab world have been very much on my mind these past weeks, Algeria and Lebanon. The former was once synonymous with anticolonial resistance and uncompromising toughness; the latter with openness, diversity, and the joy of life. Yet both places have gone through horrendous transformations. The Lebanese civil war lasted for almost twenty years, virtually destroyed the society, produced uncounted thousands of dead innocents mostly killed or massacred because of their religion, and then finally gave birth to a so-called new Lebanon in which many of the old problems have been swept under a carpet of corruption, frenzied environmentally destructive building, and deepening economic crisis. The poor are poorer, the rich richer, and all the old politicians and their supporters remain in place on almost entirely confessional grounds.

Algeria has fared just as badly, but in a different, perhaps more agonizing way. An aging political oligarchy held over from the days of anti-French struggle ruled the country for three decades after 1962, in the process bleeding it dry, extinguishing democracy, giving the army the main role in authority and political life. Then in 1992, after the Islamic Salvation Front in effect won the elections, the results of those elections were nullified by the army, and the Islamists—whose politics I have no love for—were declared outlaws, their leaders jailed, their organizations disbanded. Since that time Algeria has endured wave after wave of massacres, first the killing of intellectuals and artists, then of journalists, most recently of literally hundreds of innocent women and children killed in the most brutal and senseless way. The government's position is that all the killings are being done by renegade members of FIS or the GIA, whereas independent observers such as Amnesty International have accused government troops of taking part in the killing, or of not doing anything to stop it, even though in several instances villagers have been slaughtered right next to army posts. To make matters worse, the government has made it almost impossible for foreign journalists to visit Algeria and has turned down several offers of mediation from the Arab League, the European Union, and the United Nations.

Are these two cases unique in the Arab world? Only in degree, not in kind. Those of us who have fought for Palestinian self-determination over the years have been bitterly disappointed in the behavior of Yasir Arafat's Palestinian Authority toward its own citizens. All the human rights groups have commented on the lawlessness, corruption, and sheer brutality of PA security men, many of whom paradoxically were victims of Israel's occupation policies. I recall a young man from Gaza, who now worked for one of the security forces in Ramallah, responding to my shocked query about his activities as a spy on, and interrogator of, his fellow students at Bir Zeit university. He said that "they [meaning the Israelis] tortured me; now it's my turn." Every Arab country practices what we all denounce in Israel, namely, physical coercion in prisons, and all around Israel the signs of Arab inhumanity to Arabs are plainly evident. Take as a very simple, even trivial case, people arriving at the airport. Almost without exception they are treated harshly and in a hostile manner by their border police, as if it was assumed that they were criminals and not citizens returning to their homes. Wherever one looks, the signs of an absence of humanity in the powerful toward the weaker and the disadvantaged stands out starkly. Torture, massacres, repression, undemocratic practices: this is what we Arabs have become known for.

It is no use simply blaming Israel or imperialism for this situation, even though they can be blamed in some measure. No one denies that Zionism bears an enormous responsibility for the unhappy fate of the Palestinian people since 1948, but Arabs—collectively and individually—also bear responsibility. This was dramatically apparent

in a surprisingly frank and humane program broadcast on January 20
by ABC television. Apparently the reporter, Steve Lawrence, was sent
to Lebanon to report on the country's reconstruction but ended up
reporting on the three hundred fifty thousand (or perhaps more)
Palestinian refugees now marooned there without residence permits,
unable to work (there are ninety-five different kinds of jobs which
Palestinians are forbidden by law to undertake), unable to travel, poor,
destitute, uncared for, and generally in a pitiable, not to say dreadful
state. Lawrence focuses on one refugee family in Shatila camp. They
are completely without hope, without health, without money. The
father tells how when his week-old baby son was gravely ill he took the
child to a hospital for treatment. That hospital referred him to a
charity institution, Hotel Dieu, which had a contract with UNRWA to
treat Palestinians. There the poor man was told that he needed to pay
$3,000 before the sick baby could be treated. When Lawrence visited
the hospital to find out exactly what happened he was first told that
the baby was indeed treated free of charge; later, though, a hospital
administrator admitted on camera that "it was possible" that the baby
had been turned away because he was Palestinian. Desperate, the man
took the dying child to Sidon, fifty miles away, but there too he was
asked to pay $1,000. Because he started to cry, the hospital person
took pity and told him to leave the baby for treatment but to come
back with money the next day. Since he had no choice, the father did
what he was told; when he returned the next day his child had died but
a hospital official refused to give the body back unless he was paid
$220. As the disconsolate man and his wife say to Lawrence, death is
better than the sort of life we have to lead here.

The story gets worse. The reporter pays a visit to the prime minister who before the cameras says that Lebanon is not responsible for
the Palestinians, only Israel is. I quote verbatim from the transcript:

LAWRENCE: *Is it fair for the head of the Lebanese government to say
it's not our problem?*
PRIME MINISTER: *You know, it depends how you put it. It depends
how you put it. We cannot integrate them in the society. We cannot
give them the Lebanese nationality. We cannot consider them as*

Lebanese because they are not and, if we did so, we feel that we are
implementing the plan of Israel.
LAWRENCE: *So the refugees are stuck. Even Yasir Arafat appears to*
have forgotten them. Financial aid from the PLO has been cut. Con-
tributions from wealthy Arab nations, once generous, are next to
nothing now.

It is particularly painful to witness such a scene on American television, which is not known for its compassion for Palestinian refugees.
Certainly the brief episodes I have described do not begin to approach
the exhaustive account of Palestinian life in Lebanon, *Too Many Ene-*
mies, written by Rosemary Sayigh. But the story she tells is pretty
much the same as Lawrence's, a story for which the usual excuses and
explanations will not do. By the terms of Arab political logic what the
Lebanese prime minister says is unremarkable, perhaps even acceptable. But by the terms of normal human logic it is profoundly cruel,
which is the same attitude to be found in every Arab country with a
population of Palestinian refugees who, with the exception of Jordan,
are largely treated as nonpersons, barely tolerated, officially stigma-
tized as Palestinian aliens. The pity and tragedy of it is that even Palestinian leaders seem not to care about the destitute people they claim to
be representing in talks with the World Bank or President Clinton.

Or consider Iraq. Understandably, Saddam Hussein does not want
to submit to United States bullying. But he did invade and attempt to
obliterate Kuwait, he deliberately provoked a costly and ultimately
useless war, and by going on as he has, he has caused enormous suffering for his people, the most innocent of whom (children, the sick, and
the aged) have paid and continue to pay the price of his folly. Is the
safeguarding of Iraq's totally ineffective military assets worth such
inhumanity, such callous disregard of human life, even as more presidential palaces are built and "protected"?

There is a coarse inhumanity to public life in the Arab world that
is deeply shocking. We have not paid sufficient attention to the liberal
and humanistic education of our young people nor, alas, to the real
priorities for our national institutions. The inhumanity of colonialism
is replicated, indeed reproduced, in our societies two generations after

the end of colonialism. The distortions of Zionism have not been rectified by our various national movements, who have glorified raw
power, a blind subservience to authority, and a truly frightening
hatred of others into practices that are taking us back inexorably into
the middle ages. In the name of what? Certainly not freedom, since we
have far less of it now than we did fifty years ago. In the name of sovereignty and national unity? Certainly not: Arabs are more divided than
ever. Development and democracy? Of course not. I am afraid to say
it, but the conclusion is inescapable: in the name of inhumanity. That
is our problem, our inability collectively and individually to treat ourselves as human beings deserve to be treated, as citizens whose lives
are intrinsically important and valuable. How is the so-called peace
process going to help us achieve this basic level of decency and
humanity? Obviously it cannot, since the problem begins at home.
The sooner we acknowledge that, the better for us.

Al-Ahram Weekly, January 29, 1998
The Gulf Today, February 4, 1998
Al-Hayat, January 29, 1998
Al-Khaleej, January 29, 1998

Chapter Thirty-seven

Gulliver in the Middle East

G ULLIVER'S TRAVELS, published by the great Anglo-Irish
writer Jonathan Swift in 1727, is a classic political satire. It is
the story of an Englishman, Lemuel Gulliver, who decides to leave
England, is shipwrecked, and in the first of the four voyages he
recounts, lands on an obscure island, Lilliput, whose inhabitants are
tiny people measuring about six inches in height. The second voyage
takes Gulliver to Brobdingnag, a country whose residents are enormous giants. So whereas in Lilliput Gulliver describes his adventures
as a giant among dwarfs, in Brobdingnag he is a dwarf among giants.
Both episodes illustrate the related problems of being too big in one
setting or context, and being too small in the other. Despite his
immense size in Lilliput, Gulliver is victimized by the Lilliputians, who
draw him into their petty intrigues, and finally decide either to kill or
banish him; in Brobdingnag he is permamently disadvantaged, a tiny
human surrounded by immense creatures who are in danger of crush-
ing him by their sheer size. When he is finally allowed by the king of
Brobdingnag to say something in defense of himself and the "normal"
human world from which he comes, he launches into a long speech
about life in England, with all its peculiarities of class and privilege,
its court intrigues, its sordid politics and unprincipled national life, its
wars, conspiracies, and general violence. Far from feeling admiration
for the pitiful little being who has declaimed the speech, the king concludes instead that Gulliver belongs to "the most pernicious race of

little odious vermin that nature ever suffered to crawl upon the surface of the earth."

So disillusioned and harsh is Swift's view of political life, so uncompromising and unforgiving is its perspective, that it seems to me to be the only one capable of dealing with the recent Iraq-U.S.A. crisis in all its drama, farce, and incongrousness. Despite its immense military, economic, and political power, the United States in the Middle East has had all the success of Gulliver in Lilliput, ultimately trapped in local politics by its own illusions as to its strength and its moral authority. Size and authority are simply not the same thing. Having for years behaved like an international gangster, flouting international law, supporting its clients in the most bloodthirsty exploits, resorting to subversion and insurgency in order to destabilize its enemies, the United States under George Bush suddenly discovered the importance of United Nations resolutions. No other power has resorted to the United Nations with such cynicism and contradictory policies as the United States, which is delinquent in its back payments to the world organization amounting to about $1.3 billion. No other member state has used the veto to defend internationally condemned behavior (in this case, Israel's) as the United States, which also, like no other state, has openly vented its contempt for the world organization. Then it finds that its position vis-à-vis Iraq is best (and opportunely) expressed in a handful of resolutions passed seven years ago, and proceeds to their literal implementation, something that has never happened before in the UN's history. In the meantime a regime of sanctions has decimated the Iraqi infrastructure, and in effect murdered 1.5 million innocent Iraqi civilians. As recently as a few hours ago Madeline Albright, who lies more shamelessly than any of her predecessors in office and, along with Secretary of Defense Bill Cohen, acquitted herself disgracefully before a properly unimpressed audience of ordinary American citizens in Columbus, Ohio, proudly proclaimed her "humanity and concern," while at the same time boasting that the sanctions against Iraq were the most complete and punitive ever imposed in history. Not to be outdone, President Bill Clinton—squirming under a whole series of investigations as to his sexual and financial misadventures—has the remarkable gall to address the Arab people as if they were a collection of morons. The United States, he says, has no quarrel with the people of Iraq; the quarrel is with Saddam Hussein, who of course suffers very little under the sanctions regime while the people of Iraq continue to suffer and die. And this was offered as a justification for a possible military strike.

Nor is this all. For weeks the media have been feeding the public a diet of stories about hidden weapons of mass destruction in Iraq, which may have them for all I know, but which are neither a threat to anyone nor, in fact, have been proved by anyone to exist. The United States, reserving for itself the right to stand above all the norms of international behavior, is determined to strike if diplomacy does not work. So a massive armada of American warships, aircraft, land forces—supplemented by a tiny force of British supplies, rushed to the Gulf in an unseemly gesture of slavish solidarity with the United States—has been gathering at a cost of at least $50 million a day, billed directly to the U.S. taxpayer. Never mind that no clear war aim has emerged in the weeks of swaggering and threatening, nor any assurances that even Saddam's military forces, such as they are, would in fact fight against or be damaged by the strike. No assurances at all, any more than there was a possibility of mustering enough soldiers to attempt Iraq's dismemberment and occupation with the goal of toppling Saddam's dreadful regime. The net result of all this has been to reduce the American colossus to Saddam's stature, to make it plain that rather than a moral authority, the United States in its lawlessness and unilateral arrogance was on Saddam's level, a regional bully unable to do much more than strut and pose, like the inordinately large Gulliver pinioned by the tiny Lilliputians.

It is equally important to recall that the United States, still strapped inside its crippling Cold War mentality, has gone from one failure to another in its general Middle East policy. Benjamin Netanyahu has wreaked havoc on the remaining tatters of the peace process, which, it is important to remember, is sponsored by the United States. Having just returned from ten days in Palestine, I can testify to the fact that after fifty years of official state existence, the Zionist juggernaut is still in the process of taking Palestinian land, destroying houses, displacing people on a daily basis, nearly all of it started with new vigor after September 1993. The United States has also lost the support of even those Arab and Islamic states who are its supposed allies, so

appallingly insensitive and hypocritical has its behavior been in cod-
dling Israel and at the same time demanding compliance from the
Arabs. The November Doha summit was a fiasco, as was the more
recent attempt to mobilize Egypt, Saudi Arabia, and Jordan into anti-
Iraq military action. Above all, it is the brazen duplicity of American
rhetoric, as embodied in Mrs. Albright, who loses no opportunity to
act like a macho thug, that reveals the threadbare principles (such as
they are) of U.S. Middle East policy. How official spokesmen still can
speak with a straight face of averting violence and condemning terrorism when the United States has a long record of bloody illegal action
all over the Third World achieved by no other power simply defies
credulity. The United States after all is the country that killed 3 million
Vietnamese, that was behind the massacre of roughly 10 percent of
the Guatemalan population during the 1950s, that collaborated with
the Suharto regime both in the invasion of East Timor and the killing
of half a million Indonesians Suharto suspected of being communist,
that connives daily in the Turkish attacks on the Kurds, that illegally
engaged in the mining of Nicaraguan harbors (for which it was condemned by the World Court) and funded subversives against the Sandinistas throughout the 1980s, that invaded Panama and Granada,
that funded Afghanistani fundamentalists, that subsidizes Israeli conquest and pillage virtually without restraint. That it has done and
continues to do all this and, at the same time, arrogates for itself the
right to speak of international law to the Arabs, is nothing short of
stupefying, the modern equivalent of a Gulliver bellowing furiously at
the very same tiny Lilliputians whose tactics and presence confuse and
finally disable the lumbering giant.

Despite its size and power, then, the United States has been forced
to accept the realities of a world it does not and can never completely
control. Looking as shamefaced and embarrassed as the local bully
who has been shown up by a firm but understated schoolteacher, Bill
Clinton has in effect accepted Kofi Annan's compromise. The details
are as yet to be worked out, but all the diplomacy has deterred the
great war machine (perhaps only for a short time). But I would guess
that the great days of the United States in the Middle East are now
definitively over. It is still true that its hegemony remains potent, but
that it can continue to pretend that it can be all things to all parties;

that pose has been shown for the miserable ruse that it has always been. Like Gulliver before the King of Brobdingnag, its officials boast of its prowess in arms and intrigue, but stand revealed for the hollow sham its policy has now become, manipulated by the Zionist lobby, cajoled by a battery of journalists who still believe in the United States's imperial mission (Tom Friedman, Jim Hoagland, A. M. Rosenthal, Fouad Ajami, etc.) but try to convince themselves that they are right when in fact they have always been proved wrong.

One would wish, however, that our own part of the world had the mettle to benefit from this Gulliverian situation. Saddam, in my opinion, is too discredited and bloodied a leader to be anything more than a nuisance to his neighbors and a horror to his long-suffering people. It seems to me irrelevant whether or not in this latest confrontation he "won" or "lost": his country destroyed and set back in its development for decades, if not generations, Saddam should do the decent thing and simply quit, although he is too stubborn and cowardly to do anything like that. I fear that many Arabs now hero-worship him, despite his immense profligacy and total incompetence. Like many of his aging counterparts in the Arab world, he will limp along indefinitely until another upstart will unseat him, and start a new process either of recovery or of further slippage. Without democracy or a shared vision, the Arab leaders find themselves reduced to hushed consultations, ritual meetings, financial deals that put off even longer the massive investments needed in education, health, and democratic practices. Faced with similarly depressing actualities, Swift made Gulliver finally confront himself as an unregenerate savage, a Yahoo, as Swift calls him, lectured to not by a wise human being, but by a whinneying horse. In these dark times, it is not hard to go the whole way and condemn ourselves as a people for our congenital inability to get anything right. But, having seen the fortitude of Palestinian peasants and ordinary working people trying to fight more dispossession by Israeli settlers and army, I remain convinced that there is a battle and a cause to be served. Despite us.

Al-Ahram Weekly, February 26, 1998
Al-Hayat, March 3, 1998
Al-Khaleej, March 3, 1998
Dagens Nyheter, April 2, 1998

Chapter Thirty-eight

Making History: Constructing Reality

S EPARATED FROM EACH OTHER by well over three hundred
years and the Mediterranean Sea, Ibn Khaldun, who died in 1406
at the age of seventy-four, and Giambattista Vico, the Neapolitan
philosopher who died in 1744, nevertheless held astonishingly similar
views of history, both of which still have great relevance today. Vico's
book *The New Science,* published a year after his death, remained
relatively unknown until the late eighteenth century, and was then discovered by the French historian Jules Michelet, who translated it
into French. Since that time numerous major figures in European
thought—Hegel, Marx, Nietzsche, Croce, Freud, James Joyce, Beck-
ett, and many others—were in some way indebted to Vico's profound
insight that human beings make their own history, a history that
can therefore be understood scientifically and according to laws of
context, development, and understanding. Thus it would be wrong,
Vico said, to judge the primitive world of Homer by the more
advanced rational world of Aristotle. Humankind begins in barbarism,
moves to sociability as provided by families, and then achieves social
solidarity, what Ibn Khaldun who identified the same stages called
'asabiya. The essential point for both men is that the world of human
beings is neither the world of nature, nor the sacred world which is
made by God, but the world of history, a secular world that can be
understood rationally as the result of transformations, stabilities, and
upheavals that are governed by observable laws and human actions.

Historical understanding is the comprehension of what human doings do and what they cannot do. In a famous passage Ibn Khaldun makes fun of Mas'udi, who had an entirely fanciful idea of how Alexander first descended into the Mediterranean to frighten sea monsters so that he could then build Alexandria. In other words, historical truth has to be plausible, it must be able to place events in the proper context, it must be free of exaggeration, it must not be partisan, it must focus on what human beings did, and so on. Although this brief summary makes these two great thinkers appear simple enough to accept, the fact is that we are still struggling to grasp the consequences of their profound insights, especially in the Arab world, but elsewhere too. Notions of conspiracy, divine intervention, heroic individuals impede our capacity for understanding that history is made by human effort, not magic or mysterious forces that act mysteriously. This may seem like an unarguable reality, but if we pay close attention to some of the explanations that are passed off today as explanations for, let us say, American and Israeli behavior, we will conclude that these explanations are really quite far from rational, secular, or plausible.

In its dealings with the Arab world the United States has been governed by pressures and interests, and not simply by a Zionist plot, or an immoral disregard for Palestinian rights, which is certainly there. As I have said frequently here, it is one of the most illogical things for Arab leaders to throw themselves on the mercy of the United States just because it is powerful and seems to speak a language of official morality. That, in my opinion, is an example of fantasy, the assumption that some leader somewhere will cast aside the logic of interests and pressures, jump out of a historical context, and embrace the Arabs. A distinguished Arab political scientist in a recent study says that Oslo was simply the result of the balance of power, as if the balance of power were a fact of nature, like a tree or a mountain.

The missing factor here is the role of will in the creation of power in human affairs, which both Vico and Ibn Khaldun well understood. Will operates aggressively as well as defensively. The core idea of Zionism, as Zeev Sternhell shows in an important new book called *The Founding Myths of Israel: Nationalism, Socialism, and the Making of the Jewish State,* was conquest. This is clear in Ben-Gurion's rhetoric. It is also clear in the language of Berl Katznelson, the major

theorist of Labor Zionism, who openly proclaimed in 1929 that "the
Zionist enterprise is an enterprise of conquest." He then adds that "it
is not by chance that I use military terms when speaking of settlement." To this end, the Zionist movement sought, consolidated, and
deployed power consistently. This was as true in Palestine as it was
after 1948, when it was clear that the new state of Israel required sustained support from abroad, especially from the United States. This
will to power and conquest must be understood as the conscious, systematic creation of men and women dedicated to keeping hold of a
conquered territory. Far from it being a matter of luck, or coincidence,
or conspiracy, it was—and still is—announced as the goal of every
major Israeli leader of the Right or of the Left: in this respect Netanyahu is cruder, but really no different from Ben-Gurion or Rabin. One
of the main misunderstandings of those Palestinians who negotiated
the Oslo accords was not that they weren't aware of the balance of
power, but that they were ignorant of the detailed circumstances of
the Israeli military conquest and occupation of the West Bank, Gaza,
the Golan Heights, and Jerusalem. If they had known them, they
would have seen clearly that Oslo was designed to get Palestinian
approval for an extension of those circumstances into the heart of a
formal peace agreement between Israel and the PLO. Everything we
now know about what happened in Oslo suggests that the Palestinian
leadership believed that it was getting a state, whereas the Israelis in
fact were planning exactly the opposite. The question then is if this
situation was made by human beings, and is not an act of God or a
fact of nature, is there any way of dealing with it that does not perpetuate the injustice?

I think the answer is yes—but once again, by conscious, secular,
and rational means, not by waiting for a miracle or a great leader or
some unforeseen intervention, none of which can be expected in what
Vico and Ibn Khaldun studied as the world of the nations, the secular
world, which is governed by human effort that can be analyzed and
understood rationally and historically. The influential English cultural
critic Raymond Williams once said that no social system, no matter
how repressive, can exhaust every social alternative that might contra-
dict or resist it. The same is true of the United States where, despite
the power of the Israeli lobby and the converging interests of that

lobby with the strategic aims of the United States as characterized by the corporate and defense communities, there is an important sector of the population that is perplexed and angry that Israel should be getting away with so many infractions of what are stated U.S. policies, policies about human rights abuses, proliferation of weapons of mass destruction, illegal annexation of territory, and so on. What we need to ask ourselves is why has this alternative constituency never been systematically addressed by the Arabs and Palestinians. Why have our leaders and renowned intellectuals and political scientists always believed that one should address only the "policy makers" and "senior officials" and leave the rest of the population unattended to? Never having lived in the West or in a democracy, perhaps they do not understand the way power operates, not as the result of military force but as the result of mobilized opinion, the movement of ideas, the relationship between interests and ideas, and between institutions and values. As I said earlier, the Zionists grasped the importance of opinion in the modern world, and sought to influence the largest possible number of people in the West by bombarding them with images of Israel as a pioneering democratic state, built on empty, neglected, or uninhabited land, surrounded by violent Arabs who wanted to drive Jews into the sea. Ninety percent of the Western electorate still does not know that there is a Law of Return only for Jews, that Israel was built on the ruins of Palestinian society, and that only Jews (at the expense of the indigenous inhabitants) can benefit from the institutions of the state, especially so far as landowning is concerned.

Yes, the importance of holding on to our land is crucial, but no less crucial is the need to expose the immorality of Israel's now almost thirty-two-year-old military occupation, which is opposed by many Israelis, as well as supporters of Israel in the West. The enemies of South African apartheid did exactly that by campaigning in universities, churches, corporations, in the media; thus South Africa's discrimination against nonwhites became a public, moral cause. We have never even tried to organize such a campaign on a mass level, partly because we have not understood its importance, partly also because many of us still refuse to see the connection between power, will, and injustice, and refuse therefore to see the reverse—that power and will can be harnessed to resistance and to the cause of justice.

There is nothing else on the horizon, which is more bleak than it has ever been. We are getting weaker, we are slowly being overtaken and forgotten, our resolve is in danger of succumbing to the sullen silence of other defeated native peoples. And yet a proper reading of history teaches us that even though the balance of power is unfavorable, the weaker can overcome the stronger because of the human factor, that is, the will to resist, to seek new and ingenious ways to fight injustice, to be relentless in energy and hope. I think we should draw support from the fact that despite years of oppression and dispossession we continue to exist as a people, and our voice can still be heard. That should encourage us to go on—critically, consciously, creatively. Above all, we must always remember to read history as the record of what men and women did, and what they did not do.

Like success, failure is made, and is not simply an automatic thing: failure has to be constructed and worked at until it becomes a habit and a commitment. It is neither a matter of genes nor of "destiny." By the same token, we can commit ourselves to changing our situation not by force of arms, which we do not possess and cannot foreseeably possess in requisite strength, but by a mass movement of people determined by political, moral, nonviolent means to prevent our further ghettoization and hopeless drift. There are hundreds of thousands of Palestinians everywhere who are in principle prepared to sound the message everywhere that men and women will listen to and are interested in understanding. Because of its historical, cultural, and religious significance Palestine is a perennially renewed, open-ended symbol of the possibility of diversity, pluralism, and creative balance. To have expected Zionism to rise to Palestine's challenge on human and political grounds was idealistic, maybe even naive. But I remain convinced that if as Palestinians we make it clear that we are prepared with the Jews of Israel and Arab people in the surrounding region to make a new kind of history based on a politics of integration and inclusion, we can carry the day. It is slow, hard work, but it is doable and, I think, achievable in the best sense. To settle for less would be a terrible mistake whose consequences are evident all around us.

Al-Ahram Weekly, March 12, 1998

Chapter Thirty-nine

Scenes from Palestine

I HAVE JUST RETURNED from two separate trips to Jerusalem and the West Bank, where I have been making a film for the BBC to be shown in England on May 17, and then later in the month on the World Service. The occasion for my film is Israel's fiftieth anniversary, which I am examining from a personal and, obviously, Palestinian point of view. For our shooting in Palestine we have had an excellent crew: an English director, a young Anglo-Indian woman (whose idea it was to approach me for the film in the first place), a Palestinian cameraman, and an Israeli sound man. We concluded work on the film in New York a few days ago; all that remains is cutting, editing, and assembling the many hours of interviews, scenes from Palestinian life, etc., into a one-hour film. This is obviously the most difficult part of the job since we already have far too much material to be conveniently stuffed into a meagre fifty-five minutes. But the experience of going around Palestine and recording what I saw was so powerful for me that it seemed worthwhile to reflect here a little on the experience itself. I should say also that director and crew were immensely cooperative and helpful; even the Israeli sound engineer, who is employed by the BBC in Jerusalem, found the actual business of talking to Palestinians and a few Israelis very rewarding and, given his conventional Zionist upbringing (he is a liberal, by no means a dogmatic Zionist), enlightening and a definitive challenge to long-held and unexamined

views about Israel's history. "It is hard to be an Israeli again," he said
at the end of the shoot.

Two completely contradictory impressions override all the others.
First, that Palestine and Palestinians remain, despite Israel's concerted
efforts from the beginning either to get rid of them or to circumscribe
them so much as to make them ineffective. In this, I am confident in
saying, we have proved the utter folly of Israel's policy: there is no getting away from the fact that as an idea, a memory, and as an often
buried or invisible reality, Palestine and its people have simply not disappeared. The more Israel wraps itself in exclusivity and xenophobia
toward the Arabs, the more it assists them in staying on, in fighting
its injustices and cruel measures. This is specially true in the case of
Israeli Palestinians, whose main representative in the Knesset is the
remarkable Azmi Bishara. I interviewed him at length for the film and
was impressed with the courage and intelligence of his stand, which
is invigorating a new generation of young Palestinians, whom I also
interviewed. For them, as for an increasing number of Israelis (Professor Israel Shahak in the forefront), the real battle is for equality
and rights of citizenship. Contrary to its expressed and implemented
intention, therefore, Israel has strengthened the Palestinian presence,
even among Israeli Jewish citizens who have simply lost patience with
the unendingly shortsighted policy. No matter where you turn, we
are there, often only as humble, silent workers and compliant restaurant waiters, cooks, and the like, but often also as large numbers of
people—in Hebron, for example—who continuously resist Israeli
encroachments on their lives.

The second overriding impression is that minute by minute, hour
by hour, day after day, we are losing more and more Palestinian land to
the Israelis. There wasn't a road, or a bypassing highway, or a small
village that we passed in our travel for three weeks that wasn't witness
to the daily tragedy of land expropriated, fields bulldozed, trees,
plants, and crops uprooted, houses destroyed, while the Palestinian
owners stood by, helpless to do much to stop the onslaught, unassisted
by Mr. Arafat's Authority, uncared for by more fortunate Palestinians.
It is important not to underestimate the damage that is being done,
the violence to our lives that will ensue, the distortions and misery
that result. There is nothing quite like the sorrowful helplessness that

one feels listening to a young man who has spent fifteen years working as an illegal day laborer in Israel in order to save up money to build a little house for his family, only to discover one day upon returning from work that the house has been reduced to a pile of rubble, flattened by an Israeli bulldozer with everything still inside the house. When you ask why this was done—the land, after all, was his—you are told that there was no warning, only a paper given to him the next day by an Israeli soldier stating that he had built the structure without a license. Where in the world, except under Israeli authority, are people required to have an unobtainable license before they can build on their own property? Jews can build, but never Palestinians. This is racist apartheid in its form.

I once stopped on the main road from Jerusalem to Hebron to record on film an Israeli bulldozer, surrounded and protected by soldiers, plowing through some fertile land just alongside the road. About a hundred meters away stood four Palestinian men, looking both miserable and angry. It was their land, I was told, which they had worked for generations, now being destroyed on the pretext that it was needed to widen an already wide road built for the settlements. "Why do they need a road that will be 120 meters wide; why can't they let me go on farming my land?" asked one of them plaintively. "How am I going to feed my children?" I asked the men whether they received any warning that this was going to be done. No, they said, we just heard today and when we got here it was too late. What about the Authority? I asked. Has it helped? No, of course not, was the answer. They're never here when we need them. I went over to the Israeli soldiers, who at first refused to talk to me in the presence of cameras and microphones. But I kept insisting, and was lucky to find one who clearly seemed troubled by the whole business, even though he said he was merely following orders. "But don't you see how unjust it is to take land from farmers who have no defense against you?" I said, to which he replied, "It's not their land really. It belongs to the state of Israel." I recall saying to him that sixty years ago the same arguments were made against Jews in Germany, and now here were Jews using it against their victims, the Palestinians. He moved away, unwilling to respond.

And so it is throughout the territories and Jerusalem, with

Palestinians powerless to help each other. I gave a lecture at the University of Bethlehem about the continuous dispossession that was taking place, and wondered why those fifty thousand security people employed by the Authority, plus the thousands more who sit behind desks, pushing paper from one side of their desks to the other, cashing handsome checks at the end of each month, were not out there on the land helping to prevent the expropriations, helping the people whose livelihood was being taken from them before their eyes? Why, I asked, don't villagers go out to their fields and simply stand in front of the bulldozers, and why don't all our great leaders give support and moral help to the poor people who are losing the battle? One night I came back from filming all day and discovered that the hotel restaurant was sponsoring a Valentine's Day dinner at $38 (yes, $38) per person. I was told that since I didn't have a reservation I couldn't be served, but I insisted that as a guest in the hotel I was at least entitled to a sandwich or something equally simple. I was shown a table in the corner and duly served a plate of rice and vegetables. A moment or two later I saw a Palestinian minister enter the room with seven guests, and sit at a prominent table weighted down with the seven-course Valentine's Day menu, plus wine, and drinks for all. I was so sickened by the sight of this large, fat, smiling man who spends so much time "negotiating" with donor countries and with the Israelis, eating away happily while his people were losing their livelihood a few meters away, that I left the room in disgust and shame. He had arrived in a gigantic Mercedes; his bodyguards and driver—three of them—were sitting in the hotel lobby eating bananas, while their great leader sat in the dining room and stuffed himself.

This is one reason why wherever I went, whomever I talked to, whatever the question, there was never a good word for the Authority or its officers. Basically it is perceived as guaranteeing security for Israel and its settlers, furnishing them with protection, not at all as a legitimate, or concerned, or helpful governmental body vis-à-vis its own people. That at the same time so many of these leaders should think it appropriate to build ostentatious villas during a period of such widespread penury and misery fairly boggles the mind. If it is to be anything today, leadership for the Palestinian people must demonstrate service and sacrifice, precisely those two things so lacking in the

Authority. What I found staggering is the absence of care, that is, the sense that each Palestinian is alone in his or her misery, with no one so much as concerned to offer food, blankets, or a kind word. Truly one feels that Palestinians are an orphaned people.

Jerusalem is overwhelming in its continuing, unrelenting Judaization. The small, compact city in which I grew up over fifty years ago has become an enormously spread-out metropolis, surrounded on the north, south, east, and west by immense building projects that testify to Israeli power and its ability, to change the character of Jerusalem. Here too there is a manifest sense of Palestinian powerlessness, as if the battle is over and the future settled. Most people I spoke to said that after the tunnel episode of last September they no longer felt the need to demonstrate against Israeli practices, nor to expose themselves to more sacrifice. "After all," one of them told me, "sixty of us were killed, and yet the tunnel remained open, and Arafat went to Washington, despite having said that he would not meet with Netanyahu unless the tunnel was closed. What is the point of struggling now?" Few Palestinians from Gaza or the West Bank (i.e., from cities like Ramallah, Hebron, Bethlehem, Jenine, and Nablus) can enter Jerusalem, which is cordoned off by Israeli soldiers. Apartheid once again.

On the Israeli side, the situation is not as bleak as one would have expected. I conducted a long interview with Professor Ilan Pappe of Haifa University. He is one of the new Israeli historians whose work on 1948 has challenged Zionist orthodoxy on the refugee problem, and on Ben-Gurion's role in making the Palestinians leave. In this, of course, the new historians have confirmed what Palestinian historians and witnesses have said all along—that there was a deliberate military campaign to rid the country of as many Arabs as possible. But what Pappe also said is that he is very much in demand for lectures in high schools all over Israel, even though the latest textbook for classes on Israel's history simply make no mention of the Palestinians at all. This blindness coexisting with a new openness regarding the past characterizes the present mood, but deserves our attention as a contradiction to be deepened and analyzed further.

I spent a day filming in Hebron, which strikes me as embodying all the worst aspects of Oslo. A small handful of settlers, numbering no more than about two hundred people at any one time, virtually control the heart of an Arab city whose population of over one hundred thousand is left on the margins, unable to visit the city center, constantly under threat from militants and soldiers alike. I visited the house of a Palestinian in the old Ottoman quarter. He is now surrounded by settler bastions, including three new buildings that have gone up around him, plus three enormous water tanks that steal most of the city's water for the settlers, plus several rooftop nests of soldiers. He was very bitter about the Palestinian leadership's willingness to accept the town's partition on the entirely specious grounds that it had once contained fourteen Jewish buildings dating back to Old Testament times but no longer in evidence. "How did these Palestinian negotiators accept such a grotesque distortion of the reality," he asked me angrily, "especially in that at the time of the negotiations not one of them had ever set foot in Hebron when they negotiated the deal?" The day after I was in Hebron three young men were killed at the barricade by Israeli soldiers, and many more injured in the fighting that ensued. Hebron and Jerusalem are victories for Israeli extremism, not for coexistence, or for any sort of hopeful future.

Perhaps the high point of my experiences with Israelis was an interview with Daniel Barenboim, the brilliant conductor and pianist who was in Jerusalem for a recital at the same time I was there for the film. Born and raised in Argentina, Barenboim came to Israel in 1950 at the age of nine, lived there for about eight years, and has been conducting the Berlin State Opera and the Chicago Symphony Orchestra—two of the world's greatest musical institutions—for the last ten years. I should also say that over the past few years he and I have become close personal friends. He was very open in our interview: regretting that fifty years of Israel should also be the occasion of fifty years of suffering for the Palestinian people. During our discussion he openly advocated a Palestinian state, and after his Jerusalem recital, to a packed audience, he dedicated his first encore to the Palestinian woman—present at the recital—who had invited him to dinner the night before. I was surprised that the entire audience of Israeli Jews (she and I seemed to be the only Palestinians present) received his views and the noble dedication with enthusiastic applause. Clearly a new constituency of conscience is beginning to emerge, partly as a result of Netanyahu's excesses, partly as a result of Palestinian resistance. What I found extremely heartening is that Barenboim, one of the world's greatest musicians, has offered his services as a pianist to Palestinian audiences, a gesture of reconciliation that is truly worth more than dozens of Oslo accords.

So I conclude these brief scenes from Palestinian life today. I regret not having spent time among refugees in Lebanon and Syria, and I also regret not having many hours of film at my disposal. But at this moment it seems important that we testify to the resilience and continued potency of the Palestinian cause, which clearly has influenced more people in Israel and elsewhere than we have hitherto supposed. Depite the gloom of the present moment, there are rays of hope indicating that the future may not be as bad as many of us have supposed.

Al-Hayat, March 26, 1998
Al-Khaleej, March 26, 1998
Al-Ahram Weekly, March 1998
Panorama, March 27, 1998
The Nation, May 4, 1998
Al-Hewar, April/May 1998
Washington Report on Middle East Affairs, May/June 1998
Le Monde Diplomatique, May 1998

Chapter Forty

End of the Peace Process, or Beginning Something Else

DENNIS ROSS'S LATEST "return" from the Middle East to Washington brought the usual results: absolutely nothing new by way of advancing a moribund "peace process." Israel has refused the United States's modest proposal of an additional 13 percent withdrawal, and the Palestinian Authority has refused the refusal. As a confirmation of the hard-line Israeli position, Netanyahu declared in a speech on March 26 (reported by *Ha'aretz* on March 27) that "we are making a constant effort to preserve the maximum [in terms of land], including territories I would fight for even if they had no security value." Then he added, "The permanent settlement will follow negotiations on the territorial dimension and on the functional dimension. The functional dimension would include limitations on the powers that would accrue to the Palestinians, such as a prohibition on their concluding international alliances, using Israel's water sources, threatening Israeli air space, flooding the area with refugees." So truculent and aggressive has Netanyahu become that he seems to prefer talking exclusively to himself and to his right-wing accomplices than to anyone outside that tight little circle. The wonder of it is that he is still perceived by some American supporters of Israel—the Clinton administration among them—as making some sense. Whereas the reality is that Netanyahu lives in an Alice in Wonderland construction of his own making, sounding off like the March Hare or the Queen of Hearts with scarcely a concern for facts, possibilities, and the existence of other interests in the world besides his. I think it is obvious he believes that in the long run the Palestinian leadership will settle for 9 percent plus the 3 percent already under Palestinian self-rule, and just leave Israel alone, as if the deal had been concluded happily to everyone's satisfaction.

The Clinton administration is too concerned with the president's domestic agenda to do very much about the declining American position in the Middle East. For the time being, then, United States policy will be left to the handful of men, most of them former functionaries of the Israeli lobby, whose main purpose seems to be to keep themselves in business. Robin Cook's confrontation with the Israelis may have signaled a change in European Union policy, but it is still too early to tell. In any event there is no gainsaying the central tension, which is between Palestinians and Israelis over the land. That contest will continue, and in the absence of a credible Arab military deterrent, or a serious American dispute with Israel, it is imperative that we think of what is within our means at present.

For Palestinians, one of the first imperatives is somehow to prevent disadvantaged Palestinians from taking jobs constructing Israeli settlements. Obviously such jobs are taken out of desperation. Three weeks ago when I asked a Palestinian truck driver why he was working for an Israeli contractor, he replied, "I need to put food on my table. Find me another job, and I'll stop right away." With the cooperation of the Authority we need immediate attention to this problem, the answer to which is to set up an unemployment fund to prevent, or at least discourage, men from taking these jobs. I see no reason why the Legislative Council cannot challenge Arafat on this point, putting it in the context of the continuing debate over PA corruption. The fact is, for example, that somewhere between forty and fifty thousand men are employed in security services, most of them as informers and supererogatory guards. Why can't this expenditure be revised so as to divert money from security to land preservation? Additionally, there are four million Palestinians living abroad, quite a few of them well-off and able to contribute a monthly sum to this unemployment (or alternative employment) fund. This is an urgent necessity, which in our addiction to pointless theoretical debate over "strategy" is left out completely.

Along with restraining Palestinians from building Israeli settlements, we have to think over the whole matter of civil disobedience campaigns. I do not refer to a new intifada, since that would be to repeat something that cannot be repeated. But I do think a sustained series of peaceful marches on settlements undergoing construction, blocking traffic, demonstrations, etc., must be considered as part of a general strategy for containing Israel's daily expansionism. Since we cannot for obvious reasons reproduce the southern Lebanese situation, which has given Hizballah an important victory, we have to plan for what we can do, and more important, for what we can win. Rebuilding demolished houses falls in the same category of disobedience and resistance. But none of this can be contemplated unless the leadership, under pressure from the Palestinian population, is driven to raise these matters, forced to concede publicly that the whole Oslo process no longer has any substance, and that more urgent matters of self-preservation are our new priority.

Lastly, an international campaign must be mounted against settlements and for self-determination. This would help the European Union to determine its priorities more crisply, and at last would put the United States on notice that we can no longer tolerate the slow erosion of our territorial sovereignty as a people. I have been surprised during the past few months that wherever I have spoken or written the response has been enthusiastic: Arabs, Europeans, Americans, Asians, and Africans are waiting to hear from us, are looking for ways to support a struggle that diminishes Israel's power and extraordinary arrogance. Yet unless we once again assume the responsibility for conducting our fight against apartheid as a just one, nothing very much can happen. We have been bogged down for so long in the minutiae of a fraudulent peace process that we have been unable to utter or even recall our own first principles. Netanyahu's Israel has made no secret of wanting to fight a war of attrition against us, so surely the time has come for us to admit this and disrupt the wearying charade that has involved us in five years of fruitless haggling over less and less.

We have to be able to engage Israeli public opinion on our own terms, not as providers of security but as seekers after justice. I have no doubt that outside the main channels provided by the establishment—Labor, Likud, or religious—there are numerous avenues for communicating with Israelis who are prepared to fight against apartheid and theocracy in their country. And here we must courageously welcome such people and not hide behind Jesuistic casuistry about being opposed to "normalization." We must normalize with Israelis who share our goals, that is, self-determination for two peoples in Palestine. And we must be prepared to meet and visit with people like Daniel Barenboim—who has made no secret of wanting to perform and has performed for Palestinian and Arab audiences—who correctly perceive that the only real avenue open for reconciliation is culture, not politics, nor economic schemes. What can be wrong with having him perform in Ramallah or Cairo or Damascus, a great artist who speaks of peace and justice for the Palestinians openly? There are others like him whom out of fear and timidity we have avoided. The time has come to make justice a common topic for us and for Israelis.

The proposals I have suggested here are nothing like an answer to Dr. Haidar Abdel Shafi's question, what is to be done? But for intellectuals the important thing is to think new thoughts and open lines of reflection that convention and orthodoxy have closed to us. Ours is a very unusual set of circumstances: our Israeli opponents are unusual, our history is unusual, our future, therefore, must be unusual. Surely the end of Oslo is in fact the beginning of something else, which in the present disarray has got to be better than anything now before us. I firmly believe that Oslo and all its domestic consequences on Palestinian society have been detrimental and, in the most profound sense, corrupting. Personal interests have come first, avoiding central tasks, and looking for a quick profit by doing things as usual—all these have led us to our present impasse. Certainly Israel and the United States have played a leading part in this debilitation, but it is unacceptable to overlook our own quite central role. We represent our own most formidable challenge; unless it is met we might as well simply give up and become the Middle East's Red Indians.

Al-Ahram Weekly, April 9, 1998
Panorama, April 17, 1998
Al-Khaleej, April 10, 1998

Chapter Forty-one

Art, Culture, and Nationalism

I HAVE JUST RETURNED from a short trip to Berlin, where I participated in a weeklong festival dedicated not only to the performance but also to the discussion of great musical works associated with German nationalism, a nationalism, no one needs to be reminded, that led to the collective insanity of Hitlerian facism. The core of the musical program was a performance of Richard Wagner's opera *Die Meistersinger von Nurmberg* (The Mastersingers of Nuremberg) which he composed just after *Tristan and Isolde* and in the middle of writing his vast four-opera cycle, *The Ring of the Nibelung*. What gives *Meistersinger* its special character is the paradox that alone of all his operas it is a comedy with a happy ending, and yet, because of one of its main themes, was of particular importance not just to the Nazis but to Hitler himself. The work was originally performed in 1868, roughly three years before the unification of Germany under Bismarck, but it strangely presages the rise of a virulent German nationalism that reached paroxysms of chauvinism during the period of the Third Reich. Near the very end of the gigantic work, one passage in the opera seems to suggest that "holy German art" must be protected from foreign influences in order for it to remain "German and true." This passage alone was elevated by the Nazis to the level of doctrine. Anything that did not fit the prescription of what was traditionally "German art" was therefore considered bad and had to be expunged—or so Wagner's later disciples and interpreters suggested.

The opera is set in sixteenth-century Nuremberg, which Wagner saw as an analogy for the contemporary world in which he lived. At the core of the opera are a group of "mastersingers," that is, skilled singers who are experts in the rules and forms of traditional German choral art. They form a sort of guild, and yet at the same time, each of them is a craftsman or bourgeois citizen with a specific trade. The hero of the opera is Hans Sachs, a shoemaker as well as a skilled singer himself, who adopts the cause of a young nobleman, Walther, who wants to become a mastersinger and marry Eva, the woman offered as a prize for the best singer. Walther is a gifted musician and poet, but is impatient with the rules. His rival is Sixtus Beckmesser, the town clerk, a mastersinger and an aspirant to Eva's hand. By the end of the opera, the two men sing in a contest for the right to marry Eva, except that Beckmesser fails miserably (despite the fact that he knows the rules very well) whereas Walther wins because, thanks to Hans Sachs's help, he combines knowledge of the rules with genuine originality. After the contest is over and Walther duly crowned a new mastersinger and husband of Eva, Sachs then sings to the assembled townspeople of Nuremberg about how important it is to understand the new, and yet not to forget "the traditional German masters" and of course their genuine "pure German art."

Over time Beckmesser has been interpreted both by German nationalists and by anti-Germans as Wagner's portrait of a hated Jew, although in the opera itself Beckmesser is as German as everyone else and not at all Jewish. But because at the end of the opera Beckmesser disgraces himself, sings an ugly song, and is thrown out of the contest, it has often been assumed that what Wagner had in mind—notorious anti-Semite that he was—was nothing less than a ceremony of ridding Germany of a hated member of its society, that is, the Jew. And so the Nazis seemed to have thought: performances of *Meistersinger* during the Nazi era were used on important state occasions to celebrate Germany's cultural purity and, at the same time, to demonstrate how Jews were to be treated. Since World War II a heated debate has raged around this opera, which is acnowledged by all as a great musical masterpiece: Is it mainly a eulogy to German culture, and hence a document of the kind of rabid German nationalism that led to Nazism and Auchwitz, or is it a work of art in which ugly thoughts and frightening suggestions play a role but by no means determine the whole work's meaning? In Berlin, then, we debated this point, especially since our deliberations took place in the German State Opera right in the heart of what was the capital of the Third Reich.

It is part of Wagner's endless complexity that one can see in *Meistersinger* both the seeds of what was to come during the great Nuremberg rallies of the 1930s as well as a humane and rich work of art that tries to show the connection between culture and an evolving nation. To interpret Wagner only as a prophet of facism is, I believe, to miss what he himself also felt about the dangers of a nationalism that could go too far. What Sachs says at the end of the work, therefore, is that people should remain in touch with their collective past yet also be able to develop by recognizing new and valuable experiences that do not fit the nationalist prescription. And it is new and other experiences that keep culture from freezing into a hard set of doctrines: culture is culture only when it is renewed, re-interpreted, re-lived. The death of culture is literalism, that is, the practice of turning tradition and history into orthodoxy and authoritarianism.

A great deal of this discussion in Germany is relevant to contemporary Arab culture, which is undergoing a similar process of self-searching and re-invigoration. For us, however, our relationship to our own past, traditions, and art is complicated by our encounters with the West and Israel, both of which seem to have deprived us of various continuities and of self-confidence. In both instances these two outside presences still command an extraordinary amount of our attention, since both remain to challenge us culturally as well as politically. The result has been an astonishing contradiction between public defiance and private anxiety, between ringing declarations of official nationalism and abject collaboration with our enemies. For years, the orthodox rhetoric of Arab nationalism stipulated that Israel was an irreducible enemy, its aggression against the Arabs an unacceptable collective assault, its very presence a burden from which we needed to be liberated. Then all of a sudden it was possible not only to accept Israel, but to conclude peace arrangements with the Jewish state, and at the same time actively to solicit American mediation. Even after the various peace arrangements revealed that Israeli governments still had active designs on Palestinian land, and Israeli settlers and soldiers remained in possession of Syrian, Lebanese, and Palestinian territories, the language of the peace process continued, at the same time that America did nothing to stop Israel, but in fact supported the most extreme of Israeli governments, that of Benjamin Netanyahu's Likud.

So glaring and irreconcilable were the requirements of Arab collective orthodoxy that all sorts of amazing claims began to appear, many of them concerning Palestine. Take as an exceptionally remarkable incident the case of recent attacks on the Beirut Theater (Masrah Beirut) which organized a series of impressive events to commemorate the Palestinian side of Israel's fifty years (reported in *al-Hayat*, April 17, 1998). The principal organizer, Elias Khoury, is a very gifted novelist, editor, and intellectual who has remained committed to the secular and democratic goals of the Palestinian revolution. As a Lebanese citizen he could very easily have forgotten about Palestine, given that since 1982 the whole issue has been surrounded with ambiguities, compromises, and appallingly difficult complications for the Lebanese and Palestinian peoples. But he, and his colleagues at the theater including Fawwaz Trabulsi, among several others, have remained committed to the ideals for which all of us, Palestinian and non-Palestinian, have been struggling, the core of which is a belief in the necessity of justice, non-discrimination, and equality, precisely those qualities of citizenship which Israel has denied the Palestinian people. The argument is a universalistic one, that all peoples, regardless of religion, race, or language, are entitled to the same civil, political, and human rights. Given Israel's radical mistreatment of its "non-Jewish" citizens on the grounds of both religion and language, the only intellectually responsible position is to assert the invalidity of such discrimination, replacing it not with discrimination for Arabs, but rather non-discrimination for all.

In this respect, therefore, the Palestinian struggle has derived much of its moral argument from the support of non-Zionist Jews, especially those Jews in Arab countries like Morocco and Tunisia who have suffered precisely because they opposed the Zionism of their own communities. This was also the case with Palestinian Jews and, more recently, Sephardic Jews (from Yemen and Iraq and Egypt) whose [victimization] in Israel as non-Ashkenazi Jews has turned them into powerful critics of the Jewish state. One of the more interesting panels in Beirut was to have been made up of a group of Arab Jews, all of whom, without exception—I think particularly of the Moroccan Ibrahim Sarfaty, imprisoned for many years by King Hassan, and the distinguished writer Edmond el Maleh—have paid very heavily for their public support of radical non-Zionist ideas.

How outrageous and unacceptable, then, the hue and cry against Beirut Theater for inviting such people on the pretext that this was "normalization" with the Israeli enemy. The scheduled panel was canceled. So false and utterly specious is this notion that it returns us to the kind of discredited German nationalism that culminated in German fascism, whose main cultural argument against the German Jews was that they were not "really" German but outsiders whose presence in some way sullied and tarnished the pristine essence of what, as Wagner's character had said in *Meistersinger,* was "true and German" *(echt und Deutsch)*. The notion that pure cultures, pure identities, and pure nations really exist is supremely arrogant and without merit at all. No culture, no nation, no people is free of an enormous variety of mixes. What would Germany have been without Italy, or without Greece or France, or without the Slavs, and now the Turks and Kurds and Arabs that make up a large part of its present reality? Very little, and very little also if one says, as Hitler and Goebbels did, that even German Jews, who spoke German and considered German culture their culture, were not REALLY German, as if being really German was something that could be legislated and even created in a laboratory. Human history and reality are more complex than that, and always contain "impurities" that it would be folly to exclude or destroy. What is it, then, that we have against Israel if we say that we want a "pure" Palestine, free of Jews, free of everything that isn't pure Arab and Muslim and Palestinian? Nothing at all: we would be mimicking exactly what it is that we attack. And how ignorant and narrow-minded, how chauvinistic and racist it is to define a person not by his/her ideas and values, but by his racial origins, religion, or culture.

What I found particularly important about the German discussion is that it took place at all. Our own situation, it seems, does not permit honest discussion of that sort, as if the notion that there is a real Palestinian struggle on behalf of real freedom and democracy is something that frightens the Arab establishment, as if the idea that people demand the same respect and consideration from Israel toward the Palestinian people which it has dispossessed and oppressed is also an argument that should not be stated and restated within the Arab world. One language and universal rights, although honored rhetorically, turn out to be very dangerous things when spoken both at home in the Arab world and abroad in places like Paris and New York. The challenge is not to admit a double standard and not to use two different languages. That would be to fall into the very trap which we claim Israel has not evaded. Our struggle must present an alternative view of how culture and politics are related. We cannot say that only Arabs can speak about Arabs, and only Arab Muslims can discuss Palestine. In other words, we must either be part of the solution or, terrible as it may be to admit, part of the problem. The attacks on Elias Khoury and Beirut Theater are a scandal of hypocrisy and frenzied chauvinism. We can ill afford such nonsense: given the enormity of Israeli persecution of "non-Jews" (i.e., Palestinians), we can do a lot better than simply replicating the same bankrupt xenophobia in the midst of our struggle.

Al-Ahram Weekly, April 23, 1998

Panorama, May 1, 1998

Al-Hayat, April 28, 1998

Al-Khaleej, April 28, 1998

Chapter Forty-two

Fifty Years of Dispossession

I N THE UNITED STATES, celebrations of Israel's fifty years as a
state have tried to project an image of the country that went out of
fashion since the Palestinian intifada (1987–92): a pioneering state,
full of hope and promise for the survivors of the Nazi Holocaust, a
haven of enlightened liberalism in a sea of Arab fanaticism and reaction. On April 15, for instance, CBS broadcast a two-hour prime-time
program from Hollywood hosted by Michael Douglas and Kevin
Costner, featuring movie stars such as Arnold Schwarzenegger, Kathy
Bates (who recited passages from Golda Meir, minus, of course, her
most celebrated remark that there were no Palestinians), and Winona
Ryder. None of these luminaries are particularly known for their
Middle Eastern expertise or enthusiasm, although all of them in one
way or another praised Israel's greatness and enduring achievements.
There was even time for a cameo appearance by President Bill Clinton,
who provided perhaps the least edifying, most atavistic note of the
evening by complimenting Israel, "a small oasis," for "making a once
barren desert bloom," and for "building a thriving democracy in hostile terrain."

Ironically enough, no such encomia were intoned on Israeli television, which has been broadcasting a twenty-two-part series, *Tekuma*,
on the country's history. This series has a decidedly more complicated
and indeed more critical content. Episodes on the 1948 war, for instance, made use of archival sources unearthed by the so-called revi-

sionist historians (Benny Morris, Ilan Pappe, Avi Schlaim, Tom Segev, et al.) to demonstrate that the indigenous Palestinians were forcibly expelled, their villages destroyed, their land taken, their society eradicated. It was as if Israeli audiences had no need of all the palliatives provided for diasporic and international viewers, who still needed to be told that Israel was a cause for uncomplicated rejoicing and not, as it has been for Palestinians, the cause of a protracted and still continuing dispossession of the country's indigenous people.

That the American celebration simply omitted any mention of the Palestinians indicated also how remorselessly an ideological mindset can hold on, despite the facts, despite years of news and headlines, despite an extraordinary, if ultimately unsuccessful, effort to keep effacing Palestinians from the picture of Israel's untroubled sublimity. If they're not mentioned, they don't exist. Even after fifty years of living the Palestinian exile, I still find myself astonished at the lengths to which official Israel and its supporters will go to suppress the fact that a half century has gone by without Israeli restitution, recognition, or acknowledgment of Palestinian human rights and without, as the facts undoubtedly show, connecting that suspension of rights to Israel's official policies. Even when there is a vague buried awareness of the facts, as is the case with a front-page *New York Times* story on April 23 by Ethan Bronner, the Palestinian *nakba* is characterized as a semifictional event (dutiful inverted commas around the word "catastrophe" for instance) caused by no one in particular. When Bronner quotes an uprooted Palestinian who describes his miseries, the man's testimony is qualified by "for most Israelis, the idea of Mr. Shikaki staking claim to victimhood is chilling," a reaction made plausible as Bronner blithely leapfrogs over the man's uprooting and systematic deprivations and immediately tells us how his "rage" (for years the approved word for dealing with Palestinian history) has impelled his sons into joining Hamas and Islamic Jihad. Ergo, Palestinians are violent terrorists, whereas Israel can go on being a "vibrant and democratic regional superpower established on the ashes of Nazi genocide." But not on the ashes of Palestine, an obliteration that lingers on in measures taken by Israel to block Palestinian rights, domestically as well as in territories occupied in 1967.

Take land and citizenship. Approximately seven hundred fifty thousand Palestinians were expelled in 1948: they are now roughly 4 million. Left behind were one hundred twenty thousand (now one million), who subsequently became Israelis, a minority constituting about 18 percent of the state's population today, but not fully fledged citizens in anything more than name. In addition there are 2.5 million Palestinians without sovereignty on the West Bank and Gaza. Israel is the only state in the world which is not the state of its actual citizens, but of the whole Jewish people, who consequently have rights that non-Jews do not. Without a constitution, Israel is governed by Basic Laws, of which one in particular, the Law of Return, makes it possible for any Jew anywhere to emigrate to Israel and become a citizen, at the same time that native-born Palestinians do not have the same right. Of the land of the state 93 percent is characterized as Jewish land, meaning that no non-Jew is allowed to lease, sell, or buy it. Before 1948, the Jewish community in Palestine owned a little over 6 percent of the land. A recent case in which a Palestinian Israeli, Adel Kaadan, wished to buy land but was refused because he was a non-Jew has become something of a cause célèbre in Israel, and has even made it to the Supreme Court, which is supposed to but would prefer not to rule on it. Kaadan's lawyer has said that "as a Jew in Israel, I think that if a Jew somewhere else in the world was prohibited from buying state land, public land, owned by the federal government, because they're Jews, I believe there would have been an outcry in Israel" (*New York Times,* March 1, 1998). This anomaly about Israeli democracy, not well known and rarely cited, is compounded by the fact that, as I said above, Israel's land in the first place was owned by Palestinians expelled in 1948. Since their forced exodus their property was legally turned into Jewish land by The Absentees' Property Law, the Law of the State's Property, and the Land Ordinance (the Acquisition of Land for Public Purposes). Now only Jewish citizens have access to that land, a fact that does not corroborate *The Economist*'s extraordinarily sweeping statement on "Israel at 50" (April 25–May 1, 1998) that since the state's founding Palestinians "have enjoyed full political rights."

What makes it specially galling for Palestinians is that they have been forced to watch the transformation of their own homeland into a

Western state, one of whose express purposes is to provide for Jews and not for non-Jews. Between 1948 and 1966 Palestinian Israelis were ruled by military ordinance. After that, as the state regularized its policies on education, legal practice, religion, social, economic, and political participation, a regime evolved to keep the Palestinian minority disadvantaged, segregated, and constantly discriminated against. There is an eye-opening account of this shabby history which is rarely cited or, when it is, elided or explained away by the euphemism (familiar from South African apartheid) that "they" have their own system: it is the Report of March 1998 entitled "Legal Violations of Arab Minority Rights in Israel," published by Adalah (the Arabic word for justice), an Arab-Jewish organization within Israel. Especially telling is the section on the "discriminatory approach of Israeli courts," routinely praised by supporters of Israel for their impartiality and fairness. In fact, the report notes that, while the courts have delivered progressive and decent-minded decisions on the rights of women, homosexuals, the disabled, etc., they have "since 1948 dismissed all cases dealing with equal rights for Arab citizens, and have never included a declaratory statement in decisions regarding the protection of Arab group rights." This is borne out by a survey of criminal and civil cases in which Arabs get no help from the courts and are far more likely to be indicted than Jews in similar circumstances.

It is only in the past year or two that investigations of Israel's political makeup, hitherto assumed to be socialist, egalitarian, pioneering, forward-looking, have turned up a rather different picture. Zeev Sternhell's book *The Founding Myths of Israel* (Princeton 1998) is the work of an Israeli historian of twentieth-century right-wing European mass movements who finds a disturbing congruence between those movements and Israel's own brand of what he rightly calls "nationalist socialism." Far from being socialist, Israel's founders and subsequently the polity they established were profoundly anti-socialist, bent almost entirely upon "conquest of the land" and the creation of "self-realization" and a new sense of organic peoplehood that moved steadily to the right during the pre-1948 years. "Neither the Zionist movement abroad," Sternhell says, "nor the pioneers who were beginning to settle the country could frame a policy toward the

Palestinian national movement. The real reason for this was not a lack of understanding of the problem but a clear recognition of the insurmountable contradiction between the basic objectives of the two sides." After 1948, policy toward the Palestinians clearly envisioned that community's disappearance or its political nullity, since it was evident that the contradiction between the two sides would always remain insurmountable. Israel, in short, could not become a secular liberal state, despite the efforts of two generations of publicists to make it so.

After 1967 the occupation of the West Bank and Gaza produced a military and civil regime for Palestinians whose aim was Palestinian submission and Israeli dominance, an extension of the model on which Israel proper functioned. Settlements were established in the late summer of 1967 (and Jerusalem annexed) not by right-wing parties but by the Labor Party, a member, interestingly enough, of the Socialist International. The promulgation of literally hundreds of "occupiers' laws" directly contravened not only the tenets of the Universal Declaration of Human Rights but the Geneva Conventions as well. These violations ran the gamut from administrative detention, to mass land expopriations, house demolitions, forced movement of populations, torture, uprooting of trees, assassination, book banning, closure of schools and universities. Always, however, the illegal settlements were being expanded as more and more Arab land was ethnically cleansed so that Jewish populations from Russia, Ethiopia, Canada, and the United States, among other places, could be accommodated.

After the Oslo Accords were signed in September 1993 conditions for Palestinians steadily worsened. It became impossible for Palestinians to travel freely between one place and another, Jerusalem was declared off limits, and massive building projects transformed the country's geography. In everything, the distinction between Jew and non-Jew is scrupulously preserved. The most perspicacious analysis of the legal situation obtaining after Oslo is Raja Shehadeh's in his book *From Occupation to Interim Accords: Israel and the Palestinian Territories* (Kluwer, 1997), an important work that demonstrates the carefully preserved continuity between Israeli negotiating strategy during the Oslo process and its land occupation policy established in the occupied territories from the early 1970s. In addition Shehadeh demonstrates the tragic lack of preparation and understanding in the PLO's strategy during the peace process, with the result that much of the sympathy gained internationally for the Palestinians against Israeli settlement policy and its dismal human rights record was frittered away, unused and unexploited. "All the support and sympathy," he says, "which it took years for Palestinians to rally, returned home, so to speak, with the mistaken belief that the struggle was over. The Palestinians, as much as the Israelis, helped in giving the false impression through, among other things, the highly publicised media image of the Arafat-Rabin handshake, that the Israeli-Palestinian conflict was resolved. No serious attempt was made to remind the world that one of the main causes of the conflict after 1967, the Israeli settlements in occupied Palestinian territory, remained intact. This is not to speak of the other basic unresolved questions of the return of refugees, compensation, and the issue of Jerusalem" (131).

Unquestionably the moral dilemma faced by anyone trying to come to terms with the Palestinian-Israeli conflict is a deep one. Israeli Jews are not white settlers of the stripe that colonized Algeria or South Africa, though they have used similar methods. They are correctly seen as victims of a long history of Western, largely Christian, anti-Semitic persecution that culminated in the scarcely comprehensible horrors of the Nazi Holocaust. To Palestinians, however, their own role is that of victims of the victims. This is why Western liberals who openly espoused the anti-apartheid movement, or the cause of the Nicaraguan Sandinistas, or Bosnia, or East Timor, or American civil rights, or Armenian commemoration of the Turkish genocide, or many other political causes of that kind, have shied away from openly endorsing Palestinian self-determination.

An even greater challenge is the difficulty of separating Palestinian and Israeli-Jewish populations, who are now inextricably linked in all sorts of ways, despite the immense chasm that divides them. Those of us who for years have argued for a Palestinian state have finally, perhaps even sadly, come to the realization that if such a "state" (the inverted commas here are definitely required) is going to appear out of the shambles of Oslo it will be weak, economically dependent on Israel, without real sovereignty or power. Above all, as the present map of the West Bank amply shows, the Palestinian autonomy zones will mostly be non-contiguous (they now account for only 3 percent of the West Bank; Netanyahu's government has balked at giving up an additional 13 percent) and effectively divided into Bantustans controlled from the outside by Israel. The only reasonable course, therefore, is to recommend that Palestinians and their supporters renew the struggle against the fundamental principle that relegates "non-Jews" to subservience on the land of historical Palestine. This, it seems to me, is what is entailed by any principled campaign on behalf of justice for Palestinians, and certainly not the enfeebled separatism that movements like Peace Now have fitfully embraced and quickly abandoned. There can be no concept of human rights, no matter how elastic, that accommodates the strictures of Israeli state practice against "non-Jewish" Palestinians in favor of Jewish citizens. Only by facing the inherent contradiction between what in effect is a theocratic and ethnic exclusivism on the one hand and genuine democracy on the other can there be any hope for reconciliation and peace in Israel/Palestine.

The Guardian, May 2, 1998
Panorama, May 8, 1998
Al-Hayat, May 5, 1998
Al-Khaleej, May 5, 1998
Le Monde, May 27, 1998
Harper's, October 1998

Chapter Forty-three

New History, Old Ideas

THE FRENCH MONTHLY *Le Monde Diplomatique*, together with the *Revue d'études palestiniennes*, a quarterly journal published in Paris by the Institute of Palestine Studies, held a conference last week which I attended and participated in. Although it was announced as the first time that the so-called "new" Israeli historians and their Palestinian counterparts had exchanged ideas in public, it was actually the third or fourth time; yet what made the Paris meeting so novel was that this was certainly the first time that a prolonged exchange between them was possible. On the Palestinian side there were Elie Sambar, Nur Masalha, and myself; on the Israeli side Benny Morris, Ilan Pappe, Itamar Rabinowitch (who is not really a new historian, but a former Labor Party adviser, Israeli ambassador to the United States, professor of history at Tel Aviv University, and an expert on Syria, but whose views seem to be changing), and finally, Zeev Sternhell, Professor at the Hebrew University, author of *The Founding Myths of Israel,* a very important book in which he dispels the myths about Israeli society as a liberal, socialist, democratic state—in an extraordinarily detailed analysis of its illiberal, quasi-fascist, and profoundly anti-socialist character as evidenced by the Labor Party generally, and the Histadrut in particular.

Because it was not well promoted, the conference attracted rather small audiences on the whole, but because of the quality of the material presented and the fact that sessions went on for several hours, it was a very valuable exercise, despite the unevenness of some of the contributions. One very powerful impression I had was that whereas the Israeli participants—who were by no means all of the same political persuasion—often spoke of the need for detachment, critical distance, and reflective calm as important for historical study, the Palestinian side was much more urgent, more severe, and even emotional in its insistence on the need for new history. The reason is of course that Israel, and consequently most Israelis, are the dominant party in the conflict: they hold all the territory, have all the military power, and can therefore take their time and have the luxury of sitting back and letting the debate unfold calmly. Only Ilan Pappe was open in his espousal of the Palestinian point of view, and, in my opinion, provided the most iconoclastic and brilliant of the Israeli interventions. For the others, in varying degree, Zionism was seen as a necessity for Jews. I was surprised, for instance, when Sternhell during the final session admitted that a grave injustice was committed against the Palestinians, and that the essence of Zionism was that it was a movement for conquest, then went on to say that it was a "necessary" conquest.

One of the most remarkable things about the Israelis, again except for Pappe, is the profound contradiction, bordering on schizophrenia, that informs their work. Benny Morris, for example, ten years ago wrote the first important Israeli work on the birth of the Palestinian refugee problem. Using Haganah and Zionist archives, he established beyond any reasonable doubt that there had been a forced exodus of Palestinians as a result of a specific policy of "transfer" which had been adopted and approved by Ben-Gurion. Morris's meticulous work showed that in district after district commanders had been ordered to drive out Palestinians, burn villages, systematically take over their homes and property. Yet strangely enough, by the end of the book, even the timid literalist Morris seems reluctant to draw the inevitable conclusions from his own evidence. Instead of saying outright that the Palestinians were, in fact, driven out, he says that they were partially driven out by Zionist forces, and partially "left" as a result of war. It is as if he was still enough of a Zionist to believe the ideological version—that Palestinians left of their own accord without Israeli eviction—rather then completely to accept his own evidence, which is that Zionist policy dictated Palestinian exodus. Similarly, in his book Sternhell admits that the Zionists never considered the Arabs as a problem, because if they did they would have openly admitted that the Zionist plan to establish a Jewish state could not have been realized without also getting rid of the Palestinians. But he still insisted during the conference in Paris that although it was morally wrong to expel Palestinians, it was necessary to do so.

Despite these discordances it is impressive that when pushed hard either by Pappe or by the Palestinians, both Morris and Sternhell appeared to hesitate. I take their changing views as symptomatic of a deeper change taking place inside Israel. The point here is that a significant change in the main lines of Zionist ideology cannot really occur within the hegemony of official politics, either Labor or Likud, but must take place outside that particular context, that is, where intellectuals are more free to ponder and reflect upon the unsettling realities of present-day Israel. The problem with other attempts by intellectuals on both sides to influence Netanyahu's policies, for instance, is that, as in the case of the Copenhagen group, they take place too close to governments who have a much narrower, much shorter range view of things. If the years since 1993 have shown anything it is that, no matter how enlightened or liberal, the official Zionist view of the conflict with the Palestinians is—and this is as true of left Zionists like the Meretz party or center left people like Shimon Peres—they are prepared to live with the schizophrenia I referred to above. Yes, we want peace with the Palestinians, but no there was nothing wrong with what we had to do in 1948. So far as real peace is concerned this basic contradiction is quite untenable, since it accepts the notion that Palestinians in their own land are secondary to Jews. Moreover, it also accepts the fundamental contradiction between Zionism and democracy (how can one have a democratic Jewish state and, as is now the case, one million non-Jews who are not equal in rights, landowning, or work to the Jews?). The great virtue of the new historians is that their work at least pushes the contradictions within Zionism to limits otherwise not apparent to most Israelis, and even to many Arabs.

It is certainly true that the great political importance today of the new Israeli historians is that they have confirmed what generations of

Palestinians, historians or otherwise, have been saying about what happened to us as a people at the hands of Israel. And of course they have done so as Israelis who in some measure speak for the conscience of their people and society. But here, speaking self-critically, I feel that as Arabs generally and Palestinians in particular we must also begin to explore our own histories, myths, and patriarchal ideas of the nation, something which, for obvious reasons, we have not so far done. During the Paris colloquium Palestinians, including myself, were speaking with a great sense of urgency about the present, since, in this present, the Palestinian *nakba* continues. Dispossession goes on, and the denial of our rights has taken new and more punishing forms. Nevertheless, as intellectuals and historians we have a duty to look at our history, the history of our leaderships and of our institutions, with a new critical eye. Is there something about those that can perhaps explain the difficulties as a people that we now find ourselves in? What about the conflict between the great familes or *hamulas,* the fact that our leaders have traditionally not been elected democratically, and the fact, equally disastrous, that we seem to reproduce corruption and mediocrity in each new generation? These are serious and even crucial matters, and they cannot either be left unanswered or postponed indefinitely under the guise of national defense and national unity. There is perhaps a start of critical self-awareness in Yezid Sayigh's new book on the history of Palestinian armed struggle, but we need more concretely political and critical works of that sort, works whose grasp of all the complexities and paradoxes of our history are not shied away from.

So far as I know, the works of Morris, Pappe, and Sternhell have not been translated into Arabic. This should be remedied forthwith. Just as important, I think, is the need for Arab intellectuals to interact directly with these historians by having them invited for discussions in Arab universities, cultural centers, and public fora. Similarly, I believe it is our duty as Palestinian and, yes, even Arab, intellectuals to engage Israeli academic and intellectual audiences by lecturing at Israeli centers, openly, courageously, uncompromisingly. What have years of blanket refusal to deal with Israel done for us? Nothing at all, except to weaken us and weaken our perception of our opponent. Politics since 1948 is now at an end, buried in the failures of the Oslo process of attempted separation between Israeli Jews and Palestinians. As part of the new politics I have been speaking about in these articles, a splendid opportunity presents itself in continued interaction with the new Israeli historians who, while a tiny minority, nevertheless represent a phenomenon of considerable importance. Their work, for instance, had a great influence on *Tekuma,* shown on Israeli television as a history of the state produced for its fiftieth year celebrations. They are greatly in demand in Israeli schools as lecturers, and their work has atttracted the attention of historians and others in both Europe and the United States. It seems anomalous, not to say retrograde, that the one place they have not been fully heard is the Arab world. We need to rid ourselves of our racial prejudices and ostrich-like attitudes, and make the effort to change the situation. The time has come.

Al-Khaleej, May 26, 1998
Al-Hayat, May 26, 1998
Al-Ahram Weekly, May 21, 1998

Chapter Forty-four

The Other Wilaya

M OST OF THE great liberation struggles of the twentieth century were unconventional in that they were ultimately won not
by armies but by flexible, mobile political forces who relied more on
initiative, creativity, and surprise than they did on holding fixed positions, the firepower of conventional armies, and the sheer weight of
formal institutions and traditional establishments. During the 1968
Tet offensive the North Vietnamese risked, and lost, many men in all
sorts of daring raids inside the South Vietnamese capital, Saigon,
which is where the American general command was also located. The
purpose of these attacks was to draw attention to American and
South Vietnamese vulnerability, and this was certain to be recorded on
U.S. television. In other words the point was to influence American
audiences in America, to provoke resistance and dissent in the United
States, to demonstrate the weakness of the American political cause
whose main purpose was to impose its will on Vietnam.

During the 1954–62 war of national liberation in Algeria, the FLN
divided Algeria into six districts, or *wilayas,* each of which had its
own command structure, field of operations, fighting forces. The seventh *wilaya* was metropolitan France itself. The idea was that given
French military superiority it would be crucial for the liberation movement to conduct political operations behind the French lines, that is,
to win as much opinion and gain as much support as possible from
French civilians. And this proved to be a significant factor in the Alger-

ian victory which, to repeat, was not military but political. Influential French public figures like Jean-Paul Sartre, Pierre Vidal-Naquet, Jean Genet, and others were won over to the Algerian side, even though as French citizens they were expected to oppose the insurrection defying French colonialism.

And in South Africa, it was a major component of ANC policy to make sure that white South Africans were directly involved in the struggle against apartheid. The policy was clear. Since it was necessary to convince whites that a victory for justice was not the beginning of a new form of injustice, whites were always promised that if they stayed, they would enjoy equality with blacks in the event of an ANC victory. Therefore it was a logical necessity for whites to be directly involved in the struggle against apartheid *as members* of the ANC. Without such a policy of actually getting white men and women to fight a policy that racially favored them, the ANC could not have won the battle inside South Africa. When the movement was at its lowest ebb inside the country, its leaders imprisoned, killed, or exiled, its cadres demoralized, the apartheid government's forces in complete control, the focus of struggle shifted to the international arena and to influential whites. Similarly during the civil rights movement of the sixties in the United States, it was because the black leadership actively sought out intellectuals and public figures for their support *as whites,* going on marches, signing petitions, and so forth, that it achieved some measure of success.

Such a strategy demands extraordinary discipline and detail. A friend of mine who went to North Vietnam in the late sixties told me that when he visited the NLF's political headquarters he was astonished to see an enormous map of the United States divided into each of the five hundred congressional districts. For each district the Vietnamese had drawn up a list of congressmen as well as ten issues—domestic as well as international—that each of the congressmen had voted on. In this way the Vietnamese were able to keep tabs on every voting record and each congressman who might be persuaded to change or reconfirm a vote bearing on the war in Vietnam. And this at a time when the United States was bombing the whole of Indochina on a scale that far outstripped anything in World War II or the Korean conflict.

The South Africans during the 1980s and early '90s organized a boycott of visiting academics, journalists, sports figures, entertainers, and businessmen, but lifted the boycott in individual cases. When I went there in May 1991 as a guest of the Universities of Cape Town and Witswatersvand I had to be passed by the boycott committee, who reasoned that my presence would enhance the anti-apartheid struggle. In other words, there was never a total, undiscriminating opposition to every person assumed to be on the other side, neither in Vietnam, the United States, Algeria, nor South Africa. A subtle system of trying to involve people from the opposing camp on the side of liberation was an essential component of the battle.

Our position as Palestinians and Arabs generally in opposition to the abuses of Zionism must deal with the other side with equal knowledge and discrimination. The idea that we should boycott all Israelis as a way of opposing normalization is, in my opinion, far too blunt an instrument and in the end both impractical and self-destructive. In the first place there is practically no conventional Arab military or political force that truly opposes Israel. Even the PLO, to say nothing of states like Jordan and Egypt, have signed peace agreements with Israel. We have no credible military option of any sort, with the exception of a valiant guerilla struggle waged by Hizballah in South Lebanon. Secondly, there are many Israelis who are quite disgusted with the policies of the Netanyahu government and who can be effective in helping us with the struggle against apartheid, which currently disfigures the Israeli and Palestinian landscape. Thirdly, we have foolishly confined our "acceptance" of Israeli forces on our side only to those connected in some way to the government and establishment. This is as true of the PLO currying favor with the Labor Party as it is of independent intellectuals who are happy to meet with people like Mossad operative David Kimche in Copenhagen.

This is to fundamentally misunderstand the nature of our battle for equal rights and for self-determination. As was the case in South Africa, we cannot be ambiguous about making it clear to Israelis that our fight does not envision driving them out of the Middle East altogether. We cannot turn the clock back to pre-1917 or pre-1948 days, but we can assure them, as Mandela regularly assured the white South African community, that we want them to stay and share the same land with us on an equal basis. There is therefore an appeal to be made to Israelis on the grounds of civil, human, and political rights for all the peoples of Palestine. What we oppose is that Israelis should dominate us and continue to occupy and deprive us of our land. If we were to say to democratic elements in the Israeli population that we want the same things, equal rights and a decent life in peace and security, we can then enlist each other's help in the struggle. But we must do this with attention to the exact nature of Israeli civil society, just as the Vietnamese did with the United States or the Algerians with France.

I emphasize this notion of acting and taking into consideration the existence of other *wilayas* as a way of criticizing the ineffective notion of an absolute demarcation between us and every single Israeli or Jew. This is why in a previous article I spoke about the need for Palestinian intellectuals to address Israeli students, professors, intellectuals, artists, and other independent people directly, rather than to say that we will never talk to or deal with any Israeli. In the absence of a real military option, in the absence even of a real front dividing Palestinians from Israelis (the two populations are mixed despite the dreams of Zionism to separate them), there is no way for Palestinians to gain their rights without actively involving Israelis in their struggle. A well-organized international campaign against the settlements; a major march, including Israelis and Palestinians, on one of the settlements; public meetings in which common goals are articulated: in such efforts it is we, not the Israelis, who must take the intiative, and we must do so at the same time that we speak openly and candidly about putting our own house in order. As a people we can no longer endure quietly the tyranny and corruption of the present Palestinian regime. Make no mistake about it, the Israeli government wants a weak, corrupt, and unpopular Palestinian Authority. It has no use for democracy or a dialogue between equals. This is why we must take our cause to the very heart of the Israeli *wilaya,* to speak both of peace and of democracy for two peoples. Until we can do this and do it without complexes about speaking with "the enemy," until we can make distinctions between the real forces of peace in Israel and the Labor Party, we will continue to drift and suffer the costs of occupation and undemocractic Palestinian rule. We must speak the truth to power.

Al-Hayat, June 4, 1998
Al-Ahram Weekly, June 4, 1998

Chapter Forty-five

Breaking the Deadlock: A Third Way

NOW THAT OSLO has clearly been proven the deeply flawed and unworkable "peace" process that it really was from the outset, Arabs, Israelis, and their various and sundry supporters need to think a great deal more, rather than less, clearly. A number of preliminary points seem to suggest themselves at the outset. "Peace" is now a discredited word, and is no guarantee that further harm and devastation will not ensue to the Palestinian people. The Roman historian Tacitus says of the Roman conquest of Britain that "they [the Roman army] created a desolation, and called it peace." The very same thing happened to us as a people, with the willing collaboration of the Palestinian Authority, the Arab states (with a few significant exceptions), Israel, and the United States.

Second, it is no use pretending that we can improve on the current deadlock, which in the Oslo framework as it stands is unbreakable, by returning to golden moments of the past. We can neither return to the days before the war of 1967, nor can we accept slogans of rejectionism that in effect send us back to the golden age of Islam. The only way to undo injustice, as Israel Shahak and Azmi Bishara have both said, is to create more justice, not to create new forms of vindictive injustice, i.e., "They have a Jewish state, we want an Islamic state." On the other hand, it seems equally fatuous to impose total blockades against *everything* Israeli (now in fashion in various progressive Arab circles) and to pretend that that is the really virtuous nationalist path. There are after all one million Palestinians who are Israeli citizens. Are they also to be boycotted, as they were during the 1950s? What about Israelis who support our struggle, but are neither members of the slippery Peace Now or of Meretz or of the "great" Israeli Labor Party led by Ehud Barak, widely presumed to be the murderer of Kamal Nasir and Abu Iyad? Should they—artists, free intellectuals, writers, students, academics, ordinary citizens—be boycotted *because* they are Israelis? Obviously to do so would be to pretend that the South African triumph over apartheid hadn't occurred, and to ignore all the many victories for justice that occurred because of nonviolent political cooperation between like-minded people on both sides of a highly contested and movable line. And we must cross the line of separation—which has been one of the main intentions of Oslo to erect—that maintains the current apartheid between Arab and Jew in historic Palestine. Go across, but do not *enforce* the line.

Third and perhaps most important: there is a great difference between political and intellectual behavior. The intellectual's role is to speak the truth, as plainly, directly, and as honestly as possible. No intellectual is supposed to worry about whether what is said embarrasses, pleases, or displeases people in power. Speaking the truth to power means additionally that the intellectual's constituency is neither a government nor a corporate or a career interest: only the truth unadorned. Political behavior principally relies upon considerations of interest—advancing a career, working with governments, maintaining one's position, etc. In the wake of Oslo it is therefore obvious that continuing the line propagated by the three parties to its provisions—Arab states, the Palestinian Authority, the Israeli government—is political behavior, not intellectual. Take for example the joint declaration made by Egyptian and Israeli men (mostly men) on behalf of the Cairo Peace Society and Peace Now. Remove all the high-sounding phrases about "peace" and not only do you get a ringing endorsement of Oslo, but also a return to the Sadat-Begin agreements of the late seventies, which are described as courageous and momentous. But what does this have to do with Palestinians whose territory and self-determination were removed from those courageous and momentous Camp David documents? Besides, Egypt and Israel are still at peace. What would people think if a few Israelis and Palestinians got together and issued ringing proclamations about Israeli-Syrian peace that were meant to "appeal" to those two governments? Crazy, most people would say. What entitles two parties, one who oppresses Palestinians and the other who has arrogated the right to speak for them, to proclaim peaceful goals in a conflict that is not between them? Moreover, the idea of appealing to this Israeli government, expecting solutions from it, is like asking Count Dracula to speak warmly about the virtues of vegetarianism.

In short, political behavior of this sort simply reinforces the hold of a dying succubus, Oslo, on the future of real, as opposed to fraudulent, American-Israeli-Palestinian peace. But neither, I must also say, is it intellectually responsible in effect to return to blanket boycotts of the sort now becoming the fashion in various Arab countries. As I said earlier, this sort of tactic (it is scarcely a strategy, any more than sticking one's head in the sand like an ostrich is a strategy) is regressive. Israel is neither South Africa, nor Algeria, nor Vietnam. Whether we like it or not, the Jews are not ordinary colonialists: as a people, they suffered the Holocaust, and they are the victims of anti-Semitism. But they cannot use those facts to initiate and continue the dispossession of another people that bears no responsibility for either of those prior facts. I have been saying for twenty years that we have no military option, and are not likely to have one anytime soon. And neither does Israel have a real military option. Despite their enormous power, Israelis have not succeeded in achieving either the acceptance or the security they crave. On the other hand, not all Israelis are the same, and whatever happens, we must learn to live with them in some form, preferably justly, rather than unjustly.

Therefore the *third* way avoids both the bankruptcy of Oslo and the retrograde policies of total boycotts. It must begin in terms of the idea of citizenship, not nationalism, since the notion of separation (Oslo) and of triumphalist unilateral theocratic nationalism, whether Jewish or Muslim, simply does not deal with the realities before us. Therefore a concept of citizenship, whereby every individual has the same citizen's rights, based not on race or religion, but on equal justice for each person guaranteed by a constitution, must replace all our outmoded notions of how Palestine will be cleansed of our enemies. Ethnic cleansing is ethnic cleansing whether it is done by Serbians, Zionists, or Hamas. What Azmi Bishara and several Israeli Jews like

Ilan Pappe are now trying to strengthen is a position and a politics by which Jews and those Palestinians already inside the Jewish state have the same rights; there is no reason why the same principle should not apply on the occupied territories, where Palestinians and Israeli Jews live side by side, together, but with only one people, Israeli Jews, now dominating the other. So the choice is either apartheid or justice and citizenship. We must recognize the realities of the Holocaust not as a blank check for Israelis to abuse us, but as a sign of our humanity, our ability to understand history, our requirement that *our* suffering be mutually acknowledged. And we must also recognize that Israel is a dynamic society containing many currents—not all of them Likud, Labor, and religious. We must deal with those who recognize our rights. We should be willing as Palestinians to go to speak to Palestinians first, but to Israelis too, and we should tell our truths, not the stupid compromises of the sort that the PLO and PA have traded in, which in effect is the apartheid of Oslo.

The real issue is intellectual truth and the need to combat any sort of apartheid and racial discrimination. There is now a creeping, nasty wave of anti-Semitism and hypocritical righteousness insinuating itself into our political thought and rhetoric. One thing must be clear: we are not fighting the injustices of Zionism in order to replace them with an inviduous nationalism (religious or civil) that decrees that Arabs in Palestine are more equal than others. The history of the modern Arab world—with all its political failures, its human rights abuses, its stunning military incompetences, its decreasing production, the fact that alone of all modern peoples we have receded in democratic and technological and scientific development—is disfigured by a whole series of outmoded and discredited ideas, of which the notion that the Jews never suffered and that the Holocaust is an obfuscatory confection created by the elders of Zion is one that is acquiring far too much currency. Why do we expect the world to believe our sufferings as Arabs if (a) we cannot recognize the sufferings of others, even of our oppressors, and (b) we cannot deal with facts that nullify the simplistic ideas of the sort propagated by *bien-pensants* intellectuals who refuse to see the relationshp between the Holocaust and Israel?

But to support the efforts of Roger Garaudy and his Holocaust-denying friends in the name of "freedom of opinion" is a silly ruse that discredits us more than we already are discredited in the world's eyes for our incompetence, our failure to fight a decent battle, our radical misunderstanding of history and the world we live in. Why don't we fight harder for freedom of opinions in our own societies, a freedom, no one needs to be told, that scarcely exists? When I mentioned the Holocaust in an article I wrote last November, I received more stupid vilification than I ever thought possible. One famous intellectual even accused me of trying to gain a certificate of good behavior from the Zionist lobby. Of course I support Garaudy's right to say what he pleases and I oppose the wretched *loi Gayssot* against "historical falsification" under which he was prosecuted and condemned. But I also think that what he says is trivial and irresponsible, and when we endorse it it allies us necessarily with Le Pen and all the retrograde right-wing fascist elements in French society.

Our battle is for democracy and equal rights, for a secular commonwealth or state in which all the members are equal *citizens,* in which the concept underlying our goal is a secular notion of citizenship and belonging, not some mythological essence or an idea that derives its authority from the remote past, whether that past is Christian, Jewish, or Muslim. The genius of Arab civilization at its height in, say, Andalusia was its multicultural, multireligious, and multiethnic diversity. That is the ideal that should be moving our efforts now, in the wake of a dead and embalmed Oslo and an equally dead rejectionism. The letter killeth, but the spirit giveth life, as the Bible says.

In the meantime we should concentrate our resistance on combatting Israeli settlement (as described in an article I wrote a few weeks ago) with nonviolent mass demonstrations that impede land confiscation, on creating stable and democratic civil institutions (hospitals and clinics, schools and universities, now in a horrendous decline, and work projects that will improve our infrastructure), and on fully confronting the apartheid provisions inherent in Zionism. There are numerous prophecies of an impending explosion due to the stalemate. Even if they turn out to be true, we must plan constructively for our future, since neither improvisation nor violence is likely to guarantee the creation and consolidation of democratic institutions.

Al-Hayat, June 30, 1998
The Marxist, November/December 1998

Chapter Forty-six

The Final Stage

FOR REASONS THAT elude me, there continues to be some hope on the part of Arab governments that American impatience with Israel will soon reach the breaking point, perhaps provoking a dramatic new initiative, perhaps finally galvanizing American power into actively opposing Netanyahu's tactics. This, alas, is seriously to misunderstand what is currently taking place both in Israel and the United States, where the likelihood of any qualitative change of the sort dreamed of by Arab leaders is very small indeed. Clinton is opposed by a Congress that is solidly pro-Likud for many domestic reasons. There is an Israeli lobby, but the fact is that the Republican Party in alliance with the Christian right-wing, plus conservative foundations and business groups, and an uneducated, brainwashed public, see in Israel not only a stubborn ally forcing its intransigence on the entire world but also an international partner which the United States should emulate, doing what Israel does in thumbing its nose at the very notion of an international community. And all this has the advantage of being a slap in the face of Bill Clinton, whose corrupt, problem-ridden administration is seen by many Americans as too enmeshed in the schemes of the UN and the international community, thereby curtailing American sovereignty and its capacity for using its power unilaterally. The negative Clinton response to the recent meeting on war crimes in Rome was, I believe, designed to convince his domestic opponents that at the right time and for the right cause he was capable of acting like Israel, defying world opinion in showing that his country's perceived interests overrode even the Nuremberg principles first articulated by the United States after World War II.

At the present moment the Palestinian question has receded so dramatically in the public mind as to be nonexistent. There are occasional references to the 13 percent of West Bank territory proposed by the United States and accepted by the Palestinian leadership, but that is always hedged with discussions of Palestinian terrorism and the PLO covenant, thereby denuding the issue of land of any serious content. To make matters worse there is an almost total absence of any Palestinian information effort in the United States or in Western Europe. Gone are the academics, the students, the organizations that used to bear a message about dispossession and injustice: an immense void swallows what little is said or done on behalf of a people that has suffered the loss of its land and identity over the past century. To an outsider like myself, what is going on inside the Arab world is no less discouraging. Leaders visit each other, talk about change and important meetings, more meetings are held, more trips taken—and nothing much changes. The fact is that the Arab world is totally unmobilized, particularly inside Palestine, where the losses are the greatest, the offenses against ordinary everyday people the most egregious, and the Israeli plan most close to final realization. I understand that in countries like Egypt and Lebanon, for example, there is a serious intellectual attempt to confront the tragedy of the Palestinian people in discussions about positions that ought to be taken, petitions that should be signed, and so forth, but very little of this has any bearing at all on what Israeli troops and settlers do, which is nothing less than a concerted attempt at ethnic cleansing. The main difference between Bosnia and Palestine is that ethnic cleansing in the former took place in the form of dramatic massacres and slaughters which caught the world's attention, whereas in Palestine what is taking place is a drop by drop tactic in which one or two houses are demolished daily, a few acres are taken here and there every day, a few people are forced to leave. No one pays much attention, least of all other Palestinians, who live, say, in Ramallah, for whom the destruction of the main road out of Husan (a tiny village just west of Bethlehem) by the settlers of Efrat is scarcely perceptible or noticed.

In the meantime the prosperous Palestinian communities in London and Amman go about their daily business oblivious to what is happening to the dwindling remains of their original homeland. Huge weddings take place everyday in the luxury hotels of those capitals, young people drive their BMWs and Honda motorcycles noisily up and down the hills of Abdoun and the leafy boulevards of Holland Park, and the impression is that of a long daydream, with not much thought given either to the past or the future. Filled with pleasant interludes, school years at Harvard or Georgetown, vacations in Gstaad and Cannes, careers in advertising, marketing, investment, or construction, the privileged generation of Palestinian—and indeed Arab—youth, whose parents made their fortunes in the easy days of the Gulf oil and construction boom, go about their lives in a never-never land of tax-free spending that has made of it a class unique in the history of the twentieth century for its wastefulness and unproductivity. And it is this class that is theoretically entrusted with the future of our struggle against a ruthless and single-minded foe.

I recall that about twenty-five years ago in reviewing a book about pre-1948 Zionist settlement and colonization in Palestine I drew attention to a remark made by Chaim Weizmann to the effect that this movement was beginning small, acquiring bits of land here and there, "another acre, another goat." The idea was that such a concentrated project, however modest, never lost sight of the final goal, which was to gain all of Palestine as a Jewish state. Until 1948, Zionists controlled a little less than 7 percent of the land of Palestine. After 1948, they took over everything but the West Bank and Gaza Strip. After 1967 they conquered the rest of historic Palestine. With the Oslo agreements they consolidated their hold on the land by ceding approximately 3 percent of the West Bank (which itself constitutes only 22 percent of the whole of Palestine) to the Palestinian Authority, in return for which the Authority won the right to administer Palestinian life without territorial sovereignty. Nor is this all. With the goal of eliminating the Palestinian presence on most of the West Bank not covered by Oslo, Israel is doing two things: it is expropriating land for use by Israeli settlers and the military, and it is destroying houses. An article that appeared in the *Palestine Report* of July 15 by Muna Hamza-Muhaisen is quite bleak in its findings. I quote her: "Since the signing of the Oslo accords in 1993, between September 1993 and March 1998, 629 Palestinian homes were demolished by Israeli bulldozers; 535 in the West Bank and 94 in Jerusalem. Of the 629 destroyed homes, 268 were demolished by the Labor Government and the remaining 361 were demolished by the Likud. Under the Netanyahu government and in 1997 alone, some 233 homes were demolished. In the first quarter of 1998, a total of 57 Palestinian homes and, in the week of June 21, 1998 alone, a total of 30 homes were demolished. Today more than 1,800 house demolition orders still remain to be carried out, threatening to leave another 10,000 people homeless."

The absolute, relentless continuity between Weizmann's simple remark about the acre and the goat, made over seventy-five years ago, and what is taking place today is chilling. There has been no modification in the essential Zionist vision which condemns the Palestinian to a more precarious, less perceptible existence day by day. It is plainly there for everyone, Arab and Jew alike, to witness. No secret is made of this plan, no palliative or sugar-coating seems to be required. We are taking the land detail by detail, inch by inch, house by house. Hamza-Muhaisen concludes: "By achieving all this, Israel will succeed in isolating the Palestinian population in three or four disconnected Bantustans, a plan known in Israel as Allon Plus. This way, even if Palestinian President Yasir Arafat declares a Palestinian state in May 1999, as he is expected to, Israel would have created a new reality on the ground that would make it impossible for such a state to be territorially connected."

Unintentionally perhaps, Hamza-Muhaisen dramatizes the differences between Israeli action and Palestinian reaction: they take the land, we declare a state. As Haidar Abdel-Shafi put it in a recent interview: What is the point of declaring a state yet again, since we already declared one in Algeria in 1988? How many times does one declare a nonexistent state, and what is achieved by such repetitions? Like Dr. Abdel-Shafi I am mystified by this odd, not to say irrelevant, response to a moment of the most far-reaching emergency. Israel is taking the land systematically and we are more or less looking on, doing no more than saying "They haven't really taken it, we consider it our state." The crying shame is that this has been our strategy from the beginning. Faced with a clear, concrete, practical, systematic activity—land expropriation—for one hundred years we have been unable, or power-less, or unwilling to do anything that might reverse the process. I have seen this dialectic in action all of my life, first when I was a boy in Palestine, then most recently a few weeks ago, as I watched Israeli troops destroy the tents of Jahhalin Bedu and the village lands of farmers outside Hebron and Bethlehem. I stood and argued with the soldiers. I tried to dissuade them. I challenged them. I reminded them that sixty years ago their land as Jews was taken from them by a "superior" people, the Germans. But the fact was that I was powerless, except to watch and record only a fraction of what I saw on film. They had the bulldozers and the machine guns. I had the words and pic-tures, and nothing else.

We are an unmobilized people. We are unled. We are unmotivated. We have not been able to concentrate our minds and hearts on the problem, which is nothing less than the robbery of our land. In the past few weeks a number of Israeli organizations against house demo-litions have been formed. They have demonstrations. They protest. But there seems to be very little on the Palestinian side. It is as if we have been anesthetized as a people, unable to move, unable to act. They take the land, and we watch or, more probably, we don't even watch. We assume it is happening to someone else; we can look away, and go about our business. What is missing is a sense of public urgency embodied in mobilized Palestinians inside Palestine, in Eu-rope, North America, in the Arab world who decide that the time has come to face the Israeli threat where it is occurring, on the land of Palestine. Even the figures of demolitions and land expropriation come from Israelis. The best report on Israeli settlement activity is not by Palestinians: it comes from an American group headed by Geoffrey Aronson, who is himself Jewish.

I appeal to my readers for help. Why is it that when it concerns the open theft of our last remaining territorial possessions we seem utterly confounded by what is taking place? Why cannot we mobilize to stand in front of Israeli troops, why cannot we organize the Pales-tinian workers who are actually building the settlements to deter them from doing that work that so harms their people, why cannot our leadership get itself out from its offices and VIP cars and onto the fields and orchards of Palestine, protecting homes with their bodies,

resisting Israeli soldiers as they confiscate our land? Why this mania
for bureaucracy, for bodyguards, for cellular phones, for expensive
shopping expeditions, for fruitless, stupid negotiations that sap our
strength and our will and leave us utterly impotent as we witness our
land disappearing before us? I cannot understand our inaction and the
spineless cowardice of our leaders who prefer to engage in the harassment and abuse of their own people rather than in safeguarding their
nation and its territory. I cannot understand the paralysis of Palestinian and other Arab intellectuals for whom theorizing about the best
strategy is a higher priority than actually going to Palestine (this is
easily done by Egyptians and Jordanians whose countries are at peace
with Israel) to stand with a Palestinian family or village defying the
Israeli robbers. I cannot understand why after one hundred years we
cannot seem to focus on what is important and drop all the other nonsense. I appeal to better-informed readers for assistance. I can neither
guess at the answers nor can I provide explanations. I only know that
very little will be left of the land of Palestine by the time we wake up.
And then we will probably ask ourselves, what happened? Why did we
let the land be taken before our eyes for one century, and why did
we do nothing? This is the final, terminal stage, and it is here. Where
are we?

Al-Hayat, July 29, 1998
Al-Ahram Weekly, July 23, 1998

Chapter Forty-seven

The End of the
Interim Arrangements

As I write these lines in October 1998, the Palestinian, Israeli, and American leaders—all of them weakened by domestic crises—have just spent several days closeted together in the Wye Plantation a few miles from Washington with the announced intention of bringing the interim agreements first announced from Oslo to some sort of conclusion. This was necessary before May of next year, since that is the date when the scheduled discussions on the final settlement must take place. Bill Clinton announced at the outset that he wanted an agreement out of the Wye meetings sooner rather than later and, despite the obvious differences between Palestinians and Israelis, he certainly got it, public ceremony and all, at least enough of an agreement to show that he is still "in charge" of foreign affairs. In other words from the U.S. point of view one main requirement of these meetings is that Clinton would appear once again to be "presidential," without in any way compromising or showing himself to be less pro-Israel than he has been hitherto. The mild demurral at the end about releasing Jonathan Pollard, which was a brazen ploy by Benjamin Netanyahu to scupper the talks and get something for nothing—the idea that he wants Pollard back after the spy stole enormous amounts of U.S. intelligence including, among other things, a map of the PLO's Tunis headquarters where a few weeks later Abu Jihad was assassinated and sixty Arabs lost their lives, is by any standard a stunning piece of arrogance—left Clinton looking slightly more dignified than otherwise. My guess is that his own intelligence people put a stop to the idea, but there's no guarantee that Pollard won't be released in a short while. Clinton, after all, is Clinton.

The U.S. press as usual reported the proceedings with a flagrant disregard of the facts. No one bothered to point out, to take one example, that the 40 percent of the West Bank's surface supposedly being given to Arafat's corrupt Authority was broken down into bits and pieces that tell a very different story, all of it subject to Israel's choice of date and location of the land to be partially vacated. No settlements and no bypassing roads are to be given up: on the contrary Israel has asked the United States for an additional $1.3 billion for the redeployments. The West Bank is now divided into three areas—A, which is entirely Palestinian-run except for security, water, and exits and entrances; Area B, jointly patrolled by Palestinian and Israeli soldiers, with security, water, building permits, exits, and entrances entirely controlled by Israel; Area C, which is completely Israeli. Before Wye, these amounted respectively to 2.8 percent, 24 percent, and 72 percent of the land area. Wye gave the Palestinians an additional 1 percent from Area C, and 14.2 percent from Area B, thus putting about 18.2 percent under full Palestinian Authority control, again with the same exclusions and provisos. In addition, Israel will transfer about 13 percent more from Area C to Area B, where—to repeat—Israel really controls things, including of course the 3 percent of Judean desert land designated as a nature preserve (whatever that is supposed to mean). In effect then, the Palestinians got (if that is the right word) a total of 18.2 percent of the West Bank added to Area A, the rest to Area B. In no case did the Palestinians acquire sovereignty, control over exits and entrances, water, and overall security. In addition, as a glance at the map shows, the Palestinian areas are for the most part non-contiguous and allow no free passage between them. Of course Jerusalem remains off limits to residents of Gaza and the West Bank.

Most of the rest of the "Wye River Memorandum" is taken up with security arrangements which in effect commit the Palestinian Authority to Israel's security, not the other way round. Palestinian lives and livelihoods are not worth so much as a sentence in the memorandum's extremely dodgy language. In addition, the CIA is to play an active role in adjudicating security issues such as extradition, combatting the "terrorist" infrastructure, incitement, and the like. Israel in the meantime can do what it likes, including building more settlements, taking more land, adding to Jerusalem's area, and helping itself to all the West Bank water it wants. The fate of Palestinian human rights looks grim indeed, subject to dictatorial control by an already despotic Arafat backed up by the CIA and Israel. But the real problem with all the land transfer arrangements is not only that it gives Israel a unilateral say over which land is to be transferred: it also allows Israel a generous number of "phases" by which the transfer is to be completed, without any mechanism to enforce delays or delinquencies. Given its record since the Oslo agreements were first signed, with the free-passage provisions never implemented, no one ought to be sanguine that re-deployments of the Israeli army will take place according to schedule, especially with the egregious Ariel Sharon in charge.

The changes in the National Covenant that Israel has demanded will require a hasty convening of the group which Clinton, for reasons that do him no credit, has chosen to address. The Palestinian airport and the Gaza seaport were left suitably vague, though there was a pretty mean Israeli insistence that even Arafat's plane be searched by them before takeoff and after landing. Once again, security at the putative port and airport are to be in Israeli hands. All in all then a dishearteningly mean-spirited, niggling document without too much chance of real enforcement (technically, one Palestinian grenade will put off Israeli deployment for months) and no chance at all to change the relationship between the two sides. The Israelis will continue to be the masters, Palestinians—pardon the expression—the abject niggers.

What now? A number of things propose themselves. In the first place the Palestinian leadership should be roundly censured by as many people as possible for so disgracefully supine a negotiating performance. Arafat and company have now completely delivered themselves to the combined Israeli and U.S. intelligence apparatus, thereby putting an end to anything even resembling a democratic and independent Palestinian national life. And this, by the way, has been sacrificed to the survival of Arafat and his coterie of advisers, hangers-on, and security chiefs, for whom as a group the idea of Palestinian civil society with an independent judiciary and legislative body is a silly inconvenience to be disposed of like the land they have given up with scarcely a look back. From now on any resistance to Israeli colonization will be dealt with summarily; opponents of what Arafat and his men are doing will be considered "haters of peace." Second, the notion that thousands of Palestinian prisoners are being left to die in Israeli jails (Netanyahu gave up 750 of the 3,000–5,000 reportedly still held) is a scandal for which Arafat should personally be held responsible. Third, the deferral of later deployments, later consideration of safe passage for Palestinians, later permits for industrial parks, and the like is also scandalous. Who can believe that the Palestinian Authority has either the will or the mechanism or the leverage to press these matters?

In sum, Arafat and his people have done the usual thing: given up without very much of a struggle and certainly without the slightest trace of a strategic or moral vision. Yes they will argue that something like Wye is better than nothing. But is it? In effect Palestinians are now tied into security arrangements for Israel that continue to devalue and debase Palestinian life, to say nothing of Palestinian aspirations, which are not even mentioned. The catastrophe of 1948 has been erased, as have the conquests of 1967 and 1982. Refugees will remain refugees, and Palestinians will continue to have Israeli soldiers as their keepers. The devil only knows what the horrendous settlers are about to let loose on the largely unprotected and exposed citizens of the West Bank and Gaza. Certainly Arafat will do nothing for them, except urge them over and over to wait for "our" state, in the meantime robbing them blind, reinforcing corruption, buying off each and every potential opponent, jailing, torturing, and killing anyone who stands up to him.

An absolute imperative now is to urge Palestinians to try to deter people from attending and participating in that Council meeting which is supposed to change, cancel, or fiddle with the Charter. It's a document I don't much care for, but the idea that people should be rounded up (like the usual suspects) just to do Israel's bidding with not a whit of a change in all of Israel's highly discriminatory laws against Palestinians strikes me as totally preposterous. The only real course for Palestinians today is to urge their representatives to vote with their feet, not to attend this ludicrously unrepresentative Council meeting, and to begin once again to plan for a new Council, one whose members are neither appointed by nor beholden to Arafat. The time grows less and less before we allow this ruinously incompetent and corrupt leadership to sell us out totally, and the sooner we take steps to organize a major Palestinian meeting to take place outside the Arab world the better. The midnight hour has already struck.

Al-Hayat, November 6, 1998

Chapter Forty-eight

Incitement

B ILL CLINTON'S TWO-DAY visit to Gaza, Bethlehem, and Israel was intended to save the peace process and to make him look more noble to his impeachers. It's too early to tell about the second mission, though I must say that his speech to the Palestinians for the first time expressed a humane sympathy for what they have endured; the first was a dismal failure, despite the media hype (more misleading than usual) and the super-ignorant gushing by media commentators. As soon as Clinton arrived, Benjamin Netanyahu announced that there would be no further Israeli army troop re-deployment as stipulated by the Wye River Plantation accords of last October. Since in any event Israel was to re-deploy from a minuscule amount of land (5 percent from Israeli-controlled Area C to jointly controlled Area B, which is under Israeli security anyway), the snub was just that, designed to humiliate both the Palestinians and Clinton. The "unrest" reported in the occupied territories for the past several weeks was provoked both by Israeli cynicism in releasing only about one hundred car thieves and common criminals (the agreement having been that 750 political prisoners would be freed) and by Palestinian anger at Arafat's limitless appetite for concessions and a careless, not to say heedless, negotiating style. (Several members of his team in the past weeks have threatened to resign for that reason). Far from peace being assured, therefore, the combination of Netanyahu's arrogance, Clinton's vulnerability, and Arafat's by now barely existent support wasn't alleviated by the picturesque, hokey ceremonies patched together by the Americans and Palestinians, bagpipes, flower maidens, Mrs. Arafat, and all.

What puzzles me is how many times Arafat can bring himself and some of his people to go through the motions of repealing the notorious Charter just to satisfy Israeli demands. There was of course no real PNC meeting, since in effect that body lost its legitimacy and independence when Arafat returned to Gaza in 1994. He brought a bunch of people together in 1996 to change the Charter, but this time only made a perfunctory effort to round up officials, businessmen, and some hangers-on for the great occasion. I was invited (by mistake) to attend when a fax from the Arafat-run Palestinian Commercial Services Company came to my office asking me to present myself at Amman Airport at a given time, then to link up with a special charter flight to Gaza, to attend the meeting, then to come back by charter the same evening. I had resigned my membership in 1991. So much for the idea of a legitimate quorum and roll-call. At the same time I was also invited to a meeting of the opposition led by George Habash and Naief Hawatmeh in Damascus; through the ever-efficient rumor mills (one of the few things that still work in Palestinian politics) it was widely reported that I was in attendance.

The low comedy of the Gaza proceedings—which elicited a rapturously ill-informed piece by the *Times*'s new Israel correspondent, Deborah Sontag, about how much nicer and more democratic life is for Palestinians than for other Arabs—was belied by what was going on outside. In the first place, the expropriation of Arab land through Israeli colonization continues at a furious pace as old settlements grow, new ones expand rapidly. About 40 percent of Gaza is held by settlers and the Strip itself is surrounded on three sides by an Israeli electronic fence (side four is the Israeli-patrolled sea). Clinton seems not to have noticed how his security was assured. According to the authoritative Washington-based *Report on Israeli Settlement,* "diplomacy fails to address Israel's transformation of the occupied territories"; thus Israel's settlement policy all through the peace process "is well on its way toward achieving an objective pursued by a succession of Israeli leaders during the last three decades: to obstruct the creation of an independent, truly sovereign Palestinian political entity west of the Jordan River. Israel's objective, on the face of it, is the antithesis of popular notions about the goal of the negotiations begun at Oslo in 1993" (Sept./Oct. 1988). Each time one of the much touted summits occurs, the Palestinians fail to curtail Israeli settlement drives. Wye was no exception, as Lamis Andoni shows in *Middle East International* (December 11, 1998), since there the negotiators failed to grasp that "Israel only agreed not to carry out the expansion of settlements until all current construction had been completed, which means that 'contiguous areas' [accepted by the Palestinians] could end up including hundreds and hundreds of acres" (p. 11). A chilling account of how one such settlement, Efrat, near Bethlehem, is expanding and choking off every Arab village in its vicinity is found in *Ha'aretz* November 27; I filmed there last February, but villages like Wad Rahal and Khadr have since lost most of their land.

Second, the economics of peace have driven Palestinians into poverty, as Sara Roy shows in an impressive new study just published by the Emirates Center for Strategic Studies, "The Palestinian Economy and the Oslo Process: Decline and Fragmentation." At all levels of society, productivity is down, markets have shrunk, there is greater dependency on Israel. Unemployment is now at an all-time high, while Arafat's Authority, with its fourteen or so security services (like Topsy, they keep growing), its bloated bureaucracy, its thousands of informers and enforcers is the largest, and the least productive, employer. Each ministry now employs hundreds of managers and directors who do absolutely nothing except draw down handsome salaries. The World Bank figure for Arafat's labor force is one hundred twenty thousand people which, multiplied by the number of dependents, accounts for almost half the Palestinian residents of the West Bank and Gaza directly in thrall to Arafat. But discontent rages anyway. Thousands of refugees demonstrated in Syria and Lebanon. Four Palestinians were wounded by Israeli forces when the latter made a group of Palestinian laborers crawl on the ground. And the Palestinian rock-throwing and Israeli shooting with "rubber-bullets" continue. Still, Netanyahu rants on about incitement when a Palestinian holds up a sign demanding free access to holy sites in Jerusalem, which is off-limits to West Bank and Gaza Palestinians (as described by *Ha'aretz*, December 14).

The main burden of the Wye accords therefore was neither to give

Palestinians more freedom nor to allow the United States and Israel to "help" Palestinian independence, but quite the contrary: with the Authority's help, to increase the restrictions and conditions under which Palestinians live so that they remain docile and taken care of in the best colonial manner. A perfect symbolic example of this is the promulgation on November 19 of a presidential decree by Arafat entitled "to strengthen national unity and forbid incitement." Obviously the result of Netanyahu's remorseless obsession with Israeli security (and Arafat's reciprocal neglect of Palestinian security) the decree states that its legal references and precedents derive among other sources from "the Palestinian penal code number 74 for 1936 and its amendments." For the uninitiated, this code is nothing less than the Emergency Defense Regulations issued by the British Mandatory Authority in 1936 as a way of punishing Palestinian resistance; it was then adopted by the Israelis after 1948 for the same purpose. And now Mr. Arafat uses it to threaten his own people. For what? To interdict incitement to violence, insults, racism. The decree also forbids "illegal organizations" as well as "undermining the quality of life, agitating the masses to bring about change by illegal methods of force, incitement to civil strife, incitement to violate agreements made between the PLO and Arab and foreign countries." To implement this remarkable new law there will be a committee made up equally of Palestinians, Israelis, and (the number varies according to reports) one or more Americans who might or might not be members of the CIA. Their mandate is nothing less than every utterance—written, spoken, printed, or broadcast—made by Palestinians and (as a West Bank friend explained it to me, his voice alternately sad and cheerful) school textbooks, newspapers, and magazines.

This bizarre document has yet to be noted by the U.S., Arab, or European media, who are falling all over each other in prophesying the advent of Palestinian statehood. Never mind of course the total absence of territorial contiguity for areas of Palestinian self-rule. Never mind that Arafat has refused to ratify either the constitution or the basic law proposed by his Legislative Council. Never mind that thanks to U.S. and Israeli pressure Palestinian life is governed by state security courts which forbid the presence of witnesses, defense lawyers, or audience. Never mind that the large sums of money pledged by European and American donors are still controlled by Arafat, who answers and is accountable to no one, despite widespread evidence of massive corruption. But that Israel and the United States should require Palestinians to submit fawningly to a law against incitement—with a Stalinist-type committee to decide unilaterally what is or is not incitement—this is scarcely a forward step in the search for peace or Palestinian self-determination. Is it any wonder then that Palestinians are less than overwhelmed by Clinton's "historic" Gaza visit, or that they recognize in U.S. prescriptions for "peace" the hand of the President's advisers, most of whom, like Dennis Ross, are alumni of the Israeli lobby?

Al-Ahram Weekly, December 31, 1998

Chapter Forty-nine

West Bank Diary

I WAS LAST IN Palestine during February and March of 1998, making my BBC film, *In Search of Palestine,* which, alas, after having been shown on BBC 2 in May and then on BBC-World in late June has more or less disappeared. Although it has been screened here and there on college campuses, in people's homes, in one or two public places in Palestine and Israel, the BBC was almost totally unsuccessful in getting it on U.S. television, which is where it might have done something to rectify the ludicrously misleading and even stupid picture most Americans now have of the Palestinian people and "the peace process." [It was finally shown once, on July 5, 1999, on WNYC.] As far as I know, BBC marketing was scarcely more successful with European and Arab television services. What we were especially conscious of as we filmed in places like Hebron, Bethlehem, and Jerusalem was the mostly unpleasant quality of everyday life for the average Palestinian, whose capacity to earn money or travel has been severely curtailed since Oslo, whose land and homes are constantly threatened or seized, and whose life under Chairman Arafat's dreadful Authority (buttressed by CIA and Mossad support) has become a nightmare. At least it had been possible to render in images the tiny bit of territory—about 3 percent—that the Authority controlled, controlled, that is, except for exits and entrances, water resources, and security, all of which Israel still holds on to. The film's last scene put things very starkly—land was being expropriated on a daily basis, with no one,

certainly no one official, able to stop the dreaded Israeli bulldozers
with troops who descend on unprotected villagers and immediately
begin their destructive, ruthlessly efficient work. Palestinian workers,
believe it or not, do the actual work of construction, the most terrible
irony of all, their leaders unwilling (for reasons I can't understand) to
prevent this by offering them alternative employment. The general
impoverishment of Palestinian political and economic life is nowhere
more cruel and evident.

This time—for the eight days I was there in mid-November—the
Wye River Plantation agreement was still fresh in memory, but just as
quickly dismissed by everyone I spoke to. I had the impression that
somewhere off the main stage there were teams of Israeli and Palestinian researchers making sense of the agreement (there is now an amazing network of institutes and think tanks throughout the Palestinian
territories, most of them funded by the Europeans, singly or in
groups, many of which work together with Israeli counterparts. Since
I am neither a professional expert, nor a policy-maker, nor a journalist, nor a candidate for a job, I became aware of this rather sizable
enterprise, which employs many Ph.D.'s, out of my rearview mirror,
so to speak). Undoubtedly a great deal is invested in this peace agreement process. Preparations were already under way for the opening
of the Gaza airport—Shyam Bhatia, the *Guardian* correspondent,
almost persuaded me to go down to Gaza just to see the place, into
which over $65 million had already been poured, a staggering con-
trast with the hundreds of thousands of poor refugees eking out a
miserable living all through the Strip—and for the upcoming meeting
of the National Council which is supposed to be addressed by Bill
Clinton while it tears up or modifies the legendary Covenant for the
fourth time.

Repetition is a constant theme wherever I go. The same questions
are asked. The same things are said (e.g., Arafat's promise to declare a
state on May 4, 1999; a state was already declared in 1988). The
fraudulent National Council was to be summmoned again to do Arafat's bidding "democratically." And still the Israeli settlers are everywhere to be found, more villages threatened, more roads built, more
lands taken. Just a few days after my arrival Ariel Sharon urged the
settlers to take as many hills as possible, as soon as possible. The very

next morning, driving on the West Bank, my Jerusalem taxi driver pointed out a new settlement, half a dozen caravans parked on a hill just outside the city. Abu Mazen, one of Arafat's numerous number twos, says that Ariel Sharon is no longer the same man who invaded Lebanon, laid siege to Beirut for two months, bombed the city indiscriminately in 1982, was responsible for Sabra and Shatila, is the settlers' main backer. I was surprised that Abu Mazen didn't also defend General Pinochet on the same grounds.

I was in Palestine at the invitation of Bir Zeit University, which was holding a conference on the subject of landscape—its history, representation, geography, and the contests it provoked—in Palestine. Bir Zeit is about ten kilometers away from Ramallah, the largest West Bank city, and also the capital and seat of government for the Palestine Authority. Though privately owned, Bir Zeit is the closest thing to a national Palestinian university—secular, liberal, open, despite the enormous financial and political problems of maintaining such a place at a difficult time. As for the conference itself, by any standards, it was a remarkable affair. For one, local participants as well as a few invited foreign guests in the fields of literature, art history, geography, history, and archaeology produced one paper after another on engrossing topics such as representations of Palestine and ideology, patterns of settlements by different conquerors, landscape and memory, travelers' accounts, geographical discourse, and archaeological dispute. For another, there was an astonishingly high number of people in attendance (three hundred to four hundred people for sessions that ran from 9 A.M. till 7 P.M. with only an hour for lunch), and the level of discussion was very high. And this while all around us on the West Bank the unending battles between Israeli settlers and Palestinian residents were taking place, truly a living laboratory demonstration of the conflict over the landscape's form and destiny.

Azmi Bishara, the charismatic Palestinian Knesset member, had set up a public meeting for me in Nazareth where I was to encounter Palestinian Israelis for the first time in such a forum. A friend, Mouin Rabbani, who works in a twinning venture with Dutch and Palestinian Municipal Councils, drove me from the last lunch of the Bir Zeit landscape conference to Nazareth via Nablus, Jenin, and the Israeli town of Afula, a three-hour drive. Just outside Nablus we picked up a young hitchhiker who was going to Zabbabdeh, a Christian village about ten kilometers from Jenin in the northern West Bank. During our conversation it transpired that our passenger was a croupier-in-training at the new Palestinian casino just opened in Jericho. "Do you travel this way every day?" we asked him, the inconvenience and length of the route uppermost in our minds. "No, just until the training is over. As it is I only have to be there for a few hours a day while the casino runs on a part-time schedule. Once our training is over and the casino runs twenty-four hours a day we'll live in dormitories next to it; the Austrian manager lives in one of the nearby Israeli settlements, as do all the foreign staff." Not being a casino habitué myself I tried to find out what exactly he was being trained for. Blackjack, he said in English, which as it turned out I knew how to play, unlike poker, baccarat, or craps, in which he was next to be schooled, whose rules had always eluded me. He seemed tickled by this admission. As we entered Zabbabdeh I said something about it seeming to be a prosperous town. "We have everything here," the young man said. "Even Fee-agra." I didn't get that last one, until he explained what he had meant. Viagra. Uneven development to say the least.

In Nazareth Azmi had rented Frank Sinatra Hall for the evening. Yes, Frank Sinatra, a longtime supporter of Israel who had apparently donated the money for a sports facility to be used by Jews and Arabs (Nazareth being the largest Arab town in Israel proper); later the facility was converted into a meeting center for the Histadrut, and when we arrived there it was explained to me that it was always available to rent for meetings, "even for me," I thought to myself. I was flattered that quite a large audience (for a Sunday night) had fetched up to see and listen to me, all of them Israeli Palestinian citizens, whose number in the aggregate is about one million people, about 20 percent of Israel's population. Azmi represents the new breed of 1948 Palestinians, as they are called: he is terrifyingly fluent (quadrilingual in Arabic, Hebrew, English, and German) and has an in-your-face style with Israelis that comes from familiarity and knowledge and a total lack of fear. Above all, he is a brilliant man, admired by his constituents, who see him neither as a lackey of one of the large Israeli parties, nor of Arafat's PLO, but as an intellectual who speaks for self-determination via citizenship and equality for everyone, Jew and

Arab. As such therefore he is as much a threat to the established Arab order as he is to Israel; much courted by the media everywhere in Israel and the Arab world, he is always willing to speak his mind, and ends up by creating much debate and controversy in his wake.

In Nazareth that night he introduced me warmly to the cordial but inquisitive crowd and then asked me to relate the development of my political ideas right up to my critique of Arafat, Oslo, and the Israeli system. That done, the floor was opened to questions, and for about an hour and a half I responded to all sorts of things, including criticisms of *Orientalism* as a CIA book that had been made by a minor Syrian Marxist in the early eighties. I mentioned at some point that the event was something of a homecoming for me since my mother had been born and was brought up in Nazareth, where her father had built and was the pastor of the Baptist Church. The occasion also gave me the opportunity to say how lacking my political formation had been in any knowledge about Israeli Palestinians, who had been regarded in the Arab world as little short of traitors for remaining as non-Jewish citizens of Israel. It now struck me, I said, that Israeli Palestinians had become crucial for our future as a people, since, given their circumstances as non-Jews in a Jewish state, they dramatized the anomalies of nationalism and theocracy throughout the Middle East. Nationalism had become the dead end of our political life, demanding endless sacrifices and the abrogation of democracy for the sake of national security. This was true both in Israel and in every Arab country. In countries like Lebanon, where large concentrations of Palestinian refugees have been totally forgotten by the Oslo process, I could see a parallel with the plight of Israeli Palestinians, except of course that the latter were not homeless, only without full and national political rights. They are allowed to vote, but not to buy, lease, or sell land, 92 percent of which is held in trust for "the Jewish people." Like all Palestinians, including myself, they do not have immigration rights and are not covered by the Law of Return. Thus there has emerged a campaign on behalf of full citizenship, which was the basis of new political struggle inside Israel (among both Jews and Palestinians) and established a secular order as the platform around which we could rally, Arabs as well as Jews. I recalled that in West Jerusalem last March Daniel Barenboim and I had met with an Israeli

Jewish group who were also concerned with secularism, constitutional rights, and citizenship within the entirely Jewish context of modern Israel; for that group that evening, secularism was an imperative that saved politics from the clutches of the religious extremists.

I found it odd that even at Bir Zeit University, where I held an open meeting with the students, there were no questions or declarations by the religious people, i.e., the Islamists of Hamas and Islamic Jihad, who held a small majority of the Student Council seats and were visibly in evidence in the hall. Perhaps they were there out of curiosity, but they simply had nothing to say to or ask me. Aside from five or six questions about the Wye agreement (Why did the Americans portray it as a great achievement, and what alternative was there to it?), the issues brought up by the students ran the gamut from personal (Why don't you think about moving here, and what do you think the role of a writer in exile such as yourself really is?) to the theoretical (What are the main networks of power we can exploit, new research methods in history and social sciences generally?) to the absolutely contemporary (the role of students, problems of identity, collective memory, and the struggle with attempts to quash it). The impression I had was of a highly politicized, skeptical, and self-conscious, albeit quite various, new generation, unlike that of its teachers in its avoidance of collective cant, automatic language, ready-made sentiment. Exhilarating, but demanding stuff, I thought, vowing to myself to try the same format with Arab and Jewish students in Israeli universities when I am to return in March as a guest of the Israeli Anthropological Association. I also felt none of the deadening effects of encountering prominent members of the new political class, whose overall attitude was both submissive and aggressive: all statements, hidden agendas, and little self-doubt.

The next day, at the invitation of a young woman, Lina Jayussi, who runs a research group on "Knowledge, Secularism and Society" at the Van Leer Institute in West Jerusalem, a few meters from the house in which I was born and which has now become the offices of the appallingly fundamentalist International Christian Embassy, I found myself facing about thirty Palestinian and Jewish Israelis. It hadn't been clear to me what I was supposed to speak about, I was exhausted perhaps by illness, perhaps by the sheer emotional pressure of being in the place, and I found myself perplexed by the swirling currents of ideology and passion all round me in the country. I stammered out a few critical words on the politics of identity, the need for new visions of inclusion, and so on, and soon had provoked a series of far more interesting interventions than mine from the assembled group, all of them young, all academic, all fluent in English. I had said something about the importance of geographical thought (as opposed to the temporal variety) to my work on culture and empire—the Bir Zeit landscape conference still fresh in my mind—and this brought forth a remarkable set of responses. For the first time in about six years of intellectual exchange with both Arabs and Jews on the politics of Palestine and Israel I felt suddenly exhilarated that we had somehow gone beyond the rhetorical salvos and barricades that were always present and had entered a relatively new territory of common interest to both Israeli Jews and Palestinians. Azmi Bishara later joined this group, and although I won't summarize here the main points being made, I recall vividly that I felt a sense of shared *secular* assumptions about politics, history, and the future. No one actually defended existing Zionism or old-style Palestinian nationalism. Near the end of our discussion, which lasted for almost two hours, it dawned on me that this was an Israeli institution I was speaking in, despite the presence of Palestinians, and that I felt justified in being able to speak openly and in an unrestrained way about the moral responsibility borne by Israel for the Palestinian *nakba,* or catastrophe.

I came away from this short sojourn with a newly strengthened resolve that it was important for us as Palestinian intellectuals, committed to our self-determination as a people, determined not to give up fighting against the injustice meted out to us by Israeli-Zionist policy, that (a) we should devote more of our time to Palestinian students and (b) we should take our message into Israel, Israeli universities, Israeli institutions, etc. I recall mentioning this to several of my Palestinian friends the next day, and then the day after when I was in Egypt for a student's dissertation defense at the University of Tanta (a grimy, bustling, and overcrowded Nile Delta city of two million people midway between Cairo and Alexandria). A brilliant young man, he had worked with me on Conrad for a couple of years in New York; the event itself was memorable as much for the enthusiasm of students and teachers as for the vivacity of the discussion. Anyway, when I brought up my Jerusalem and Nazareth experiences with Egyptian friends of unimpeachable nationalist credentials, I was immediately warned against "normalization," that is, having relationships with Israelis, especially on an institutional level. Even though Egypt has formally been at peace with Israel for almost twenty years, very few Egyptian intellectuals, artists, or writers of note has visited Israel, engaged in dialogue with nongovernmental or non–Labor Party Israeli intellectuals, and so forth. Palestinian universities as a matter of course do not invite Israeli academics or students to participate in conferences or seminars, even those Israelis known to be sympathetic to the Palestinian cause. One of my friends told me that given so many incursions by the Israeli army into campuses, Palestinians feel that visiting Israeli faculty coming to places like Bir Zeit or al-Najah universities would be seen as extensions of, or protectorates of, the army. Unacceptable. Not having lived through these traumas myself, I kept my own counsel, whereas in Egypt I was a good deal more forthcoming.

To some of my Egyptian friends, all of them well known as writers and intellectuals, I said that Palestinians suffered a great deal from the isolation of their confinement within territory all of whose exits and entrances were controlled by the Israeli army. The response I got was that it was a matter of national commitment not to go through Israeli checkpoints, not to get passports stamped or apply for Israeli visas, not to show any sign of "normalization" with Israel so long as it remained an occupying force. To this conundrum I repeated the answer Palestinians gave me: such Arab intellectuals wouldn't be coming to "normalize" with Israel, they would be there to express their solidarity with our struggle for Palestinian self-determination, to help in our institutions, to give readings, lectures, and the like to our students, to make appearances whose goal would be both to raise morale and also to get to know our problems as Palestinians at close hand, concretely, intimately. Besides, I added, your position leaves out entirely the Palestinian population of Israel: don't they have a right to be heard and seen by you? I don't think I quite made the impression I wanted to with my argument, but I did sense here and there the glimmering of a possibly new attitude, always among students and younger people, who struck me powerfully as vastly freer in their thought than their teachers and senior leaders. As for my own position, I have made it clear that because of our disproportionate weakness vis-à-vis Israel we have to undertake bold initiatives to carry our message to precisely those Israelis who for years have thrived on our absence and our silence.

This is risky, of course, for all sorts of reasons, physical as well as political. Breaking barriers after all is a two-edged sword. But I am firmly convinced that that is what we diaspora Palestinians need to do, despite the difficulty and unpleasantness of confronting diehard Israeli nationalists in their intellectual sanctuaries where the whole question of Palestine is now just a matter of separation (as the relation between blacks and whites had been in apartheid South Africa), of Israeli security, of tactical fixing. Connected to the whole history of post-War and post-Holocaust politics, the injustice done to us as a people has yet to be taken up. And unless we bring it up, as the kids of my children's generation constantly do, refusing to hide behind the historical forgetfulness accepted by Arafat and his tiny band of col-laborators, we will continue to live through its agonies. This is as true for Israelis as it is for us. The consequences of 1948 just won't go qui-etly away, partly because our conflict with Zionism is such a special one, because in the main our situation in the fifty years since 1948 has festered, has only cosmetically changed, remains basically unrectified, under-analyzed, morally and politically unacknowledged by most Israeli liberals and Israeli supporters. More interesting, though, is the impression I had that beneath the official and the institutional status quo, a vast but healthy disorder bubbled away amongst young people who were very close to total impatience with the manifest failure of the present generation. Incite them, I was urged by a senior UN diplo-mat in Palestine, there is no other hope. He's right, I now think.

London Review of Books, January 7, 1999

Chapter Fifty

Truth and Reconciliation

SINCE THE SIGNING of the Oslo peace accords in September 1993 an extraordinary disparity has developed between the rhetoric and the actualities of that peace. Because the United States, the world's only superpower, has been the sponsor and the keeper of the "peace process," as it has come to be known, the arrangements agreed to by Yasir Arafat and three Israeli prime ministers (Rabin, Peres, Netanyahu) have become synonymous with "peace," the only game in town, and the real problems on the ground either papered over or ignored. To be critical of or dissatisfied with Oslo and its aftermath thus means to be against peace, and to be roughly in the same disagreeable camps as the "extremists" (Hamas and the settlers) of both sides, "haters of peace," as Bill Clinton has called them. Therefore the "peace process" has become the only game in town: governments work with and for it, so do institutions like the World Bank, the UN, and an impressive number of donor countries, and of course the media treat it as an undisputed fact, which of course in most ways it is. But what if, according to all the signs and indications of unrequited nationalism and mounting hostility, this isn't and cannot be the peace to bring peace between Palestinians and Israelis? What if the "peace process" has in fact put off the real reconciliation that must occur if the hundred-year war between Zionism, Jewish nationalism, and the Palestinian people is to end?

Oslo brought one significantly new thing, namely, the first-time official admission by an Israeli prime minister that there was a Palestinian people (approximately 7.5 million in number) with its own representative. Beyond that, the terms of the agreement exactly reflected the huge difference in power between the two sides. Nothing was said about Palestinian sovereignty and self-determination. No end to the presence of the settlements was mentioned. (As Netanyahu said to CNN, September 17, 1998: "Rabin, in fact, who was my predecessor and who signed the Oslo accords, boasted that he could build settlements under the agreement. In point of fact, he expanded the population of the settlements by 50 percent. We're [Likud] nowhere near there.") Annexed to Israel in 1967, East Jerusalem remained under Israeli control: Oslo passed that over. The refugees expelled in 1948 were left as they have been for the last fifty years, homeless and uncompensated, despite numerous international and UN covenants and resolutions. Nothing was said about the tremendous losses endured by Palestinians as a result of thirty-two years of military occupation, the destruction of houses, of whole economies (in Gaza and the West Bank), thousands and thousands of acres of expropriated land, not to mention Palestinians deaths, long detention, torture (Israel being the only state today that officially sanctions torture).

Prior to 1993, one major problem in all discussions of this terrible conflict has been the irreconcilability between the Zionist/Israeli official narrative and the Palestinian one. Israelis say they waged a war of liberation and so achieved independence; Palestinians say their society was destroyed, most of the population evicted. A careful contemporary reading, however, shows that this irreconcilability was already quite obvious to several generations of early Zionist leaders and thinkers, as of course it was to all the Palestinians. "Zionism was not blind to the presence of Arabs in Palestine," writes the distinguished Israeli historian Zeev Sternhell in his recent book, *The Founding Myths of Israel*. "Even Zionist figures who had never visited the country knew that it was not devoid of inhabitants. . . . If Zionist intellectuals and leaders ignored the Arab dilemma, it was chiefly because they knew that this problem had no solution within the Zionist way of thinking" (p. 43). Ben-Gurion, for instance, was always clear: "There is no example in history," he said in 1944, "of a people saying we agree to renounce our country, let another people come and settle here and

outnumber us." Another Zionist leader, Berl Katznelson, also had no
illusions that the opposition between Zionist and Palestinian aims
could ever be surmounted. And certainly binationalists like Martin
Buber, Judah Magnes, and Hannah Arendt were fully aware of what
the clash would be like, if it ever came to fruition, as of course it did.

Vastly outnumbering the Jews, Palestinian Arabs during the
period after the 1917 Balfour Declaration and the British Mandate
always refused anything that would compromise their dominance. It's
hard to gainsay that attitude now by berating the Palestinians retrospectively for not accepting partition in 1947. Until 1948, Zionists
held only about 7 percent of the land. Why, the Arabs said when the
partition resolution was proposed, should we concede 55 percent of
Palestine to the Jews who were a minority in Palestine? To make things
worse, neither the Balfour Declaration nor the Mandate ever conceded that Palestinians had *political,* as opposed to civil and religious
rights in Palestine. The idea of inequality between Jews and Arabs was
therefore built into British, and subsequently Israeli and United States,
policy from the start. We now have enough evidence from Zionist
sources (through archival work done by the Israeli New Historians)
that most of the claims put forward in the official narrative of the state
of Israel's birth were largely untrue and disproved over time. No, the
Palestinians did not flee because they were told to by their leaders, but
because one of the war aims was to rid Palestine of as many Arabs as
possible; no, Britain did not oppose Zionism, it carefully encouraged
it; no, the Arab armies did not all try to destroy Israel in 1948, since
Jordan in particular, which wanted and got the West Bank, acted in
collusion with Israel; and no, the Arabs were not opposed to peace
after 1948, since every major leader sued for formal peace treaties but
was rejected by Ben-Gurion.

In short, then, the conflict is intractable only to the extent that it
was always a contest over the same land by two peoples who believed
they had valid title to it and who hoped that the other side would in
time give up or go away. One side won the war, the other lost, but the
contest is as alive as ever. I know this is true for us Palestinians. Why,
we say, should a Jew born in Warsaw or New York have the right to
come and settle here (according to Israel's Law of Return), whereas
we, the people who lived here for centuries, do not have the same

right? The Israeli line used to be: Go and live in some other Arab state, let the Jews have *this* one. After 1967, the issue between us was exacerbated. Years of military occupation have created in the weaker party anger, humiliation, and implacable hostility. To its discredit, Oslo did little to change the situation, since Arafat and his dwindling number of supporters were perceived as enforcers of Israeli security while Palestinians were forced to endure the humiliation of dreadful and non-contiguous little Bantustans that are only about 9 percent of the West Bank and 60 percent of Gaza. Oslo required us to forget and renounce our history of loss and dispossession by the very people who have taught everyone the importance of not forgetting the past. Thus, ironically, we are the victims of the victims, the refugees of the refugees.

Israel's raison d'être as a state has always been that there should be a separate country, a refuge, exclusively for Jews. Oslo itself was based on the principle of separation between Jews and others, as Yitzhak Rabin tirelessly repeated. Yet the entire history of the past fifty years, especially since Israeli settlements were first implanted on the occupied territories in 1967, has been in fact to involve Jews more and more dramatically with those of non-Jews. The effort to separate has occurred simultaneously and paradoxically with the effort to take more and more land; this policy of land aquisition in turn has meant acquiring more and more Palestinians. In Israel proper, Palestinians number about one million, almost 20 percent of the population. Between Gaza, East Jerusalem, and the West Bank, which is where the settlements are the thickest, there are almost 2.5 million more Palestinians. In the relatively small area from Ramallah in the north, Bethlehem in the south, 800,000 Palestinians and Israelis live hopelessly interlocked lives. Elsewhere, Israel has built an entire system of "bypassing" roads, designed to go around Palestinian towns and villages, connecting settlements and avoiding Arabs. But so tiny is the land area of historical Palestine, so closely intertwined are Israelis and Palestinians, despite their inequality and antipathy, that clean separation simply won't work. It is estimated that by 2010 there will be demographic parity. What then?

Clearly, a system of privileging Israeli Jews will satisfy neither those who want an entirely homogeneous Jewish state nor those who

live there but are not Jewish. For the former, Palestinians are an obstacle to be disposed of somehow; for the latter, being Palestinians in a
Jewish polity means forever chafing at inferior status. Israeli Palestinians also feel that they are already in their country, and refuse any talk
of moving to a separate Palestinian state, should one come into being.
It is also clear that the impoverishing conditions imposed on Arafat
will not subdue, much less satisfy, his highly politicized people of
Gaza and the West Bank, people whose political aspirations for
self-determination have remained steadily constant and, contrary to
Israeli calculations, show no sign of withering away. It is also evident
that as an Arab people—and, given the despondently cold peace
treaties between Israel and Egypt and Israel and Jordan, this fact is
important—Palestinians want at all costs to preserve their Arab identity as part of the surrounding Arab and Islamic world. The problem
is that Palestinian self-determination in a separate state is unworkable,
just as unworkable as the principle of separation between a demographically mixed, irreversibly connected Arab and Jewish population
in Israel and the occupied territories. The question, I believe, is not
how to devise means for persisting in trying to separate them but to
see whether it is possible for them to live together fairly and peacefully.

What exists now is a disheartening, not to say, bloody, impasse.
Israelis and Zionists elsewhere will not give up on their wish for a
separate Jewish state; Palestinians want the same thing for themselves
despite having accepted much less from Oslo. Yet in both instances the
idea of a state for "ourselves" simply flies in the face of the facts: short
of ethnic cleansing or mass transfer, as in 1948, there is no way for
Israel to get rid of the Palestinians or for Palestinians to wish Israelis
away. Neither side has a viable military option against the other,
which, I am sorry to say, is why both opted for a peace that so patently
tries to accomplish what war couldn't. The more that current patterns
of Israeli settlement and Palestinian confinement and resistance persist, the less likely it is that there will be real security for either side. It
was always patently absurd for Netanyahu's obsession with security
to be couched only in terms of Palestinian compliance with his
demands. On the one hand, he and Ariel Sharon crowded Palestinians
more and more with their shrill urgings to the settlers to grab what

they could. On the other hand, Netanyahu expected such methods to bludgeon Palestinians into accepting everything Israel did, with no reciprocal Israeli measures. Arafat, backed by Washington, is daily more repressive. Improbably citing the 1936 British Emergency Defense Regulations *against* Palestinians, he has recently decreed, as I said earlier, that it is a crime to incite not only violence, racial or religious strife, but also to criticize the peace process: Palestinians, Israelis, one or several Americans will implement the decree, going through radio broadcasts, pamphlets, schoolbooks, for examples of "incitement." There is no Palestinian constitution or basic law. Arafat simply refuses to accept limitations on his power in light of American and Israeli support for him. Who actually thinks all this can bring Israel security and permanent Palestinian submission?

Violence, hatred, and intolerance are bred out of injustice, poverty, and a thwarted sense of political fulfillment. Last fall hundreds of acres of Palestinian land were expropriated by the Israeli army from the village of Um el Fahm, which isn't in the West Bank but inside Israel. This drove home the fact that, even as Israeli citizens, Palestinians are treated as inferior, as basically a sort of underclass existing in a condition of apartheid. At the same time, because Israel does not have a constitution either, and because the ultra-Orthodox parties are acquiring more and more political power, there are Israeli Jewish groups and individuals who have begun to organize around the notion of a full secular democracy for *all* Israeli citizens. The charismatic Azmi Bishara, an Arab member of the Knesset, has also been speaking about enlarging the concept of *citizenship* as a way of getting beyond ethnic and religious criteria that now make Israel in effect an undemocratic state for 20 percent of its population.

In the West Bank, Jerusalem, and Gaza, the situation is deeply unstable and exploitative. Protected by the army, Israeli settlers (almost three hundred fifty thousand of them) can and are able to live as extraterritorial, privileged people with rights denied to resident Palestinians (e.g., West Bankers cannot go to Jerusalem, and in 70 percent of the territory are still subject to Israeli military law, with their land available for confiscation). Israel controls Palestinian water resources and security, as well as exits and entrances. Even the new Gaza airport is under Israeli security control. One doesn't need to be an expert to see that this is a prescription for extending, not limiting, conflict. Here the truth must be faced, not avoided or denied.

There are Israeli Jews today who speak candidly about "post-Zionism," insofar as, after fifty years of Israeli history, classic Zionism has provided no solution to the Palestinian presence. I therefore see no other way than to begin now to speak about sharing the land that has thrust us together, sharing it in a truly democratic way, with equal rights for all citizens. There can be no reconciliation unless both peoples, two communities of suffering, resolve that their existence is a secular fact, and that it has to be dealt with as such. This does not mean a diminishing of Jewish life as Jewish life or surrendering Palestinian Arab aspirations and political existence; on the contrary, it means self-determination for both peoples. But it does mean being willing to soften, lessen, and finally give up special status for one people at the expense of the other. The Law of Return for Jews and the right of return for Palestinian refugees have to be considered and trimmed together. Both the notions of Greater Israel as the land of the Jewish people given to them by God and of Palestine as an Arab land that cannot be alienated from the Arab homeland need to be reduced in scale and exclusivity.

Interestingly, the millennia-long history of Palestine provides at least two precedents for thinking in such secular and more modest terms. First, Palestine is and always has been a land of many histories; it is a radical simplification to think of it as principally, or exclusively, Jewish or Arab, since although there has been a long-standing Jewish presence there, it is by no means the main one. Not only the Arabs, but Canaanites, Moabites, Jebusites, and Philistines in ancient times, and Romans, Ottomans, Byzantines, and Crusaders in the modern ages were tenants of the place which in effect is multicultural, multi-ethnic, multi-religious. In fact, then, there is as little historical justification for homogeneity as there is for notions of national or ethnic and religious purity today. Palestine is an irreducibly mixed place. Second, during the inter-war period, a small but important group of Jewish thinkers (Judah Magnes, Buber, Arendt, and others) argued and agitated for a binational state. The logic of Zionism naturally overwhelmed their efforts, but the idea is alive today here and there among Jewish and

Arab individuals who, frustrated with the evident insufficiencies and depredations of the present, require a new or revived binational vision. The essence of that vision is coexistence and sharing in ways that require an innovative, daring, and theoretical willingness to get beyond the arid stalemate of assertion, exclusivism, and rejection. Once the initial acknowledgment of the Other as an equal is made, I believe the way forward becomes not only possible but attractive.

The initial step, however, is a very difficult one to take. In their culture and ideas of history, Israeli Jews are insulated from the Palestinian reality; most of them say that it does not *really* concern them. I remember once when I drove from Ramallah into Israel, commenting it was like going straight from Bangladesh into southern California. Yet it is crucial not to forget that reality is far less than neat. My generation of Palestinians, still reeling from the shock of losing everything in 1948, find it nearly impossible to accept that their homes and farms were taken over by another people. I see no way of evading the fact that in 1948 one people displaced another, thereby committing a grave injustice. The great virtue of reading Palestinian and Jewish history *together* not only gives the tragedy of the Holocaust *and* of what subsequently happened to the Palestinians their full force, but also reveals how in the course of interrelated Israeli and Palestinian life since 1948, one people, the Palestinians, has borne a disproportional share of the pain and loss.

Religious and right-wing Israelis and their supporters have no problem with such a formulation. Yes, they say, we won, but that's how it should be. This land is the land of Israel, not of anyone else. I heard those words from an Israeli soldier guarding a bulldozer that was destroying a West Bank Palestinian field (its owner helplessly watching) in order to expand a by-pass road. But they are not the only Israelis. For others, who want peace as a result of reconciliation, there is dissatisfaction both with the religious parties' increasing hold on Israeli life and with Oslo's unfairness and frustrations. Many such Israelis demonstrate energetically against their government's Palestinian land expropriations and house demolitions. So one senses a healthy willingness to look elsewhere for peace than in land grabbing and suicide bombs. For some Palestinians, because they are the weaker party, the losers, giving up on a full restoration of Arab Palestine is

giving up on their own history. Most others, however, especially my
children's generation, are skeptical of their elders and look more
unconventionally toward the future, beyond conflict and unending
loss. Obviously, the establishments in both communities are too tied
to present "pragmatic" currents of thought and political formations
to venture anything more risky, but a few others (Palestinian and
Israeli) have begun to formulate radical alternatives to the status quo.
They refuse to accept the limitations of Oslo, what one Israeli scholar
has called "peace with Palestinians," while others—in particular an
impressive young Palestinian couple from Nazareth and Haifa—tell
me that the real struggle is over equal rights for Arabs and Jews, not a
separate, necessarily dependent and weak, Palestinian entity.

The beginning step is to develop something entirely missing from
both Israeli and Palestinian realities today: the idea and practice of citizenship, not of ethnic or racial community, as the main vehicle for
coexistence. In a modern state, all its members are citizens by virtue of
their presence and the sharing of rights and responsibilities. Citizenship therefore entitles an Israeli Jew and a Palestinian Arab to the
same privileges and resources. A constitution and a bill of rights thus
become necessary for getting beyond square one of the conflict, since
each group would have the same right to self-determination; that is,
the right to practice communal life in its own (Jewish or Palestinian)
way, perhaps in federated cantons, a joint capital in Jerusalem, equal
access to land, and inalienable secular and juridical rights. Neither
side should be held hostage to religious extremists.

Yet so massive is the weight of the past and the decades of a more
and more intense sense of persecution, suffering, and victimhood that
it is nearly impossible to think around it, to launch political initiatives
that hold Jews and Arabs to the same general principles of civil
equality while avoiding the pitfalls of us-versus-them formulae that
continue the waste and insecurity. I believe Palestinian intellectuals
need to express their case directly to Israelis in public forums, universities, and the media. The challenge is both to and within civil society,
which long has been subordinate to a nationalism that has now developed into an obstacle to reconciliation, certainly not its enabler.
Moreover the degradation of discourse—symbolized by Arafat and
Netanyahu trading charges while Palestinian rights are compromised

by exaggerated "security" concerns—impedes any wider, more generous perpective from emerging. The alternatives are unpleasantly simple: either the war continues (along with the onerous cost of the current peace process) or a way out, based on peace and equality (as in South Africa after apartheid) is actively sought, despite the many obstacles. Once we grant that Palestinians and Israelis are there to stay, then the decent conclusion has to be the need for peaceful coexistence and genuine reconciliation. Real self-determination. Unfortunately injustice and belligerence don't diminish by themselves: they have to be attacked by all concerned. Now is the time.

New York Times Magazine, January 10, 1999
Al-Ahram Weekly, January 14, 1999
Al-Hayat, February 1, 1999

PERMISSIONS ACKNOWLEDGMENTS

These essays originally appeared under the following titles in the following publications:

"The First Step": *Al-Ahram Weekly,* May 25, 1995.

"How Much and For How Long?": *Al-Ahram Weekly,* August 24, 1995. *Al-Hayat,* August 26, 1995.

"Where Negotiations Have Led": *Al-Hayat,* October 1, 1995.

"Where Do We Go from Here?": *Al-Hayat,* November 8, 1995.

"Reflections on the Role of the Private Sector": *Al-Ahram Weekly,* December 7, 1995. *Al-Hayat,* December 12, 1995.

"Elections, Institutions, Democracy": *Al-Ahram Weekly,* January 18, 1996. *Al-Hayat,* January 19, 1996.

"Post-Election Realities": *Al-Hayat,* March 1, 1996.

"The Campaign Against 'Islamic Terror' ": *Al-Ahram Weekly,* March 21, 1996. *Al-Hayat,* March 24, 1996. *Dagens Nyheter,* April 13, 1996. *The Progressive,* May 1996.

"Modernity, Information, and Governance": *Al-Hayat,* July 3, 1996.

"Total Rejection and Total Acceptance Are Equivalent": *The Gulf Today,* July 5, 1996. *Al-Hayat,* July 3, 1996. *Al-Khaleej,* July 5, 1996.

"Mandela, Netanyahu, and Arafat": *Al-Hayat,* July 27, 1996.

"The Theory and Practice of Banning Books and Ideas": *Al-Hayat,* September 4, 1996. *Al-Khaleej,* September 4, 1996. *The Gulf Today,* September 6, 1996. *The Nation,* September 23, 1996. *Courrier International,* October 17, 1996.

"On Visiting Wadie": *London Review of Books,* September 5, 1996.

"Uprising Against Oslo": *The Observer,* September 29, 1996. *The Gulf Today,* October 1, 1996. *Al-Hayat,* October 1, 1996. *Al-Khaleej,* October 1, 1996. *Al-Ahram Weekly,* October 3, 1996. *El Pais,* October 1, 1996.

"Responsibility and Accountability": *Al-Hayat,* October 29, 1996. *Al-Khaleej,* October 29, 1996. *The Gulf Today,* October 30, 1996. *Al-Ahram Weekly,* October 31, 1996.

"Intellectuals and the Crisis": *Al-Hayat,* November 5, 1996. *Al-Khaleej,* November 5, 1996. *Al-Ahram Weekly,* November 7, 1996. *The Gulf Today,* November 7, 1996.

"Whom to Talk to": *The Gulf Today,* December 4, 1996. *Al-Khaleej,* December 4, 1996. *Al-Hayat,* December 4, 1996.

"The Real Meaning of the Hebron Agreement": *Al-Ahram Weekly,* January 23, 1997. *The Gulf Today,* January 27, 1997. *The Guardian,* February 15, 1997. *Journal of Palestine Studies,* Spring 1997. *Al-Khaleej,* January 27, 1997. *Al-Hayat,* January 27, 1997.

"The Uses of Culture": *Al-Ahram Weekly,* February 13, 1997. *The Gulf Today,* February 14, 1997. *Al-Khaleej,* February 13, 1997. *Al-Hayat,* February 13, 1997.

"Loss of Precision": *The Gulf Today,* February 24, 1997. *Al-Ahram Weekly,* February 27, 1997. *Al-Khaleej,* February 24, 1997. *Al-Hayat,* February 24, 1997.

"The Context of Arafat's American Visit": *Al-Hayat,* March 17, 1997. *Al-Khaleej,* March 17, 1997. *The Gulf Today,* March 20, 1997. *Al-Ahram Weekly,* March 20, 1997.

"Deir Yassin Recalled": *Al-Ahram Weekly,* April 17, 1997. *The Gulf Today,* April 25, 1997. *Al-Khaleej,* April 25, 1997. *Al-Hayat,* April 25, 1997.

"Thirty Years After": *Al-Hayat,* June 19, 1997. *The Gulf Today,* June 20, 1997. *Al-Ahram Weekly,* June 26, 1997. *World Times Focus,* July/August 1997. *El Pais,* September 16, 1997.

"The Debate Continues": *The Gulf Today,* May 7, 1997. *Al-Ahram Weekly,* May 8, 1997. *Al-Hayat,* May 7, 1997. *Al-Khaleej,* May 7, 1997.

"The Next Generation?": *Al-Hayat,* May 21, 1997. *Al-Khaleej,* May 21, 1997. *Al-Ahram Weekly,* May 22, 1997. *The Gulf Today,* May 22, 1997.

"Are There No Limits to Corruption?": *The Gulf Today,* July 2, 1997. *Al-Hayat,* July 2, 1997.

"Reparations: Power and Conscience?": *Al-Hayat,* August 10, 1997. *Al-Khaleej,* August 11, 1997. *Al-Ahram Weekly,* August 7, 1997. *The Gulf Today,* August 11, 1997.

"Bombs and Bulldozers": *Al-Ahram Weekly,* August 14, 1997. *The Nation,* September 8, 1997. *The Gulf Today,* August 19, 1997. *Inter-*

national Herald Tribune, September 11, 1997. *Al-Hayat,* August 19, 1997. *Al-Khaleej,* August 19, 1997. *Le Monde,* September 5, 1997.

"Strategies of Hope": *Al-Khaleej,* September 25, 1997. *Al-Hayat,* September 25, 1997. *The Gulf Today,* October 1, 1997.

"Israel at a Loss": *Al-Hayat,* October 21, 1997. *Al-Khaleej,* October 23, 1997. *Al-Ahram Weekly,* October 23, 1997. *The Gulf Today,* October 23, 1997. *Dagens Nyheter,* December 10, 1997.

"Bases for Coexistence": *Al-Hayat,* November 5, 1997. *Al-Ahram Weekly,* November 6, 1997. *Jeune Afrique,* December 16, 1997. *Dagens Nyheter,* December 11, 1997.

"Iraq and the Middle East Crisis": *Al-Hayat,* November 25, 1997. *Al-Ahram Weekly,* November 20, 1997. *Al-Khaleej,* November 25, 1997. *Against the Current,* May/June 1998. *The Gulf Today,* November 29, 1997. *The Yemen Observer,* March 16, 1998.

"Isaiah Berln: An Afterthought": *Al-Hayat,* December 9, 1997. *Al-Khaleej,* December 9, 1997. *Al-Ahram Weekly,* December 11, 1997.

"Palestine and Israel: A Fifty Year Perspective": *Al-Hayat,* January 6, 1998. *Al-Khaleej,* January 6, 1998. *Panorama,* January 9, 1998.

"The Challenge of Israel: Fifty Years On": *Al-Hayat,* January 12, 1998. *Al-Khaleej,* January 12, 1998. *Panorama (The Gulf Today Magazine),* January 16, 1998. *Al-Ahram Weekly,* January 15, 1998. *The Progressive,* March 1998.

"The Problem Is Inhumanity": *Al-Ahram Weekly,* January 29, 1998. *The Gulf Today,* February 4, 1998. *Al-Hayat,* January 29, 1998. *Al-Khaleej,* January 29, 1998.

"Gulliver in the Middle East": *Al-Ahram Weekly,* February 26, 1998. *Al-Hayat,* March 3, 1998. *Al-Khaleej,* March 3, 1998. *Dagens Nyheter,* April 2, 1998.

"Making History: Constructing Reality": *Al-Ahram Weekly,* March 12, 1998.

"Scenes from Palestine": *Al-Hayat,* March 26, 1998. *Al-Khaleej,* March 26, 1998. *Al-Ahram Weekly,* March 26, 1998. *Panorama (The Gulf Today Magazine),* March 27, 1998. *The Nation,* May 4, 1998. *Al-Hewar,* April/May 1998. *Washington Report on Middle East Affairs,* May/June 1998. *Le Monde Diplomatique,* May 1998.

"End of the Peace Process, or Beginning Something Else": *Al-Ahram Weekly,* April 9, 1998. *Panorama (The Gulf Today Magazine),* April 17, 1998. *Al-Khaleej,* April 10, 1998.

"Art, Culture, and Nationalism": *Al-Ahram Weekly,* April 23, 1998.

Panorama (The Gulf Today Magazine), May 1, 1998. *Al-Hayat*, April 28, 1998; *Al-Khaleej*, April 28, 1998.

"Fifty Years of Dispossession": *The Guardian*, May 2, 1998. *Panorama (The Gulf Today Magazine)*, May 8, 1998. *Al-Hayat*, May 5, 1998. *Al-Khaleej*, May 5, 1998. *Le Monde*, May 27, 1998. *Harper's*, October 1998.

"New History, Old Ideas": *Al-Khaleej*, May 26, 1998. *Al-Hayat*, May 26, 1998. *Al-Ahram Weekly*, May 21, 1998.

"The Other Wilaya": *Al-Hayat*, June 4, 1998. *Al-Ahram Weekly*, June 4, 1998.

"Breaking the Deadlock: A Third Way": *Al-Hayat*, June 30, 1998. *The Marxist*, November/December 1998.

"The Final Stage": *Al-Hayat*, July 29, 1998. *Al-Ahram Weekly*, July 23, 1998.

"The End of the Interim Arrangements": *Al-Hayat*, November 6, 1998.

"Incitement": *Al-Ahram Weekly*, December 31, 1998.

"West Bank Diary": *London Review of Books*, January 7, 1999.

"Truth and Reconciliation": *New York Times Magazine*, January 10, 1999. *Al-Ahram Weekly*, January 14, 1999. *Al-Hayat*, February 1, 1999.

INDEX

ABOUT THE AUTHOR

Edward W. Said is University Professor of English and Comparative Literature at Columbia University. He is the author of eighteen books, including *Orientalism*, which was nominated for the National Book Critics Circle Award, *Culture and Imperialism*, *Representations of the Intellectual*, *The Politics of Dispossession*, and *Out of Place: A Memoir*.